Spinning Plates

Sophie Ellis-Bextor

Spinning Plates

CORONET

First published in Great Britain in 2021 by Coronet
An imprint of Hodder & Stoughton
An Hachette UK company

This paperback edition published in 2022

1

A CIP catalogue record for this title is available from the British Library

Paperback ISBN 9781529363814
eBook ISBN 9781529363791

Typeset in Times New Roman by Hewer Text UK Ltd, Edinburgh
Printed and bound in Great Britain by Clays Ltd, Elcograf S.p.A.

Hodder & Stoughton policy is to use papers that are natural, renewable
and recyclable products and made from wood grown in sustainable
forests. The logging and manufacturing processes are expected to
conform to the environmental regulations of the country of origin.

Hodder & Stoughton Ltd
Carmelite House
50 Victoria Embankment
London EC4Y 0DZ

www.hodder.co.uk

For My Family Who Are Friends,

FAMILY

And For My Friends Who Have Become Family.

Captain von Trapp: Do you mean to tell me that my children have been roaming about Salzburg dressed up in nothing but some old drapes?

Maria: Mmm-hmmm. And having a marvellous time!

The Sound of Music (1965)

Contents

Contents

1

Introduction – 'Hello Hello'

Not my real nose or eyebrows, but they are my real teeth.

So hello, blank page. I've wanted to write to you for a while now. It's funny, I found a message I'd written to someone the other day about starting my book. It said, 'I'll start next week when the kids are back at school,' only that was a month ago and since then loads of other stuff got in the way and stopped me starting. Just now, I thought I'd start but first I had to tidy the Playmobil and reply to some emails and sort the washing and put shoes back in the cupboard and tidy the bathroom after bath time and put some kids to bed and any other of the normal stuff – I know it's normal – that sometimes gets in the way of me and work.

Anyway, this isn't a complaint book. It's about how my priorities have shifted and how I've changed. I started a podcast earlier in the year called *Spinning Plates* about the feeling a lot of us have when you're in your thirties and forties and beyond and still trying to push on and build a future but you're also dealing with a lot in the here and now. What's changed for me in the last twenty years? Primarily, it's the five small humans that Richard and I have introduced into the world, but also it's the things I care more about now and the things I care less about now . . . if we were to list the way my priorities have shifted over the years into a chart rundown it would go something like this:

In at number one – thinking about the kids!
Down thirty places – being cool
Up five – being kind
Down ten – any kind of toxic relationship
Down fifty – time for myself
And it's a non-mover for finding my own jokes funny

Anyhoo, I do spin plates, but over the years I've let a few joyfully smash and hopefully I've learnt a bit too – but there is still so much to learn. This book is a place for me to think about all of the above and I'll impart any wisdom as I go. If you don't find any, I do apologise, but hopefully I'll entertain you while we're together.

I feel I should add I've been a little bit tricked into inadvertently writing an autobiography with this book. I was never going to write one at all. When I was a teenager and already believed I was destined to become famous (cringy to write but also true – I used to doodle my autograph over all my friends' schoolbooks, determined to find the best way to do it), I was sure I'd never write an autobiography. I thought Madonna had the right idea – have them written about me, but never by me.

Well, I'm not Madonna and I'm not that famous, so here it is.

I suppose broadly speaking this book is 'stuff that has happened to me and what it taught me', but it's also a little historical document for myself, to remind older me what younger me had going on. It's such a busy life but a happy one overall. I hope I do pass on a little wisdom but if I don't then that's OK, too. It's nice to be able to put it all out there in any case. Thanks for lending me your eyes and giving me your time. Are you ready? You're about to get to know me a whole lot better . . .

Tour life with baby in tow . . . from the Song Diaries orchestral
tour with a four-month-old Mickey. It was all very wholesome.

2

ME: Early Years – 'If You Can't Do It When You're Young'

Mama Ellis and Papa Bextor with a pretty fresh SEB.

I have never been a fan of autobiographies that start way, way back in the past. I get a bit bored. Maybe you do too? I'll try to keep it brief – I was born on 10 April 1979 in the outskirts of West London to a twenty-five-year-old dad, Robin Bextor, and twenty-three-year-old Janet Ellis. Quite sweetly, on the same day in the same hospital another baby girl was born, Maria. She's one of my best friends but we didn't meet until we were eleven. Anyway, back to my folks. They had met at my dad's eighteenth birthday party when my ma was only sixteen. She kept diaries of her teen-age years written in tiny, near-illegible but still very beautiful handwriting in tiny page-a-day diaries. The smallest you can buy. They live on the bookshelf on the landing next to my old bedroom at my mum's, so I could find for you, pretty easily, the page entry where my mum first met my dad at his party. 'I got off with the party host himself,' she wrote. 'He looks a bit like a lion,' and there she's made a tiny drawing of a man's face with a lion's mane and a bit of a lion's nose, so we knew what she meant. My dad did have hair like that back then. Hey, it was 1972.

They married when my mum was just twenty-one. I have a photo of them from their wedding day in my sitting room now. They look very young. My mum is wearing the dress that I would dress up in years later, but after she'd dyed it purple and sewn on sequins for a role she had in a play. See, sequins were around me from the start. It was after they'd split up, but I don't think my dad loved that she'd done that.

My mum was a Central School of Speech and Drama actor and my dad a journalist and TV director. My surname – a little cumbersome and often misspelt and mispronounced – is the meeting of their names. I'm pretty sure I'm the only Ellis-Bextor out there, but I'll happily be introduced to another if you know one. I used to joke that I'd know I'd made it when my name wasn't ever misspelt (it's most commonly Bexter or Baxter) but that day is still to come and I doubt it ever will. I don't mind . . . I've always quite liked the fact it's an unlikely surname for a pop star. I didn't give it to any of my kids so they can be spared the bother of spelling such a long name and all that, but I didn't change my name when I got married. Partly because I'm not really into that, but also because I don't mind having a different surname and it helped me still feel like 'me' in amongst being someone's wife and someone's mother.

My mum went back to work pretty much straight after having me. She acted in *Dr Who* when I was about seven months old, *The Sweeney*, theatre plays and then by the time I was one, she had a regular job presenting a children's TV show called *Jigsaw*, which she did all the way up to 1983. Not everyone who grew up in the eighties like me remembers *Jigsaw* but for me it was quite formative. It was a sort of game show with puzzles to solve and my tiny two- and three-year-old brain couldn't make sense of much of it. There was a lot of vaguely freaky fun like a talking jigsaw piece, a character called Nosy Bonk who was played by a man with a strangely shaped white mask, a pterodactyl and a huge giant, although the only part of him you'd see on screen was an enormous foot.

Mirroring the wonky psychedelia of my mum's day job, at home I was being introduced to lots of music and music videos. My dad is a passionate music fan and he wanted to spark something similar in me. Ideally, I would have been a tiny Pink Floyd fan (they were my first gigs, aged nine and again aged eleven, and both with Papa Bextor as my date. Now that's very cool, I know, but at the time I was a bit . . . sorry to admit . . . bored). My dad used to play me stuff from his vinyl collection constantly . . . the Beatles, the Who, the Doors then later the B-52s, Pet Shop Boys, Air and Julie Cruise.

When I was small I was more hypnotised by music videos though, so my dad made a VHS compilation for me which I used to watch on repeat. 'Bedsitter' by Soft Cell, 'Hey Mickey' by Toni Basil, 'Stand and Deliver' by Adam and the Ants and 'Fish Heads' by Barnes and Barnes. The latter song was probably a novelty record of sorts – it was literally a song about being friends with the head of a dead fish – but that was way over my toddler head. I just thought the song was catchy and sad and weird, which I quite liked. The Soft Cell one had a similar sadness but was electro synth fun, too. It slinked along and made me want to dance but it was 'Stand and Deliver' and 'Hey Mickey' which both made me jump around the most. I loved Adam Ant dressed as the highwayman. So confident and camp and flamboyant. He performed with real intensity and slightly mad eyes. The most dazzling of them all was Toni Basil. In the video she had bright blue eyeshadow and red lips, wore a majorette costume and danced like no one was watching – even though she was a trained choreographer so the quirky jerky dancing in the video was incredibly poised and rhythmic. I thought she looked incredible.

Music laced its way through all my early memories and provided a soundtrack to my parent's divorce and their subsequent new relationships with my step-parents. Their marriage fell apart when I was four. My mum was a new *Blue Peter* presenter by then. She joined the show in 1983 and stayed until 1987 so it was throughout my early childhood. I think when I was four my dad also started directing *That's Life*, a big Saturday night panel show with Esther Rantzen as its host. It dealt with consumer affairs and funny stories sent in by the viewers, like the time the show went to film a viewer's dog because it could say something that sounded like 'sausages'.

I don't really have any memories of my parents happy together, which maybe sounds quite sad, but actually it meant I was never one of those kids hoping for their folks to get back together. I could see pretty clearly that they shouldn't be a couple anymore. I think they got together so young and, as my mum says, you can't have a passionate marriage without a passionate divorce, so I think that my existence, the last four years of their eleven years together, really saw them in the slow breakdown of things.

I have a few snapshots in my head of the time when I had a mum and dad under the same roof – the time when our cat had four kittens under my parents' bed – the childminder, Margaret, whose house my mum and dad used to drop me off at (she had a son called Stephen who was a little bit older than me. He had a used ice-cream tub filled with erasers shaped like different things. I thought that little collection of funny rubbers was so exciting and when my parents split I used to think I would have liked a big brother called Stephen with stuff like that I could play with). I remember having barbecues in the garden with my mum and dad at the little brick barbecue my dad had built, and I remember climbing into their bed halfway through most nights, usually after I'd wet my bed. Then I'd get in their bed and wet that, too. Looking back it probably chimed with feeling a bit worried as their relationship fell apart. I don't know loads about what happened and who did what, but I know that it all came to a head when my dad and I flew to meet my mum on a *Blue Peter* work trip in Kenya.

My mum had already been there for four weeks when we arrived. My dad and I were there for the final two weeks of her trip and then we were all going to fly home together. As soon as we got there, the mood was not great between them. We were staying in a beautiful wooden house set within an incredible garden. We had a local man staying with us who looked after the house and cooked us supper. He was quite a serious man who never smiled at me and I found that unnerving. One night he showed us the live lobster he was cooking for our supper. I didn't know how to feel about this. The lobster was moving around and opening and closing its claws as the guy held it firmly by the body. It scared me to think it was about to die but I was also fascinated to see this circle of life so close up.

When we weren't being shown live animals before mealtimes, I would play in the garden. I vividly remember one day picking beautiful bright petals to make a dress for my toy, a little doll called a flower fairy, while I could hear my parents arguing inside the house.

One of my strangest memories of the stay was a day trip we went on with the film crew. We travelled to a village where one of the women in the community had been killed by a hippo when she was washing clothes in the river. As dusk fell, we were taken by boat to see where the local men had taken their guns and shot any hippos they could find. As the guide shone his torch across the dark brown water, he occasionally lit up the bodies of the hippos, floating on their sides, and one time I saw one floating on its back with a bloody stump where its fourth leg used to be.

By the time my dad and I had been there for ten days, tensions were so strained that my mum flew home. My dad and I stayed on and went on a safari. We travelled there by train and wild giraffes galloped alongside the track. My dad told me, 'Remember this moment . . . take a photo with your mind so you can always remember the giraffes running.' It worked.

Back home, things disintegrated pretty quickly and by the time I was five, my parents' divorce was official. They lived five minutes' walk from each other. My mum and I were in a little flat on the same road as my school and my dad was in the house that he had bought with my mum, where he stayed until I was twenty.

Their homes were either side of a railway line which had a little bridge over it. I used to imagine the railway bridge was the halfway point between them and picture myself sitting there, equidistant from the two most important people in my life. I found it hard to go from house to house. Originally they had split their time with me 50/50 but after a bit of to-ing and fro-ing it changed to my being with my mum most of the time and my dad every other weekend. Every memory I have of anything related to custody invokes feelings of guilt and stress. I didn't mind when it was out of my hands, but the school holidays were split equally and when there was an odd number of nights in that holiday, arguments ensued about who would have me for that extra night. I know it is the mark of loving parents that they wanted me with them, but I felt incredible pressure not to upset them by showing any preference. When my stepmum, Polly, became part of the picture, she wanted to help my dad see more of me but I just found the conversations about spending time with one parent over another upsetting and confrontational. I didn't want either parent sad or unhappy, so I would hide how I felt and say what I thought they wanted to hear. I am not playing any small violins here – I know I am lucky to have had a lot of love around me – but I didn't find the bit of my childhood when I was still an only child particularly happy. Or rather, it was quite serious and grown-up a lot of the time.

I kept most of the sad on the inside. I used to regard crying in public as having lost some kind of challenge. I think broadly this came out of guilt . . . I didn't want whichever parent I was with to see that I had mixed emotions about where I was. I also think it came about because my parents didn't actually seem sad that they had split. I suppose there was a period of mourning for each, but by and large it just felt like a 'happening'. There was no alternative version of my life where they stayed together. The only person bringing 'sad' to the party was me, so I tried to hide it.

I used to wish I had a sibling so that another human was experiencing what I was experiencing – another barometer of how I show feel about it all – but it was just me. I remember even sad films were something I would try not to cry at. When I was taken to see *ET* at the age of four, I made it all the way through the movie before sobbing my eyes out when my mum took me to the loo after it had finished. I had tried so hard not to crumble, but who can resist that sweet little departing alien?

Throughout my early childhood and teenage years I was frustrated when my friends would cry at things. I didn't want them to. Maybe I felt a bit jealous of their emotional freedom and the attention that would follow it, but in any case I would resist any urge to cry in front of people. When I left my little primary school to go to secondary, all my friends were going to the local state comp (where I wanted to go) and I was one of only a handful heading elsewhere. They were all beside themselves with teary grief, while I was saying, 'Why are you all crying?! I'm the one who's not going to see any of you anymore!' Now I cry pretty easily at anything and my kids see me cry, but I still carry the association a little that I don't want to be someone who cries openly and freely in front of strangers and I think small me might have still been a little horrified knowing I now let the tears roll way before the end credits when I watch *ET* with my kids.

Looking back, I think I might have been quite an anxious child. It came out in odd ways like chewing off all the feet of my Sindy dolls (I can still remember the way the rubber tasted! I liked doing it but after their hobbling, the dolls did not look their best) and I often found it hard to sleep. At my dad's house my room was up the first flight of stairs but in a direct line from the front door. I was convinced someone was going to break in and head straight for my room. The adrenaline fizz of that fear would keep me up for what felt like hours, long after my dad and Polly had gone to bed and the house was quiet. I would potter around my room, playing with odds and knick-knacks until I fell asleep. But if the worry got really bad I might even take my pillow and lock myself in the bathroom for a while.

I had similar fears at my mum's house. One fateful night, I must have been eleven or twelve, I had sat on the stairs after I was supposed to be in bed and watched the TV through the small crack in the door. My mum and John were watching *Crimewatch* and there was a horrific tale of a family killed in their own home. I became convinced something similar would happen to us. It was a lonely and specific adrenaline-fuelled fear that would inhabit me by night. I would wait to hear a window being smashed or the front door being forced in. As I grew, my nocturnal life continued and I learnt how to distract myself when I couldn't sleep. By eleven, I had a little black and white telly in my bedroom at my mum's. I'd watch *Twin Peaks* on it. My dad let me watch it with him – in fact, he introduced me to all kinds of wonderful cinema too, including my favourite films: *Rosemary's Baby*, *Don't Look Now* and *Jaws*. But *Twin Peaks* was formative. I loved the aesthetic, the atmosphere, the strangeness of the dialogue and the characters. Other programmes try to emulate it but they always lack the humour – *Twin Peaks* could be funny – and also the way David Lynch would sometimes include something really odd and you wouldn't know if it was part of the main storyline or not. Sometimes it was just there for the hell of it. How brilliant.

The other thing I watched a lot (and remember, kids, this was when it was only five channels) was snooker. Turns out you can hone your ability to watch snooker on a black and white telly if that's your best option at 1 a.m. on a school night.

11

My parents were creative and outward-looking but were still figuring it all out and probably sad that the life they thought they'd be living together wasn't the one they were living anymore. My mum was only twenty-seven when she was single again. She'd been in a relationship since sixteen, was now in her mid-twenties with a great job and ready to start the next chapter. For my dad, he was working hard, and though sad it hadn't worked out with my mum, he too had the confidence of doing a job he loved successfully. But I felt a bit lonely in the middle of it all. Very few of my parents' friends had kids so I spent a lot of my time with them in adult company. The birth of my brother Jackson when I was eight, combined with my mum's happiness in her new relationship with the man who would become my stepdad, John, probably sowed all the seeds for the flock of kids I'd have later on. Small babies represent whole-some, happy new beginnings for me and have done ever since that day.

It's funny, but until recently I didn't really consider that those three years I spent with my mum in the flat were me being raised by a single parent. I think it's because it was just the two of us, so the dynamic felt comfortable. We have always been close and I think that time probably formed the bedrock of our relationship. I learnt about being resourceful and independent. I could see my mum's excitement about the future she would now have and she was always loving and unsentimental about what had happened. I share my mum's mindset of shaking off any inklings of regret about anything and always looking forward. We are both prag-matic in that way.

I think my parents both did a good job of keeping things pretty consist-ent in terms of where I'd come home to and the life I was leading. I stayed in my same school with the same friends all the way through until my dad and mum both remarried. They were always reliable and I never doubted that they loved me. Nor did it ever occur to me that their split was my fault, so credit to them for that, too. I always say that out of one unhappy marriage I got two happy ones, so I'm glad they found John and Polly. As a kid it felt logical they would find new partners, but as a grown-up I can see things don't always go that way. I honestly feel I've been raised by four people, not two, and strange as it may sound I can see bits of all four of them reflected in me sometimes. Nature and nurture all at once.

Blue Peter was like the sibling I didn't have. Between the ages of four and eight, it had a huge presence in my life. The show was broadcast live twice a week to an audience of millions and I would come in from school in time to tune in, too. There would be my mum interviewing Kenneth Williams or making a bathroom for a Sindy doll, jumping out of a plane or speaking to my grandpa who was working as a special effects designer – he helped build the Daleks for *Dr Who*. It was magical and surreal that she was talking to so many children all around the country but then coming home to me. Sometimes she'd bring home the thing she'd made, but not too often, so I wouldn't say I was spoilt by it. I honestly think the main thing I learned wasn't what to do with sticky-backed plastic but my mum's incredible work ethic. She had to learn the script off by heart as there wasn't any autocue back then. The script was delivered the day before and my mum would read it and memorise it. Impressive, right?

She was up for whatever challenges the show threw at her, too. I watched my mum wheezing with her inhaler halfway up Ayres Rock in Australia and training for solo freefall jumps. This resulted in my mum becoming the first British woman in history to do a ninety-second freefall jump with the RAF. This was after she'd broken her pelvis on another fall. In total she did nearly forty solo parachute jumps.

No wonder she got a tattoo during those years. One day she came home – I was about seven – and as it was nearly bedtime, she had a bath with me. On her back, on her left shoulder, was something covered with cling film. 'What's that?' I asked. My mum grinned at me. 'It's a tattoo. A hummingbird.' A little bird of freedom and a little nod to the need to rebel sometimes. I like that about my tattoo, too. I have heart with a ribbon on my arm. The ribbon says 'family'. It tells people that maybe they don't know everything about me – like my ma, on the surface I probably don't seem the type to have a tattoo. I love it. It's empowering doing something a bit selfish like that.

Blue Peter wasn't only a source of inspiration, but also a source of economic growth. I used to sell *Blue Peter* badges in the playground. I fancied myself as a little bit of an entrepreneur and was always trying to find ways to get extra cash. I could rake in 50p per badge or £1 if I sold it with my mum's autograph. This wasn't the only bit of Del-Boy-style business I chased back then. I used to draw and paint and, whilst I liked it, I also saw an opportunity and would sell the paintings for £5. If my mum took me out for supper with her friends I would do little pencil drawings for £1. I could see that, if you're a kid, people are more likely to buy it even if it's a bit crap. They think that it's the best you can do and feel a bit pressured to look like a nice person in front of their friends, so most of my mum's friends bought something. In fact, the night my mum met John, I was with her. We'd gone for a Chinese in a big group and there was a Lazy Susan – a spinning platform in the middle of the table to get the food around easily. I used the Lazy Susan to spin my art around and whoever it landed on would be expected to cough up.

It didn't stop there. When my mum and John became a couple, they lived at John's flat in Edgware Road. I slept on the sofa while we stayed there for a short time before they bought their house together. John's flat was accessed from the street through a big front door that led to a common staircase. His apartment had a window that overlooked the internal staircase. One day he came home from work to find me leaning out of the window with my recorder. I had placed a little Tupperware box next to the bottom of the stairs with 'money for the recorder player' written on it. I didn't make a penny, but you had to admire my spirit. I wasn't demotivated by the fact there were no people going in or out of the other flats, or that I couldn't play the recorder.

During those early years, I spent a lot of time with my parents at their work. I had a love–hate relationship with TV studios. On the one hand I liked the atmosphere. It always felt quite exciting and live TV is still something I like much more than pre-recorded. It may be more nerve-racking, but at least it has a tight schedule. What I didn't like was its self-importance. It was as if nothing else in the world was more important than the TV programme that was being made. Still, I watched along with all my peers when *Blue Peter* was on and I found it a reassuring part of my life.

It wasn't until I was halfway through primary that I started to realise that not everybody's parents worked in that sort of world. I was about five or six when I came to understand my mum was famous and that this wasn't how it was for every family. What's more, when my mother was out and about and being mobbed, it was by a crowd the same height as me. Other children were excited to see my mum and that made me feel a little jealous. I was also curious about the effect my mum could have on other people. I started experimenting with it. One time we were in a supermarket and I picked up some baked beans. In my loudest voice I asked, 'Would you like some baked beans, Janet Ellis?'

I was a fairly shy child, not overly anxious but certainly not overly confident. But I worked out soon enough that if I wanted another kid to like me, dropping the fact my mum was on *Blue Peter* into the conversation sure sped the process up. I wasn't too subtle. It was literally, 'Hello my name's Sophie and my mum's on *Blue Peter*.'

Good thing is, that kind of brazen straight-talking really works on young kids and before you could say, 'But I watch *Magpie*,' I'd have a new chum. Or at least, for a minute or two I would. Then the novelty would wear off and I might have overplayed my hand so that the new friend would decide, 'Hang on a minute, I don't want to be friends.' This got really bad in infant school where the imaginatively titled 'Against Sophie Club' was born (my mum jokes she still gets the monthly newsletter). Like I said, kids like straight-talking.

The club tried to drop stones on my head by putting them in a little tree in the playground and shaking it as I went past and then tried to flummox me with linguistical trickery like talking to each other with every word starting with a 'b' even if it didn't really. 'You're just saying things with a "b"!' I said angrily. 'Bo. Bit's bot brue,' they replied.

So my years in single figures, when my mum was on *Blue Peter*, were laced with the excitement of the fact my mum was famous, which had a certain currency with folk, but also with loneliness and a tricky family. It's funny because I didn't realise until years later that *Blue Peter* spanned the gap in my childhood when my parents were single. By the time my mum left, she was pregnant with Jackson and happily settled with John.

But before that, there was a bit of dating. I used to watch with fascination as my mum got ready for dates. I can remember the smell of her make-up and the rustle of her gold lamé skirt with big velour polka dots. I thought she looked so glamorous and as I hardly met any of her suitors, there was a lot of mystery surrounding the dates. 'Please can I meet whoever you're going on a date with?' I'd plead. 'No,' my mum replied, 'you'll only meet them if it's serious.'

I am glad I didn't get introduced to all the dates. I know I'm making it sound like my ma was seeing lots of people, but it was understandable. She was so young, she needed a bit of freedom. One guy I did meet was a ballet dancer who kept two spider monkeys in his conservatory. I can still remember the feel of their little feet on my arms as I fed them bananas. I'm glad I got to meet that guy. Good monkey memories.

*

Being a step-parent – just like any relationship between a child and an adult – is not a role that everyone finds easy. When John had started dating my mum I was not sure about him at all. He knew no other children apart from me and I found his adult way of talking to me and his dry northern humour quite disconcerting. I was seven when we met and we had our first Christmas together when my mum and John had been dating about three months. His present to me was a packet of balloons with 'Happy Birthday Jane' written on them. He thought this was completely hilarious. I didn't get it. I wrote to my mum on a little bit of paper, 'I dont like John' (yep I forgot the apostrophe). She laughed then told me, 'He's a kind man. Give it time.' Looking back, my mum was probably already pregnant with Jack by then (we Ellis girls don't mess about). I'm glad she reacted in such a gentle way and also, she was right. After those early days, John and I found our way to be together. He never once said anything negative about my dad (a word to any step-parent – NEVER SLAG OFF THE OTHER PARENT. It doesn't sway the kid's view, it just upsets them), he was funny and calm and strong in a subtle and constant way. My mum and John never seemed to argue, or if they disagreed it was without any shouting or pettiness. Mainly, they laughed. And always wanted to be together. Happy to have a little plan or adventure and walk a lot.

My dad was dating too but as I wasn't living with him I wasn't as aware and only met one girlfriend before Polly. My stepmum Polly was on the scene from the time I was about six. She was interested in me and would chat to me about all my favourite things. I was a bit intimidated at first as Polly seemed to be good at everything. She could draw really well and could even do amazing cartwheels. I think it was hard for my dad as he wanted us to bond but it took a little time to find our feet. Being a stepmum is hard and so is being a stepdaughter, but we got there. By the time Mum and John were together, Dad and Polly were very serious, too. There was stability on both sides and that made a massive shift in the dynamic, crystallised most in my becoming a big sister when I was eight.

I was obsessed with my new baby brother. Obsessed. I would carry Jack on my hip all day, give him his bottle at night, stroke his head until he fell asleep. Jack was the new beginning and the happily ever after. He's thirty-three now but I still feel more protective of him than any other sibling. It's hardwired. When Jack started working with me, at first I wanted to step in and give him special treatment, but he gently pushed back. He's properly brilliant at drumming, which helps. It's lovely he's been able to work with me so much.

When I was eleven, my mum and John moved to Hammersmith, to the house my mum is still in now. It's always been a happy home. Like me, my mum is a maximalist and there's colour and life everywhere . . . little knick-knacks, art on the walls, sometimes graffiti too. We have a wall where we – my brother, sister and I – have all written things. I was sixteen so I did meaningful stuff like an Emily Dickinson poem and the lyrics to Pulp's 'Disco 2000'. I was allowed to paint murals on my wall so I painted a woman on a horse, an angel with some pillars and a mermaid, all with a childlike naivety (a style I have maintained – my drawing has not improved since I was twelve. I still draw people standing face on with their feet pointing out). The mermaid remains on the wall to this day. She still looks pretty happy about life with her smiley face and her boobs which I painted like this: .)(. rather than the other way.

Soon after we moved in, my mum became pregnant again and I started my secondary school. In our old area I'd gone to the very sweet local state primary; now I was going to a private all-girls school in West London. I was like a fish out of water at first. I was introduced to a new type of girl – the posh kind – and it probably didn't help that on my first walk round the school, the other new pupil on the tour was wearing a cloak. On the first day of term everyone I met seemed to have learnt several languages, went skiing, could ride horses and one girl even had a lift in her house. Our form teacher was a French woman with a fantastically thick accent. On reading the register, it turned out three girls in the class were called 'Roubicca'. 'Wow,' I thought, 'must be a posh-girl name.' It turned out that's just how 'Rebecca' sounded with her accent.

Though it didn't happen overnight, by and by, I made friends. There was the obligatory queen cow in our year who made my life pretty miserable, but the scales were just about tipped in favour of girls I liked over girls I didn't and I ended up meeting a group of girls who would become lifelong friends. Enter Becca and Helen, who were in my class when I started. The school has some posh archaic system of class names which made no sense to me then or now, come to think of it, and so I found myself in Upper Three H, slightly in awe of Helen and Becca. They were already good friends and I became a bit of a third wheel at first.

Becca was popular and effortlessly cool. Being a teenager suited her – she looked like an extra from *Twin Peaks*. We both watched the show and would compare notes on the previous night's episode while we sat by the lockers eating peanut butter and jelly sandwiches. Obviously they were actually peanut butter and jam, but Becca was raised by American parents (she had the glamour of two passports) and so this added to her cool and she could legitimately use Americanisms.

Joined at the hip to her was Helen. Helen would later be the person to convince me that *Strictly* was a good idea. She was an unusual girl – her childhood bedroom housed a shelf full of *Wisden* annuals. To the uninitiated, that's books on cricket. She told me then, aged eleven, that she planned to be a cricket journalist when she grew up. She actually went on to work for Sky Sports, directing live cricket coverage. Isn't it cool when people have such a clear idea of where they are headed in life from an early age?

I was much slower to fall into music. At eleven, I was pretty set on acting. I thought that I was good at it and signed up to any school play going. Sadly, in hindsight, I was pretty rubbish. I remember in that first year of school we did a play where the cast was on stage the whole time. I was playing Mrs O'Lafferty, a drunk. Whenever the action was focused on other characters, I would wave at my parents in the audience. I suppose that could have made me look drunk, but really I was just crap and unprofessional.

Also in that first classroom was Ruth, who later became a clubbing companion. We loved a lot of the same music and have had many adventures over the years. In those early years of friendship, Ruth was obsessed with Robert Downey, Jr. She pasted photocopied pictures of his face on her ceiling so a smiling Robert looked down on her while she slept. When she grew out of this infatuation, no matter how much white emulsion her dad painted over him, Robert could still be seen peering at her through the paint.

It's hard to think of this time in my life without a soundtrack running in parallel to the memories. When, aged fifteen, Ruth joined me and my family on a road trip holiday to Cornwall, I'd made a cassette compilation for the car with songs like Dodgy's 'Staying Out for the Summer' and 'Cigarettes and Alcohol' by Oasis. When I sat chatting with Becca and Helen during school lunchbreak, we'd sing songs from Annie Lennox's album *Diva* as we gossiped. It's all so fundamentally interlaced in my head that I can time-travel to my teenagehood whenever I hear the right tune. You're so open to it all then and all discoveries are so visceral. It's as if you hear the songs with all your senses, or at least that's how it felt to me.

Later on, my close friendship with Maria took shape. Maria was in a different form to me so our paths didn't cross too much initially but by Lower Fifth (there's that antiquated class system again . . .), when we were fourteen, we had some classes together and we started hanging out. At six-foot-one, Maria was a gorgeous, funny girl and I liked her company immensely – still do. She could always make me laugh but she's also very smart and philosophical about life. One of my earliest memories of our friendship is lying on our backs on the green near where I live now (I made the decision to move back to where I grew up about twelve years ago – fifteen-year-old me would have been appalled). It was close to midnight and as we gazed at the stars we talked about the infinity of death. I used to worry about dying all the time and I passed that worry onto Maria. I can still recall when it first hit me: the fact that one day I'd be dead and that was forever and the end of consciousness. I sat bolt upright in bed with the fear making a huge chasm in my stomach. I could see it in my head: death was like the darkest, blackest sea either side of the tiny bit of time above the surface of the water and alive; just long enough for one gulp of air before heading back into nothingness. It seemed to me the most terrifying thing I could imagine.

Then came the mad cow disease outbreak in the mid-nineties, which played into every aspect of this fear. The government had allowed cattle to eat meat and bonemeal made using remains of diseased cattle. This had resulted in some humans developing a terrible incurable disease which at one point seemed to be possibly dormant in anyone who had eaten any beef in the eighties. Very much 'We're all gonna die!' territory. I remember travelling to school and all the newspaper headlines were shouting about the ticking time bomb of symptoms. My head was shouting, 'Why isn't everyone running around screaming?' My history teacher, Mr Davies, when seeing how freaked out I was, told me, 'Nothing is going to happen. You are not all going to get mad cow disease,' and though Mr Davies was not a scientist, he seemed so sure and I found that reassuring. Whenever I started to panic I would tell myself, 'Mr Davies says I'm not going to die,' and feel calmer. In the end I think I grew out of the fear or at least I grew out of it dominating my thoughts.

Maria and I spent a lot of time speaking about thoughts big and small that floated through our teenage brains. I can still remember her saying, 'The thing is, I've just realised that all those ages we imagine as a sort of abstract idea . . . our thirties, or being forty-two, or whatever . . . those ages are actually going to happen. One day that will be us!' As I write now, Maria and I have just spent the last weekend in that same park with our little boys. We are now forty-two. Yes, those days do come.

*

By the end of the first term, my mum was six months pregnant with Martha. One night I was playing the piano while John sat watching TV (which, looking back, was pretty tolerant of him. I'm not the world's best piano player). Suddenly, my mum came running in. 'I think my waters have broken.' I remember stopping playing the piano like someone on the ivories at a Wild West saloon.

That night, my thirty-week pregnant mum went to hospital. John was worried sick, manifesting in the fact he couldn't eat all of his McDonald's Happy Meal he'd bought for our unexpected supper. I was clearly in a calmer state as I finished his supper too. I wasn't worried about the baby, I just wanted my mum to be OK. Martha was born ten weeks early the next day. I had left for my dad's for the Christmas holidays that morning and didn't meet Martha until she was two weeks old. Dad and I had gone on a trip to America – he was good at taking me away on adventures and this one was pretty cool. Just the two of us in Florida for ten days including a fun but surreal Christmas Day at the Universal Studios theme park. When I returned to the UK, I remember going into the neonatal unit at Queen Charlotte's Hospital and being wary about looking at the incubators until I knew which one was Martha. I was worried that if I looked at the wrong baby first I might bond with them by accident.

Luckily, I bonded with the right one. Martha was the happiest of small people and I adored her from the get-go. As Martha is eleven years younger than me, we've never once had an argument. I think she's wonderful and in my head she's still sort of six. A very bright, tenacious, gorgeous and talented six, but six all the same. Sometimes people in your family just kind of crystallise in your emotional connection at a certain age and there's not much you can do about that.

At that time – from eleven to probably fifteen – I was still chasing the acting dream. It's not charming to say aloud, but I think somewhere in me I always thought I'd end up being in the public eye. I don't mean I was obsessed with the idea (although I did design an outfit when I was eleven that I thought I'd wear to collect my Oscar – the little image I drew shows a dramatic black dress with the mannequin's hand clutching the small golden man), and even now I have the idea of 'fame' itself held slightly at arm's reach. Fame in itself isn't particularly alluring and although it's sometimes quite fun, I think I'm quite suspicious of it – maybe because I saw from a young age how it made people react differently once they realised my mother was famous. The thing about being famous is, it doesn't mean much without context. Someone recognising you without being positively or negatively affected by the work you've done is only that – they know your face from somewhere. But I did sort of think it might be part of my life. I experimented with calling myself 'Sophie Michell' to see if that formed a more beautiful autograph, but when I started writing it 'S. Michell', my teacher said, 'Who's Smichell?' with disdain in front of the whole class, so I dropped that. Thus I started writing my own name over and over until it had the right flow and flourish. Now it's an unintelligible mess, but that's not the point. It's not very becoming to say, 'I always thought I'd be famous,' and that's not exactly right, but I found it didn't surprise me. Maybe you have to have a little of that feeling in your tummy to run towards it anyway?

*

I begged and pleaded with my mum to get me an acting agent. I was desperate to get started. Finally, at about fourteen, my mum capitulated. She took me and my angelic little brother Jackson – all blond ringlets and big blue eyes – to meet an agent. Yes, reader, we were both signed up. Jackson, then aged six, worked pretty much non-stop for the next few years. He was in films with Christian Slater, Stephen Fry, Tara Fitzgerald, Helen McCrory and Keira Knightley. His gorgeous face meant he was mainly in period dramas. Essentially, he wore little black suits and ran after famous actors calling 'Papa! Mama!' Except for the time he played it cool and was cast as a young Jarvis Cocker in their video for 'A Little Soul'.

And me? I got two acting jobs. One was playing the part of Peter Howitt's daughter in a police drama called *Frontiers*. The most cringy bit saw me lying on a sofa when my policeman dad arrived home late. Five-foot-eight fifteen-year-old me then had to thrust my hands into the air and call out, 'Daddy, carry me up to bed!' The other job was a very strange experience. It was a one-day shoot for a German police series. The actors in the scene were speaking German but my lines were in English. I was going to be dubbed out later. Good for morale. I played the part of a violinist being attacked on her way home from a concert. Whilst I was attacked, I had to hit the poor actor as hard as I could with my violin case and simultaneously remove one of his gloves to give to the police for evidence. To put the cherry on top of the whole 'Eh?!' nature of the thing, I was told to mime shouting 'Help!' as we were filming in a residential area and couldn't make any actual noise as it was night-time.

I got my best experience of acting through the National Youth Theatre course I signed up to in the summer of 1994 when I was fifteen. It was a week-long course and I got to spend it all in a university hall of residence in North London. Being away from home like that blew my tiny mind. I probably learned some acting skills, but mainly it was the first time I ever got drunk. One can of Diamond White and I was away. I still remember how wonderful it felt. I was immediately a fan of the little tin of cider's powers. As the world went a little soft round the edges, my main thought was, 'Why on earth did I not do this sooner?' I phoned home the next day. 'Mum! I got drunk!' 'Did you?' she laughed. 'Well . . . be careful.'

Thank you, NYT. I never became an actress but I did take that new alcoholic experience forward into what would become my profession in the music industry. A lesson well learned.

Once I fell into the band (more of which later), the role music had played in my life up until then all made sense. I had been passionate about singers and bands since I was tiny. I loved learning the lyrics to songs and working out the stories within them. Even now it can surprise me when I hear a song I haven't heard for a decade or two and the lyrics pop up in my head, fully formed. Imagine if school lessons were all put to music? That would have really helped. I can't remember anything about my history of art A-level thesis but if 'I'd Rather Jack' by the Reynolds Girls comes on the radio, I'd be able to sing along. Pop stars like Boy George and Adam Ant were part of my earliest memories . . . watching the videos and trying to emulate the dances. Whilst I loved the routines, it was the determination in their eyes that fascinated me most. I love that look of conviction . . . it's so hypnotic and powerful.

I suppose the alter-ego creations of those pop stars in the eighties and nineties were to me what drag culture represents to the teen generation now. We all have our insecurities, but the things that make us feel like outsiders can be celebrated when you can sing on stage with a call to arms. I can track each year of my childhood by what I was listening to. Singing was always something I enjoyed. I knew I could carry a tune but for some reason having it as my day job just never occurred until it was put right under my nose with my band theaudience. Up until then I had sung around the place, harmonising to songs I loved and would idly wonder about becoming a backing singer. I used to sign up to any school musical going and loved the music side of it so much. I must have been fairly confident in my ability as I put myself in for a school music competition when I was about fourteen. I sang an Annie Lennox song, 'Precious', accompanied by the aged piano teacher who sped up considerably as I sang. Out of three entrants, I didn't win. Pride must have led me to tell people afterwards I came second, even though only first place was announced. I guess I'm a little competitive underneath it all.

I never had singing lessons and I don't remember anyone ever talking too much about my voice. It wasn't as if I took part in one of those musicals or that competition and someone said to me, 'Oh my! Your voice!' I think I just knew I could sing and that was that. I also tried my hand at a bit of piano and guitar but ultimately I am lazy and because it takes practice to get good, I decided they weren't for me. It sounds ridiculous now but I remember thinking that somewhere out there was an instrument I was just going to be able to play. I suppose that's what singing was to me . . . but then again, I haven't tried every instrument. Quick! Someone hand me a hyperbass flute! (A weird massive rare flute I've never seen in real life but I might be able to play it amazingly.)

*

As I entered my teens I remember a kind of . . . disappointment about myself. I was getting tall and I felt ungainly and slightly like a sideshow attraction. I outgrew my mum, stepdad and stepmum before I was fifteen and I felt galumphing. I didn't look cute like Jack and Martha. Photos of me between thirteen and seventeen are a rarity. I was awkward and spotty. I looked at myself in the mirror and tried to be as pragmatic as possible. My boobs weren't as big as I'd hoped, my tummy was chubby, my face was awkward, I hated my jaw and I was taller than I wanted . . . but my thoughts were matter-of-fact. So I wasn't going to be one of life's beauties but maybe I could be funny and interesting instead? Boys my age were not interested in me at all. If I ever got close to a teenage boy his most likely comment would be that he'd grown up fancying my mum. I don't recommend the feeling that I got from that.

The most meaningful relationship I had in my early teenage years was with the actor River Phoenix, after he sadly died way too young. I was fourteen when it happened. His death really got to me. I became a little obsessed. I thought he was so beautiful. I think the fact that he was, sadly, not of this world meant it was the perfect place for me to put all my teenage passions. To try out all those emotions. I would write letters to him and set fire to them outside my window in the hope the ashes would fly up to wherever he was. With that kind of crush, there's no fear of rejection. When I said his name under my breath at the stroke of midnight on New Year's Eve of 1994, so it would be the first words of the new year, ghostly River might have been able to hear me. It was an unchallenging relationship with no chance that the reality of daylight would cast ugly shadows on my feelings and make me sad. It was already sad, of course, but with poetry, not heartbreak. The unrequited love between a dead man and me felt full of romantic poetry that suited my early teenage heart perfectly.

I felt out of step with my peers when it came to boys and social confidence. When my friends started going to parties, snogging and drinking, I just wasn't ready. I turned up to one party aged about fourteen and when my friend opened the door with a beer in her hand I said, 'You look stupid doing that.'

I had changed my tune by fifteen, but at thirteen and fourteen I just felt clunky and uncomfortably prim. I eventually had my first kiss at a party aged fifteen. I felt like the last one in the pack to cross this hurdle, though I doubt I was. Anyway, he dumped me the next day. There followed many experiences like that including one corker where the boy dumped me because I was too spotty. Oh, to be young again!

It was at fifteen that I got in the most trouble with my mum. I was passionate about music by this stage and was obsessed with bands and gigs. I wasn't alone – in the nineties, teenage culture was centred around music. Our teen magazines and TV programmes were fixated on music, too. But even then – when every girl I knew was plastering the walls with boys in bands – I knew my love affair with music would last me a lifetime. In the meantime, my love affair with music would make me do something duplicitous. I had to lie to my ma to make sure I was at the Bluetones' *NME* gig at the Astoria on a school night. I am not trying to be mean, but it pains me to write that the other band on the bill were also a draw, and that band was Menswear. I won't make excuses for my poor judgement. I was very young.

My friend Alison was my date for the night. She, like me, was music-obsessed and equally willing to risk it all for this night out. Later on it was Alison's boyfriend who owned the four-track used to record what would become my demo tape. It is Alison who I always think of when I look back to the early days of my song 'Murder on the Dancefloor'. It was her favourite when I played her the demo. My friends are a good sounding board.

But – they can also lead me astray (actually no, I think it was pretty much my idea). We were both game and it would be worth it. On the day of the gig, Alison and I told our mums that we needed to stay at the other's house. I wrote a note to my mum explaining that Alison was going through a tough time and needed a friend. I always over-elaborate when I lie, dammit. When the school bell rang, the ill-thought-out plan was set in motion. I went to Alison's house where we got ready. The plan was to return to my house after the gig. We headed to Tottenham Court Road where we bought tickets from a tout. They were £25 each, which took pretty much all our money in one go. I don't actually remember the gig, but somehow Alison and I found ourselves in the bar with Menswear afterwards. I remember standing by the bar and mean Chris Gentry (who was in the band) came over to play a trick on me. He started chatting to me and when the bartender came over, he asked me if I'd like a drink. 'Ooh, yes please.' I turned to the woman behind the bar, 'Gin and tonic please,' but when I turned back Chris had run away and was laughing with mates that he'd tricked me into buying myself a drink I couldn't afford. Chris – that was crappy and humiliating.

With our little funds Alison and I somehow made it back to mine at 4 a.m. very drunk. I was tipping my bag out on the garden path searching for my keys when my mum, clad in dressing gown and angry face, opened the door with the immortal line, 'Well, I hope it was worth it.'

As my mum lectured me in the kitchen, I was tipsy enough to alternate between a sad face for her and a triumphant, happy one for

Alison. Unbeknownst to us we'd been rumbled early on when my mum had realised there was going to be filming going on in our kitchen the next day (Nerys Hughes always seemed to be filming in our kitchen during those years) and so my mum had wanted to warn me in case I came home for lunch. She'd called Alison's house to tell me and together our mothers had worked it out. My mum was brilliant in her telling off. She didn't shout, just went for the emotional conscience angle. 'I'm going to always keep that letter you gave me where you told me you needed to be at Alison's house, just so I have a reminder of how you can lie to me.' Ouch. I have to admit, though, going to school the next day still drunk was flipping amazing. Probably the best school day I had.

Things had started to turn around with my confidence when I discovered music and a life outside of school. By the age of sixteen and seventeen, my schoolfriends and I were going out every Friday and Saturday night – mainly to indie clubs – and it gave me life.

Looking back, my parents were fairly relaxed about my gallivanting. Maybe it's because they could see how determined I was and, given my later escapades heading to see my boyfriend, their instinct was right. I think if there had been a global pandemic in my teenage years, the subsequent lockdown would have been very welcomed by my dad. He couldn't really stop me from going out but I know my choice of boyfriends was hard for him. The music side, though, the clubs and the gigs, I think that resonated with him. He was probably that teenager a bit, too. Festivals and live music made sense to him and he was always keen to know what I was listening to. It wasn't hard to find out. One glance at my bedroom wall would have shown black and white photos of everyone from Madonna to Blur. I had music idols on my wall from a very early age. Even aged seven or eight, I had a *Smash Hits* poster of Michael Jackson by my bed. I used to kiss that poster goodnight before I went to sleep. Yep, I know. Then the Madonna crush was a very real, very dominant fixture for a long time. I thought she was incredible. I loved that not only did she have so many great pop songs, she was also exciting to follow. She called no one boss and I thought that was brilliant. Her image was cool, too. In tribute I wore a huge crucifix necklace until one day, when we went to visit my step-grandma, Grandma Betty, in Huddersfield, she asked me when it was I'd found God. I never wore it again.

But the adulation of female music artists continued and as I approached my teenage years I added to the tribe Björk, Belinda Carlisle, Annie Lennox, Shirley Manson, PJ Harvey . . . they all inspired me. I wasn't so into manufactured pop when I was small (I must have been such an annoying little snob in the primary school playground when most kids were running around singing Stock-Aitken-Waterman-produced songs and I'd be standing there with my arms crossed claiming, 'I prefer the original'), but I did love pop music. For nineties me, pop music and indie music were closely entwined. Songs like 'Girls and Boys' by Blur was as catchy and shiny and fabulous as any eighties pop song.

When I found myself with a microphone in my hand at my own early gigs, I was as much looking to stray away from the classic female indie singer as I was trying to emulate my favourite performers. Typically, female-fronted guitar bands in the late nineties saw girls in midriff-exposing vest tops with baggy jeans, short hair and a bit of attitude. I probably would have done that except my tummy was not going to be introduced to anyone. Plus, I liked looking more feminine and dressed up than that. I didn't feel confident being a tomboy. I wanted to copy the grubby glamour of Courtney Love in her silk nightie rather than the deadpan cool of Justine Frischmann. I think it's a good idea to play to your strengths rather than the fashion, and there are some things I just don't think suit me – being androgynous is one of those things, even though a lot of indie girls carried it off really well.

*

I'm grateful – honestly – that my parents put so much into my education. And they took it well when, having spent thousands of pounds on my school, I turned around at the end and said, 'Thanks for all that but sod Further Education, I'm going on tour with the *NME*.' The best thing I got out of school was my friends – that core group of girls I've known since I was eleven (and one I've known since I was four) and who are still among my favourite people.

'Look around the room . . . see how many friends you have. You will never have this many friends again for the rest of your life.'

I knew, at sixteen, when my English teacher said this to the class, that it was complete bollocks.

By then, with A-level exams and the end of school on the horizon, I had already planned the five girls I was going to stay friends with post school. I was quite happy to leave. School can be so brutal and I definitely didn't sail through it. Finding my tribe both within school and then without it was my saving grace. I think in any situation if you can find your people, hold on to them tightly. Plus, if I ever have doubts over whether or not I'm a half-decent person, I only have to look at my amazing girlfriends to know that if I can have people like that in my life I can't be all bad. I have happily added to this clan throughout my adult life and have a small tribe of wonderful women who support me through every twist and turn.

I take being a friend fairly seriously. All relationships take work and you can't rest on your laurels too much. I wrote the song 'Young Blood' about how romantic relationships can keep you young in each other's eyes but I think friendship can be the same. When I hang out with old friends we can cry laughing at the things we've done together – or at the terrible hairdos I used to have. Don't worry, I will share this hairdo horror with you, too.

When it came to my family, it still hadn't finished growing but it didn't grow as fast as was hoped for. Polly and my dad had been trying to have a baby throughout my teenage years. I can recall Chinese herbs frequently being boiled on the stove to help, and tension and sadness when the much-longed-for baby didn't come. In fact, I found out later that fertility issues were a big part of what was going on behind the scenes in both households. My stepmum Polly was having IVF while my mum was trying to have another baby after Martha. I knew about the IVF but not about my mum. She didn't tell me at the time. She actually had ten miscarriages (my mum has spoken publicly about this, which is how I found out). I spoke to my mum about it later, wondering why she hadn't told me. 'Simple,' she replied, 'I didn't want you to think that having a baby sometimes wasn't easy. At that age – when you were fourteen, fifteen . . . the idea of a miscarriage was as unknown to you as the idea of having quads. It just wouldn't have been a helpful association for you.' I think she also knew how very sad it would have made us kids and wanted to protect us from that.

Eventually, Dad and Polly saw a senior specialist who told them they wouldn't have their own children. He wasn't kind, telling them, 'I don't know why you're still trying.' When I was sixteen they began the process of adopting my sister Dulce, who was born when I was seventeen. This is no revelation but it is a truth: blood does not make the family. As someone with step-parents and an adopted sister, I can confirm this. Dulce is my sister and was from the moment she came to us. She's now in her twenties and works with primates, which is so flipping cool. When Dulce was only nine months, Polly discovered she was four months pregnant, naturally, with twins. Maisy and Bertie entered the world when I was nineteen and I found myself with a tally of three sisters and two brothers. That's quite the leap from the only childhood I'd had for my first eight years. I didn't grow up in a house with Bertie, Maisy and Dulce, but I did go round to see them all the time and with three kids under two, it was the norm that when I turned up I'd have a baby in my arms within seconds. Sometimes I'd bring Martha with me because she was eight when they were born and baby-obsessed. She'd come and play with them and I liked having most of my siblings all in one place. My littlest siblings were only six and seven when I had my first baby, so they are close in age. I love the fact my family ended up so big and sprawling. I like having so much going on. It suits me and taught me how things can evolve. I started my days as an only child of two parents and ended up the eldest of six with four parents and friends I would call family, too, not to mention my own contribution to the family pot. Good job my tattoo on my arm just says 'family' and not the names of those within it. The list would be down to my wrist by now.

I'm probably about 10 here . . . rocking the Madonna look until
grandma Betty mistook my references and though I'd found God.

3

MUSIC: The Beginning –
'A Pessimist Is Never Disappointed'

Dean, me, Kerin, Patch, Billy and Nyge = theaudience. Weirdly, I don't remember
this being taken. You'd think the sheep would have been pretty memorable . . .

Theaudience was my first band and though I don't talk about them a
lot, my experience in that band during the four years it existed
taught me pretty much all I needed to know about the highs and the lows
of the music industry. Through that band I experienced the first flush of
success, the outright disappointment of the reality behind the record
company doors (so much less exciting than I ever dreamt), the absurdities
of in-band fighting and the necessity to stand up for what you believe in.
Plus a healthy dollop of clichéd record company politics – sixty-year-old

white male record-company boss tells teenage singer how it's gonna be. Oh, and perhaps most importantly of all, the cruel lessons of failure. Feeling high and dry by twenty was crap and I'd wish it on no one, but it stood me in good stead.

The band came into being when I was sixteen. I'd begun going clubbing every Friday night at an indie club called Popscene. I was music-obsessed and living for the weekend. It was me and the same school friends every week. We'd all go round to one house or another and get ready together. It was often the best bit of the night. I can still remember the clothes I would wear . . . I had a gorgeous bright red cheongsam dress from Chinatown, a black Lycra mini dress that I'd wear with a vintage striped shirt on top (I'd changed the buttons from plain ones to little acid house yellow smiley faces), a little blue suede A-line skirt with silver poppers down the front from Topshop. Under these clothes would be a Wonderbra – the choice of underwear for any non-self-respecting female teen. The bra was handy as not only did it do weird squishy things to your boobs (I never looked like the photo on the box – that model was looking down at her boobs with such happy delight) but also it had a little pocket each side with a padded cushion to add even more 'wonder', I guess. I'd take the cushion out and use the pocket for storing my cash for the night. At the club I had to do a weird leaning-forward shimmy to get the right change when I got to the bar. In my make-up bag you'd find a black kohl eye pencil (of course), Rimmel Black Cherries lipstick, Maybelline green-and-pink-packaged mascara and the wrong-coloured concealer. It took me years to realise that concealer came in more than one colour. I think I used to run into Boots, hurriedly buy it and scurry out again. I had terrible skin as a teenager and looking back, rather than concealing it I probably just painted all my spots orange. I used no eyebrow pencil as, at the time, I hadn't worked out how flattering it was to do your eyebrows. Instead it was fashionable to tweeze them into a ridiculously thin line, making us all look permanently surprised. I also had some little sequin stars I could glue to my face with eyelash glue.

The memories of those teenage nights of freedom, aka nights that weren't school nights, are still vivid in my mind. I remember counting out my coins to account for: a ten-pack of Marlboro Lights, the tube fare to get to the club, one tonic, which could be topped up with vodka we'd sneaked in, and the night bus fare home. Entry to the club was the most expensive bit – £5 with a flyer but I think sometimes they'd let us in for free. I remember the excitement of anticipation. The possibility the night held . . . the idea in your peripheral vision that maybe, just maybe, something might happen that night that would change your life.

I later found out that Richard had been going to the same club at that time but we never met. I suppose if we had, that would have been one of those 'change your life' nights.

The club itself was an indie club and I think only our teenage selves can get so excited about – addicted to, even – growing the umbilical cord that leads you back to the club you love every week. Popscene meant everything to me. It was just a Britpop club but I felt as if, while I was there, I was starting to grow myself and expand. I guess it's the rush of adolescent hormones . . . I loved the music so much and would request the same songs from the DJ each week. 'Supersonic' by Oasis and 'Connected' by Elastica. I'd then stand at the front of the stage with my mates and dance away . . . I felt like a different person. At school I was quite shy and fairly introverted. I wasn't awkward exactly but I never felt as if I was in with the 'in' crowd. I had a nice little bunch of mates but would sometimes rub up against the most popular girls in the year. I always felt as if the social side of school was a stage I had to get through.

But the club and the music made me feel more . . . three-dimensional. I could slightly reinvent myself there and it made me more confident. Not overnight or anything like that, but it was reassuring to be in a room where the songs that were special to me were special to everyone on the dance floor with me.

One night when I was at Popscene, dancing away on the front of the stage, an older guy in glasses approached me. I couldn't hear what he was saying too well but it seemed to be something about the music newspaper *Melody Maker*. Now, I was an avid reader of *Melody Maker* and the *NME* and I was definitely interested in hearing whatever this guy was going on about. I followed him into the stairway of the club but it was still hard to hear him (looking back he might have been slurring or talking too fast or something) so I ended up going into a sort of supply cupboard with him (I can be incredibly naive and clueless sometimes) whereupon he said his name was Paul Mathur and he was a journalist for *Melody Maker* and might I like to do work experience there? He also had a friend who was looking for a singer for his band and might that be something I was interested in, too? I later found out that Paul and another journalist called Tony had spotted me dancing when they were standing at the bar. Tony bet Paul £5 he couldn't get my number. I gave my number to Paul pretty easily as I really liked the idea of working at *Melody Maker* (at that point I had 'journalist' on my list of things I might do when I left school).

I still have the handwritten note – written in block capitals – from Paul, which he scribbled in biro on a bit of cardboard torn off a light bulb packet in that storeroom.

SEND ME A LONG LETTER WITH 5 SECRETS I'LL TELL YOU 5 AND I'LL TRY AND GET YOU WORK EXPERIENCE (EVEN IF YOU DON'T TELL ME THE FIVE THIS IS A GENUINE RAMBLE NOT JUST BULLSHIT PROMISE. SEND ME A TAPE.)

Then his phone number and address. He told me the friend with the band was running a club night the next night. It was upstairs at the Garage, a music venue in North London.

Looking back I don't know how I was allowed out again the next night at sixteen. It was a Saturday, but still, my mum usually had quite clear ideas about nights out. Well, I must have caught her good side as out I went to that venue armed with a friend and a little demo tape of me singing. A friend from school, Alison (the same friend I had got in massive trouble with when we snuck out to watch the Bluetones on a school night), was going out with a boy, Jamie, whose dad was in the Beatles cover band, the Bootleg Beatles. He had a little four-track recorder, so one day Alison, Jamie and I decided to have a go at recording something. We recorded four Oasis songs . . . Jamie on guitar, me singing and Alison doing handclaps. I can't remember all the songs but I know the B-side 'Talk Tonight' was on there.

As I arrived at the club I mainly felt . . . confused. I walked into the busy room and went straight up to Billy – he was the man who was looking for the singer – but I didn't know that. He was DJing his vinyl behind the decks but to me it looked like the bar. I walked straight over and asked for a gin and tonic. Gin and tonic was the drink of the day for sixteen-year-old Britpop girls like me because Liam Gallagher had used it as a lyric in the song 'Supersonic' ('I'm feeling supersonic, give me gin and tonic'). As I looked over the 'bar' and saw the decks I remember fleeing back into the crowd, embarrassed. Then my friend gave me a panicked look, 'Oh my god, someone just told me this is Uncle Bob's wedding reception . . . have we gatecrashed a wedding?!'

This was mortifying. Here I was, mistaking the DJ for a bartender and crashing a private party. Looking around, though, and maybe asking some folk, we realised no, the club night was called 'Uncle Bob's Wedding Reception'. It wasn't a wedding but the DJ was the guy I needed to give my demo to. I walked back over to Billy and squiggled myself behind the decks to talk to him. As I gave him my tape, the music in the venue ground to a halt. People started booing. The final humiliation of the night – I looked down to see my boobs had pushed up against the record player and had stopped it spinning. I had stopped the music. This was all too much for me. I left Billy the tape and scurried away back into the night.

I think he called me the middle of the next week and soon after I went to his flat in Twickenham, where I met his lovely wife, Helen, and their cat, Polly. Billy already had a pretty fully formed idea of what he wanted for the band and the soundscape we'd inhabit. Essentially, the majority of our first (and only) album was already written. As the first gig approached, Billy contacted musician friends of his to form the band. Most of them were around Billy's age: the keyboardist, Nigel ('Nige'), and the drummer, Patch, were in their thirties. Bassist Kerin was nearer my age at about twenty-one and guitarist Dean was in his late twenties. Billy was the lynchpin who brought us all together. No one knew each other outside of their relationship with Billy before the moment we found ourselves in a band together.

It turned out Billy, who was about thirty when we met, was working at a little label called Fire Records whose biggest claim to fame was releasing the first three Pulp albums before Island released their successful ones. Billy loved Krautrock bands like Neu! and obscure sixties French pop and jangly Britpop . . . he introduced me to a lot but most of it wasn't my bag at that time and I probably told him so. At that time I had very strong ideas of what I liked and didn't like. I guess that's par for the course when you're a teenager. Your likes and dislikes define you and set you apart from your upbringing. It's your way of setting out your stall and finding your people.

Billy was a kind and quirky presence in my life. He made me laugh and I found his observations about the music world interesting and different. Billy was the expert and so I listened to all he had to tell me about his plans for the future of the band. His music taste was different to mine and it was like entering a new world. He'd reference obscure French seventies pop records as if I'd already know them. It was good for me to learn more and expand a bit – even if the majority of the vintage arthouse

German music he introduced me to stayed out of my record collection. Despite the way it all came about, I never once felt that our working relationship was odd, mainly because Billy and Helen understood that it could have been misconstrued and were always keen to put me at ease. I later found out that Billy had, fairly early on, asked permission from my dad for me to be in the band. They lived nearby and so Billy popped over to chat to my pa and reassure him about the ideas he had for developing the band. I'm glad he did – it probably eased the path when I finished school and went on the road instead of going to university as my dad had previously hoped. I think both my parents could see that I was enthused, focused and ready to have this adventure with the band. Record deals straight out of school don't happen every day and they probably felt excited to see where it would lead.

*

Billy had written a ton of songs but we didn't have a name at that point. We floated a few ideas before we decided on theaudience. I don't know whose idea it was that the band's name be written like that, but it wasn't mine. I could see it was quite annoying, but that almost seemed to be the point. I did like the fact that theaudience played a bit with the idea of fame and why we should be up on a stage when we had solidarity with our audience. Or something.

I met Dean, Kerin and Patch at the same time. Kerin was a great songwriter. He only wrote one song for the album but it was gorgeous and I know he'd written more that didn't get used. Dean wrote some good songs too. Drummer Patch was around Billy's age and he was the most experienced musician as he'd been in the band the Sundays (if you're not familiar, their album *Reading, Writing and Arithmetic* is beautiful). They were all lovely guys and I would call them all friends even though I haven't seen them for years. I'd also apologise to Dean for the teasing he got in the band. Dean was a gentle soul but also sometimes pretty gullible.

When we toured the UK we told him he needed a passport to cross into Scotland. He believed us to the extent that he hid in the back of the bus not just on our way to the gig, but back over the border into England on the way home.

We had a lot of fun and I was learning so much every day with them all. Not just the process of rehearsing, refining and recording the songs, but also how to work in a band dynamic. When I met Nige – the sweetest guy and a brilliant artist as well as keyboardist – I was my usual outspoken self. I didn't get the synth keyboard sound then . . . for me the eighties was not a cool reference (although now my back catalogue would show how my allegiance has changed), and so in his first rehearsal I kept saying I thought the keyboard sound was 'naff'. Billy took me to one side and said, 'Look, this is my mate and I've asked him along so he can help our sound. You can't keep saying what you're hearing is naff. It's rude.' He was right, of course.

Initially we didn't do any gigs. Billy's plan was this: we would record three demo tapes, each with six songs. We would release them strategically and send them to various labels. Once everyone was interested in the band, we would do our gigs. I think Billy perhaps even thought we should do the tapes and no gigs and get a deal that way, but no one would have signed us without hearing us live so I might have made that up.

All this was happening in the autumn of 1995. I was going out a lot and was hungry to meet people. I had a kind of fizz in my tummy about getting out of school life and finding the wider world. At school I'd thought about being an actor or a writer – maybe a lawyer as I loved to argue my point – but nothing had stuck. When I was asked to join the band I had only said yes as I thought it was something I was supposed to do, a rite of passage. I remember thinking, 'It'll be a good story to tell my grandkids'.

The year I turned seventeen I have pretty well documented. I have never really kept a diary, but in January of 1996 I had two calendar diaries in which I scribbled all my plans. It's fairly exhaustive reading and I won't bore you with the majority of it except to say I had a dentist appointment on March 26th and I think my friend Sarah still owes me £6.75.

It's also very revealing. I can see my obsessions – boys, music and getting out the house. Probably pretty typical stuff, but I was clearly set on being part of a scene. Whenever money would allow, I'd go to gigs and whenever I could I'd go to places where I might meet someone . . . journalists, folk in bands, the movers and shakers and hangers-on. It was addictive. Suddenly I was being written about in the gossip columns of *Melody Maker* and even though it was pretty small fry, I felt seen and a bit special. At school and at the parties I'd gone to, I'd felt invisible. Not cool enough or slim enough or pretty enough, but when I was hanging out in the music scene with older exciting people, I felt as if there was another life for me. I think I was wowed by anything and everything touched by that scene. I once went to a club night and a band called Northern Uproar was there. I wasn't a fan, but when one of them accidentally burnt my arm with his cigarette it was OK because, hey, it was a burn from someone in a band. I knew the names of all the labels, the producers, the recording studios, the journalists . . . they were all rock stars to me. I often felt intimidated and naive but it was intoxicating to become part of that world. I started 1996 pretty innocent and green and by the end of the year I had more of a handle on things . . . or so I thought. On the inside I was still pretty insecure but the momentum from the band distracted me from that a bit. I started to hang out with a different group from school and it was liberating. Even though I didn't form any hard-and-fast life-long friendships with that new group, it felt good to be seen through fresh eyes. I was still prone to embarrassing myself, though. One particularly memorable humiliation was when there was a journalist who used to like to wear headdresses and things stuck onto his bald head. I always got the impression he didn't like me very much. One night he wasn't there and I said to someone over loud music, 'How is (insert name of guy) and his headpiece?' Next time I saw him he hauled me into the club corridor to tell me off: 'What's all this about you asking how I am and my herpes?' I don't think he believed me that I'd been misheard. Mortifying, again.

Anyway, back to theaudience and our ascent through the A&R world to the heady heights of being offered a deal. After three demo tapes had been sent out, we were under pressure to do a gig. In the autumn term of the last year of school, on a Tuesday night in October, we played our first ever show at an eternally glamorous art centre in Staines. I was a bit grumpy about the location. Even before Wikipedia was a twinkle in anyone's eye I knew I didn't want my first gig to be in Staines. But there we were on a rainy school night. My family all came, my little sister Martha aged six wearing her fave dungarees and my dad with his video camera. We started the gig and I was super nervous but we got through the first couple of songs. I had already begun my awkward onstage ramblings of telling bad 'knock-knock' jokes every time there was a stall in the proceedings. By about our fourth or fifth song, another embarrassing turn of events: just as we got to the chorus there was a loud beeping sound – a fire alarm going off throughout the arts centre. At first we kept going, then it became apparent we were going to have to leave, so I found myself getting off the stage and leaving through the fire exit with the audience. Theaudience and the audience, out in the rain, together. Not at all humiliating.

*

Whilst I loved indie and Britpop in the nineties, the 'ordinary' aesthetic of it didn't appeal too much. I wasn't scared of looking a little different from the pack. I learnt to celebrate what did suit me because I had to come to terms with all the things that didn't. Tanned skin and blonde hair – so perennially popular – definitely didn't suit me so I had to look elsewhere for inspiration. That was why, when I became a solo artist in 2001, I was keen to carve out my own look and drew inspiration from the leading ladies of 1950s and 1960s musicals, which wasn't original but it was different from the denim-clad blonde female pop star look of the time. I felt happier doing my own thing in a vintage dress rather than trying to look like Britney. I never could have anyway.

For that first performance with theaudience I wore a satin slip skirt (it was all the rage to wear underwear as outerwear back then) and wow, let me tell you, that stuff really catches the light. A couple of days later my dad played me the footage of the pre-fire drill bit of the gig. I took one look at my fat face, fat body, unflattering satin skirt, and after hearing my awful voice, I burst into tears and ran out of the room. My poor dad didn't get it but I couldn't stand what I was seeing. Watching the footage of the gig back, all I could see was how the skirt made my tummy – the bit I was most self-conscious about – look as if it was glowing and round. I was horrified. How could I fail at this first hurdle? Stage wear is supposed to make you feel Teflon-coated, not draw attention to the bits that you feel insecure about. At school it felt as if all my friends had flat stomachs and everyone knew the waist circumference of every model in the magazines (the goal was 25″ or, for a gold star, be like Kate Moss – 23″). Remember, these were the days of the fashion movement's 'heroin chic'. My squidgy body simply didn't fit in. Seeing my perceived flaws up there on the stage made me feel vulnerable and I think after that I was a lot more careful with what I chose to wear. Even now I hardly ever watch anything I do afterwards. It's invariably better left in your head as a memory. I've noticed how, on a night out you can leave the house feeling as if you look awesome then catch your reflection in the bar mirror or whatever and suddenly – oh my god I look knackered! From then on you can just feel so flat . . . so now I don't really look at myself. Once in the morning and then on I go. I'd rather build a positive image in my head and not dismantle it later with my eyes.

After the gig at the arts centre, amazingly, we got an offer from a record label. I still applied to university (to study English and drama), but by Christmas it was looking more likely that I was going on tour rather than going to a halls of residence.

Over the next few months, up until my eighteenth birthday in April 1997, theaudience played six gigs and received six record deals. It was pretty extraordinary. Billy seemed to have such a clear plan in his head. He used all his contacts and all his experience in music to give our band the best chance and it seemed to work. Our band ended up with a lot of hype around it. Billy was slightly conflicted at times . . . he'd spent a long time feeling excluded from the more successful parts of the scene. The charts and the record deals and that heady flush of being the one folk wanted to talk to, it had all eluded him up to now. Suddenly, with the band, he was right in the epicentre. The deals we were offered seemed ridiculous, plus publishing deals too. So many six-figure numbers being thrust at us.

I don't remember what I thought about any of that but I do remember feeling excited that another life was unfolding for me. All my friends were going off to university but as soon as I'd started singing on stage I knew I'd found the thing I wanted to do. It was as if all the different strands of what I'd loved were combining. I'd always enjoyed drama, and now the lyrics I was singing gave me the best script. I'd always wanted to perform, and this gave me a way to do it on my own terms and in a more introverted way than an all-singing, all-dancing kind of performer. I'd always loved music and singing along to stuff, but the idea of singing for a living, well, it just hadn't occurred to me. Now I could combine it all and suddenly I couldn't really think of a plan B. As luck would have it, my first band swept me up and away.

As my eighteenth birthday was approaching, Billy decided we should wait to announce who we would sign to. If we signed before that, then my folks would have to be co-signatories, but if I was eighteen, I could do it alone. We used this as an excuse to buy time to play the labels off against each other and for me to be wined and dined a little and to be given sackfuls of free CDs. I took them gladly. My little music collection quadrupled overnight. It felt great.

I was not really aware of the discussions going on with each label and with the publishers. We did have a lawyer who probably did try and explain it all to me but I tend to zone out a little bit when the paperwork is happening, so I didn't really pay attention to the fact that the publishing deal (the deal you sign solely for the songwriting royalties) was being signed by Billy and me, even though only Billy had done any of the writing.

We had a gig and a birthday party for my eighteenth at a little venue in Central London called the Borderline. The gig was on the 9 April 1997 and I turned eighteen at midnight (i.e., on the 10th. This is an important fact as I am the sort of person who tells everyone when it's their birthday. I firmly believe the world is split into people who tell everyone when it's their birthday and people who don't tell anyone. I am the former. You won't be out with me, ever, and accidentally find out it was my birthday the day before, or the next day. I will tell you. Of this you can be sure.) So, at midnight we announced we had decided to go with Mercury Records. Mercury is part of Universal and is a big label. The A&R man, Alan Pell, had come along to the club night with a load of presents for my birthday. One was a large pink plastic piggy bank. He must have panic-bought.

The deal itself was finalised in May. I was one month away from my A levels and so the deal was signed on a Friday as I had a half day from school that day. I took two school friends along with me. I still have a Polaroid picture of that moment. As Billy signed, there were the usual jokes about Faustian pacts and signing away your soul. I guess there's an element of truth there and some of that chat was a little close to the bone. Only a year and a half later, Billy would leave the band. But you do have to make peace with the fact that signing a deal is going to mean some difficult choices and decisions made by committee. There are two elements at the heart of any music career when you sign a deal, and art and commerce make for uneasy bedfellows. The musicians (the art) often want to run free and trust in instinct, but for the label (the commerce), there are spreadsheets and facts and data and everyone at the label is looking for the big sales. Once you accept these two things are always a bit jarring, it makes it easier I think.

While the ink was drying, the label (based in Hammersmith – conveniently about ten minutes' walk from my mum's house and my school) took me and my mates Helen and Becca to the very gorgeous and fancy restaurant the River Café, where I'm pretty sure I had lobster. It was a Friday but we had a free afternoon from school. Afterwards I remember walking back along the Thames with my two girlfriends and a bottle of champagne before we got in a taxi home. On the radio, 'MMMBop' by Hanson was playing. We all sang along and I found it extra intoxicating as Hanson were signed to Mercury too. We were a bit tipsy but all happy and excited. I'm glad I got to do that with friends. I'll always try to involve my mates at any juncture. It keeps it fun and fresh and reminds me how lucky I am to do what I do. For a little while, when I first started singing in Russia, it would be the fashion to book me with a band who would mime while I sang live. It's tricky to mime guitar but no one can see what the keyboard-ist's fingers are up to, and so a whole host of my non-keyboard-playing girlfriends would come on jolly little trips with me to Moscow to mime the keys. They got free vodka and I got a friend to have fun with. It was a good set-up.

After signing the deal, it was back to school and A levels. I had to focus a little. A very little. But still, I was at an academic school and for the whole time I'd been there, the end goal was to do OK in your final exams. I had done what I was supposed to do. The exams came and went. I deferred my place at university and it was time to get the album done. I was eighteen and felt liberated to have finished school. I'd felt so out of place there for so long, as if there was so much of me that the school didn't see. Maybe everybody finishes school feeling that way.

The album was pretty much written when we signed so it was time to get it recorded. We went to RAK Studios in North London. It's a gorgeous studio that was founded in the seventies by the producer Mickie Most. He was still alive when we went to record and one day he popped his head into the studio to say hello. My dad was there that day and he and Mickie exchanged notes on how both of their daughters had done in their A levels. I'm sure as they chatted I looked on with an expression of 'Good conversation topic, Pa!'

Being in the studio introduced me not only to the feel of singing and recording in a place steeped in history, it also introduced me to a thing known as 'demo-itis', which is basically when you have grown so used to the way the demo of a song feels that it's hard to update and improve it. While I tried hard to emulate the feel of the original vocals and improve them, most of the songs on theaudience album ended up using the original vocals I'd put down. The first single was 'I Got the Wherewithal' which had vocals I'd sung when I was sixteen. It was a classic example of the band's more experimental side and Billy's love of angular indie. I don't think I've sung the word 'unctuous' in another song since. I actually always loved 'Wherewithal'. It's dramatic and brooding and was fun to perform live as it builds into a real crescendo. I used to find the high notes at the end a bit tricky on tour though . . . I was always staying up too late and then those notes would go missing. It's a weird thing when you lose that register and a weird 'nothing' sound comes out . . . I always called them 'glass notes' as it sounded a bit like running your finger along glass to me.

The video for 'Wherewithal' was shot by my dad, who is a director. As a massive music fan he was really enthusiastic about making the video just right. It was low-budget, but stylish. We filmed it in an empty school and it's essentially close-ups of my face interspersed with shots of the band playing. I think I do a fairly good job of not letting on that I kept forgetting what 'unctuous' meant. In a few shots you can see the guitar that Billy had had made for me – a Fender copy painted baby pink with a

Dalmatian-print fretboard. I'd had guitar lessons as a teenager from a slightly pervy teacher who would occasionally smack my thigh and call me cheeky if I got something wrong. I had to learn 'Blowing in the Wind' – I don't think he was very interested in teaching me Oasis. I certainly didn't learn enough to be great at guitar. At one gig, I played my guitar part in completely the wrong key. Afterwards our guitarist Dean was complaining about bad sound during that song, so after that I kept my volume turned off and just went for it. I didn't bother looking to see if my fingers were near the right dots.

For the video I wore a Biba shirt I'd bought on a shopping trip with a stylist which the record company had organised, with £500 to spend. This was heaven. The stylist who went with me was called Polly and was the girlfriend of Tony, the journalist who had bet Paul Mathur he couldn't get my number. Together Polly and I bought some cool bits and bobs and I was over the moon to have an all-expenses-paid shopping trip. For the video I wore the Biba shirt with a rubber skirt I'd bought for £3 in Covent Garden market.

Now the record company wanted all the artwork for the album. At that point I hadn't spent tons of time in the record company building but I can say that I found it ... underwhelming. No, more than that, I found it disappointing. I'd always imagined record companies as such exciting, finger-on-the-pulse places, but instead they were rather dry. The creative side of things was so disappointing to me as a teenage music fan – the album cover was some not-very-good shots of the band on a white background. It looked like amateur Photoshop to me. As someone who saved up pocket money to buy music from the bands and artists I loved, I knew how fans loved to pore over every single detail. I knew they would want extra angles and gems to reveal themselves long after purchase day. Favourite album covers become classic album covers. It's often the first thing you look at when you're getting to know an artist. It informs you about them and the context of the work. The album art for theaudience ended up better than the first images I saw, but I still felt it didn't convey much personality.

In the end they used a still from my dad's 'Wherewithal' video for the cover and on the back is a photo of me taken not long after I'd had one of the worst haircuts of my life. A £5 short haircut from Mr Toppers on Camden High Street. Forever immortalised. It was even made into a life-size cardboard cut-out. Joy.

'I Got the Wherewithal' was released as a limited edition single, intended to spark interest in theaudience before we got going with the more mainstream stuff. It was so exciting to release a song. It came out in October, four months after I left school, and I was a bit blown away that I was a real signed musician in a band. The single's B-side was 'Je Suis Content', which Billy had me singing in French. He was introducing me to lots of music I'd never heard of before and I liked that Billy had such a strong vision for the band's sound while I was just working out what kind of frontwoman I wanted to be. I had lots of inspiration . . . women like Shirley Manson from Garbage who I'd seen live and who was unapologetic and a bit fierce. I'd also seen PJ Harvey at a festival the band did in France. Off stage we said hello and she was smiley and sweet and shy, but on stage she became this confident and sexy singer in her fuchsia-pink catsuit. I also loved Bjork who was musically exciting and unpredictable. These were women who seemed to own themselves on stage and I took a lot of heart from their confidence.

What a fun thing at that stage in my life to be thinking about an onstage persona. I was pretty shy and insecure but I loved feeling transformed when I went on stage. I've changed a lot over the years in that I'm a lot more relaxed now – the me on stage is more like the me off stage now – but I've always felt powerful performing to a room full of people. I remember when I thought I wanted to act and my mum talked about that feeling of power when she was on stage. I realised later that made complete sense to me but with music, not drama. That's not to say I find it easy and I certainly respect my crowd and want to earn the right to their attention, but there's a big part of me that feels a little bit of a headmistress up there and I don't fear being disliked at the beginning. It's my job to win you over.

*

I remember getting my first instalment of money from the record deal. I went from small amounts of pocket money and cash from Saturday jobs and babysitting to having four figures in my bank account. I was actually a bit freaked out. For weeks, I couldn't spend any money. Well, I think it was weeks, but knowing me, it was days. I do know that I spent the first £70 of it on two skirts from Marks and Spencer and it felt like a Big Deal . . . but then I was away, shopping happily for vintage clothes and meals out. What a privilege to have that choice. I love Madonna's quote that money doesn't buy happiness but at least you can afford to rent it for the evening. It's true.

The first time I heard myself on radio I was at my dad's house, staying over for the night. I was in my old room and XFM was on the radio. They played 'Wherewithal' and it was pretty electrifying. There's nothing quite like hearing one of your songs on the radio. It's magical to me. Even now, there are so many songs to play and I know how lucky I am if one of mine is chosen. I don't think that feeling will ever get old.

We also had our first photo shoot. It was with Rankin, still a big mover and shaker in that world, and I still cross paths with him. I also used to see Lauren Laverne at club nights. Her band, Kenickie, was part of the same scene and they were also releasing albums. I always liked Lauren – she was smart and funny and I had a feeling she was going to be around for the long haul. I also had one of my first ever interviews with Caitlin Moran when I was about seventeen and she was nineteen. She was another person I immediately warmed to. Smart women are the best.

With the first 'soft release' out the way, we moved on to releasing 'If You Can't Do It When You're Young'. Again my dad made the video but this time my little sister Martha, who was then aged seven, played a mini me as we performed the song surrounded by oversized props from the film *The Borrowers*, which had just been made. The B-side to the single was a cover of 'There are Worse Things I Could Do' from *Grease*. Billy called it 'the slapper's lament' but I think Rizzo was just a misunderstood girl who liked sex and what's wrong with that?

The first single charted at 170, but this one went to 48. It was all going fairly according to plan from what I understood. It was 'A Pessimist is Never Disappointed', the third single, which was intended to be our first 'proper' release. By now we'd spent a lot of our time since signing on tour. Not long after we'd finished the album and released 'Wherewithal', we'd been sent out on the *NME* Brat Bus Tour in January 1998. We were the first on of four bands with the Stereophonics headlining. As first support, we'd often perform our set to an empty venue where the people running the merchandise stall were still stapling T-shirts to the back wall. I think I was pretty relieved. I was still working out what kind of frontwoman I wanted to be and I'd poke fun at the whole idea by signing any autographs with 'charismatic frontwoman' after my name. The other bands on the tour were the Warm Jets and Asian Dub Foundation. Everyone was very nice from what I remember, but I still found it a little intimidating. Firstly, of all the musicians on the tour, I was the only female. This was especially significant as I'd gone to an all-girls secondary school and so I simply hadn't hung out with that many boys or men at that point. I always felt envious of girls who had brothers or lots of male friends as I felt as if my awkwardness was a failing.

Also, the other bands were a lot more experienced than us, so singing to empty venues was a good way to relax me. The whole idea of being on an *NME* tour was a big deal, and this meant my nerves massively reduced. An empty venue is not a hard crowd to win over. Plus I was still struggling a bit with how to talk to the crowd (if there was one . . .), so on the whole, I didn't. It's a sign of how far I've come that now I rarely shut up when I'm on stage. Well, I say how far I've come, but I mean how much I've changed. It's not for me to say one is better than the other and I know which version my kids would vote for.

The year unfolded with more tours (we supported James and Monaco) and the singles 'Pessimist' and 'I Know Enough'. The plan from the label was to release four singles and then the album in the autumn. 'Pessimist' charted at 27. We had our biggest TV appearance with that single when we performed it on Chris Evans' Friday-night show *TFI Friday*. My excitement was dampened by the fact I had awful tonsillitis on the day. It was live and all day leading up to the show I was lying on the sofa at the TV studios with a fever of well over 100. The TV nurse told me I shouldn't really be there, but it was too big a deal to miss. I sang with my shoulders hunched, leaning into the microphone with my eyes closed. Maybe it made me look kind of intense, I don't know, but I got through it. The guys at the record company seemed pleased with us so far. The band wasn't a runaway success, but things were moving in the right direction. As we moved into the summer months and our first few festivals, it was hoped our next single would be the hit we needed.

It felt amazing to be singing at the festivals I'd only been to before as part of the crowd. My first Glastonbury rolled into view and with it the obligatory introduction to a field full of mud. I was dressed wrongly and can still recall the way it felt when the muddy water gushed into my train-ers as I stood ordering noodles from a food truck. The gig was really fun though. I wore sparkly silver peep-toe stilettos and my tour manager had to carry me from the dressing room to the stage so they wouldn't get muddy. As it happened, I didn't play Glastonbury again until 2014 after my folky album *Wanderlust* came out, which prompted me to wonder aloud on stage if I was one of the few performers to have played Glastonbury in two different but non-consecutive decades.

As the months rolled on, so too came the Phoenix Festival and the Reading Festival and I was probably too nicely distracted to take much notice of the disappointment from Mercury when our first single, 'I Know Enough', only charted at 25. It hadn't done much better than 'Pessimist' and this was the single which should have launched the album well. I was also probably distracted by that awful hairdo as well as the weight I'd gained on tour. The world of eating at motorway services and enjoying Ginsters pasties on the road was a total revelation and made me the largest I've ever been in my life. I caught sight of my reflection in a hotel room one night and was shocked. I vowed to get back to my usual size, but as the band disbanded over the next eighteen months I took it too far the other way, becoming overly controlling of what I ate as everything around me started to go wrong.

Tensions were forming within the band. Billy was a talented songwriter but he had put the band together and he wanted full control. He was starting to find it difficult that the band was made up of individuals who all wanted different things. To me, it felt as if he thought he could move us like pawns. I remember thinking, after one conversation where he was telling me what he wanted to happen next and how he was going to make it happen, 'Maybe I am stupid and he's smarter than me, but even a stupid person knows to take offence when they are called that name.' That's how I felt – as if I was being talked down to and muted.

Looking back, it must have been hard for Billy to know how to deal with these new fractures in the band and everyone's ideas of what to do next. Billy had written the songs and had drafted us all in thinking it would be OK for him to continue to steer the ship. But band relationships are like any relationships – they take patience and time and respect and ultimately sometimes it just doesn't work out for the long term.

By the time we got to the summer of 1998 – only one year into our record contract and a month before we were releasing our album – Billy took some time out. The rest of the band continued to promote and tour but without Billy. We had a slightly traumatic Reading Festival performance: we'd been drafted in at the last minute to go onstage in the slot billed as belonging to the alternative rock duo Curve. As we took to the stage in front of a baffled crowd who had been waiting for another band, things started to get a bit tetchy. I addressed the crowd, 'Look, we're not Curve so you can either stay and watch theaudience or you leave and grumble outside.' The packed tent emptied a bit but we were left with a decent crowd and from what I remember it was quite a good gig.

But things were starting to break down further than we could repair. When the album came out in August, it charted at 22. This was not what was supposed to happen. We got a scathing 4/10 in the *NME* and the other reviews were patchy. I didn't write the record so I can be objective here and say I think the album is good. But I think it counted against us that the songs were intellectual and wordy, which probably rubbed some folks up the wrong way, and we were so hyped that the relative lack of chart success made our demise more of a likelihood. It's hard to come back from that.

Meanwhile, Billy was gone and having a difficult time. I think he was finding it all quite a strain. He told me one time that he'd seen the devil and he had the face of our A&R man, Alan. There was also the rumour that he once went to our publishers armed with an axe demanding payment. I don't know if it's true but I did notice there was a big chunk out of the skirting in their office when I next visited.

Billy had shown me so much and it had been a crazy ride with the band, but I was unhappy being in a group with him. I felt he spoke down to me and it could be nasty. We've since made amends and I'm fond of BIlly, but things were not great between us at the time. The audience embarked on what was to be our last ever tour and Billy was not due to come with us. He called me from London in the morning while I was in the hotel in Glasgow getting ready for the first gig that night. He wished me well on the tour.

Then, at our soundcheck, he walked into the venue. He must have hotfooted it to the airport straight after we spoke. He begged me to let him back in the band but I was done. When someone hurts me, I have to let the barriers come down. I'll take it as far as I can, but once a line is crossed, that's it. I felt absolutely terrible having that conversation. I don't run on drama and hate conflict, but enough was enough.

The band stumbled on through the unremarkable tour. After that the label wanted us to start work on the next album. There were clashes within the band about our next direction . . . everyone had their own idea of what it should be. We were all writing songs – some collaboratively, some alone – and it was a bit of a mess. Not all the songs were bad, but none of them had the feel of our first sound. In typical major label fashion, thousands of pounds were spent during 1999 on studio time with different producers to try and get the album on track. We worked with Stephen Street who had done the Blur album (I was super excited about this as a big Blur fan) and then another producer who was a big name at the time. This second guy was a talented producer but had a different vibe to me as he'd done a lot of hallucinogenic drugs and I hadn't. He was so relaxed that occasionally I'd turn up to the studio just as he was leaving. 'Ah hello, Sophie! I'm just off to Portobello Market with the family! See you later!'

By the end of the year, we'd been dropped. The label let us go and I felt . . . relief. It had been so painful to try and get a new album together with no clear vision. What I didn't realise was that the band was no more. I thought the audience would regroup and start again, but no. In an interview I did that year with the *NME*, the journalist said I should ditch guitar pop and head for stardom in the pop world. I could see he was saying it with kindness but I felt misunderstood. I was an indie singer without a band, maybe, but still an indie singer.

Even seeing that article in black and white didn't wake me up to the reality of being high and dry with no band and no prospects. I had a lunch with my publisher James who said, 'No one cares about theaudience. It's old news, done. Go off and have a gap year. Go travelling. Do anything else. It's over.'

He was right, it was over, but I didn't have a plan B. It was music or nothing. I felt sure the highlight of my career was behind me. I was done and dusted before I'd even turned twenty-one.

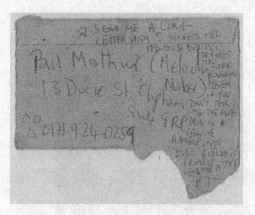

This is the bit of cardboard (an old light bulb packet) that was given to me by Paul Mathur from Melody Maker. It changed everything. I never did tell him any secrets.

4

MUSIC: Sexism in the Workplace – 'Crying at The Discotheque'

Just 18 and feeling Yo! (on my t-shirt) but not sure where to go after that . . .

In the late nineties, when I was in my late teens, there was a new cowgirl in town. She called herself a 'ladette'. She drank pints and had one-night stands, she could talk the talk and walk the walk, she wore a Wonderbra and could banter with the boys. She was who I was supposed to be.

My first introduction to how to be a grown woman, nineties style, had been through the pages of *More!* magazine. I bought a load of old magazines from a car boot sale and I used to hide them inside the pages of my old *Smash Hits* when I was about thirteen or fourteen. *Smash Hits* had been my previous source of education, with the pull-out lyric sheets in the middle of the magazine. It was essential reading. How else was I going to learn the words to 'Americans' by Holly Johnson? Plus *Smash Hits* was witty and pop-obsessed; I read it cover to cover. Now, though, my new teacher was *More!* magazine. So familiar were the pages that, when my mum told me we were getting new neighbours and one was called Collette, I immediately thought of a model called Collette who was regularly used in photo stories in *More!* It actually turned out to be the same Collette who moved next door.

More! was released every two weeks and they had a section called 'Position of the Fortnight'. Now, obviously the editor of *More!* was not imagining fourteen-year-old me reading it, but I was young and impressionable and thought I needed to be able to recall and act out any of the positions they showed in those pages. I also read about one-night stands and blow jobs and how to be sexually confident. Except I missed a bit – that it only counted as true sexual confidence if it was what you wanted, not if you could do it all 'well'.

At the beginning of the nineties, the Wonderbra advert's slogan was, 'Say Goodbye to your Feet'. By the middle of the decade it was not a model looking down at her aggressive cleavage, but out towards an unseen viewer. Now, the slogan was 'Hello Boys'. Being sexy was about attracting men, not looking a certain way for yourself. This era saw the emergence of TV shows like *The Girlie Show*, which was on late on a Friday night in what is known as the post-pub slot. It was hosted by ballsy women and it was intentionally controversial and chaotic. I hated it but obviously watched it. Not just because there were only five channels, but because it was one of the only places I could hear women talking about sex. I was sixteen when it was on and I was fascinated. Is this what I was supposed to be like in a few years' time? Binge-drinking, calling out wankers, sexually dominant and entirely cynical about romantic commitment? And so many women in the public eye at the time seemed so good at being like that. Of course they might have been riddled with insecurity, but they seemed so comfortable and unflinching when they spoke about shagging and boozing and doing it all over again the next night.

Not long after this, I found myself being interviewed in the music press. It was the era of the (mainly) straight white male journalist baiting the young female singers. You were supposed to be able to take it. If women wanted to match the lads drink for drink then they had to take the chat and that involved being asked inappropriate questions, which you had to answer without stumbling over your answer, or you lost the game.

The thing is, I understand where the ladette culture came from. Women wanted to be able to be free to do whatever they wanted and that included acting like 'a bit of a lad' too. If women wanted to sleep with whoever without judgement then she should be able to do it. A woman should be able to drink as much as she wants without judgement too. Men can sleep around and it's all high fives; women do the same and they are a slut. This was not a new chain to break and I'm not sure the ladette movement truly broke it, but I understand the impetus.

As a teenager, though, I hated it. I thought it was reductive and frustrating. It looked like women wanted equality, but they wanted to be equal to the worst kind of guy: someone who was selfish and acted without caring too much about how he was functioning or who he was hurting. I didn't want to be a ladette. It looked like wonky feminism to me.

Still, I did believe that to be a successful young woman you should be able to have casual sex and match male company drink for drink, as that's what you did in 1998. This was the bawdy world I entered when I started talking to journalists and going on telly in the late nineties. It was intimidating and I felt way out of my league.

I'd not spent much time in male company. I'd had no real boyfriends growing up and was jealous of girls who found it easy to hang out in male company. And, as I've said, at eleven, I went to an all-girls school. This meant two things – I was not distracted by boys (good thing) but it also meant that boys were suddenly BOYS, i.e. very exciting and strange other beings who I did not know how to act around. Every time we went to the boys' school for any reason (I always signed up for musicals because you did that with the boys' school and this was Very Exciting), I would bite my lips and rub my cheeks to make them both rosy. I'm sure it worked a treat and I looked very alluring, not at all wind-chapped and sore. One thing is for sure – I was never anything like casual. Around the opposite sex I felt awkward and ill at ease and this simply wouldn't do when it came to being interviewed by music journalists. The music journos were tough and their pens were tougher. You had to keep up.

My first interviews teased me with questions about how I'd react to coming home and finding my boyfriend in bed with another man, my sexual preferences and comments about my boobs . . . I was eighteen. It was daunting but I also learnt to sink or swim so I got on with it. I watched back the episode of *Never Mind the Buzzcocks* where I was teased about *Blue Peter*. Now, I never had a problem with *BP* being part of my life but of course the teasing wasn't affectionate. It was meant to humiliate and undermine me. 'You're not cool, you're just your mother's daughter.' It was intended to make me look daft. On the programme I'm ridiculed by my own team captain and the host over and over. After the recording, they were all nice to me, but that wasn't the point. The main thing was – take the abuse. If you want to run with the big boys, better keep up, little girl.

Watching the recent Britney Spears documentary brought the mood of that era back to me. Of course, she experienced that culture in the extreme, but young women in the public eye were fair game. If your look or figure wasn't what was expected of you, you were taken to task. Young women were given the hardest ride. Particularly in pop music. You weren't edgy or cool so you could be pulled apart at any time and if you couldn't hack it then you should move on. Casual misogyny was commonplace.

The other day I was clearing out a cupboard at home and I stumbled across some old newspaper clippings from interviews I'd done when I was in theaudience. I was shocked how sexualised some of the questions were. In amongst the 'Where do you see your band in five years?' (to which the only answer a fresh new band can give is 'world domination'), there were questions like 'What's your favourite position?' and 'Would you be willing to give up sex if you could have sensual and erotic dreams every night?' I know I was an adult, but I was still a teenager. This was in print and the journalists were older than me and all of them were men.

This was accompanied by many articles that detailed and debated my looks. Is she young? Old? Ugly? Beautiful? This was shocking to me. I didn't want to know the conclusion. I'd never wanted to put it out there for debate. I felt weird-looking and awkward. I didn't know it then, but this would become part of the conversation when it came to critiquing the band I was in.

At the time, my parents were looking out for me as I entered the public eye, but the sexism was so rife I don't think it occurred to any of us to call it out. So many things have changed since then. Some subtle things like questions I was asked or ways I was addressed on TV programmes just wouldn't happen now . . . but some of the stuff is actually no longer legal. On one occasion I was doing a day of promotion for my second album and as I left the house I realised my dress had an ugly VPL. It was pretty out of character for me (I'm a 'big knickers' type of gal), but at the last minute I whipped my pants off so that the dress looked better. One journalist from Norway took photos as we chatted, and it was only when those photos were printed in the newspaper he worked for that I could see what he saw – a photo taken straight up my skirt. Way to go, smarmy man. The trouble is, I just felt like an idiot for not realising I was sitting badly in my outfit rather than thinking that he was a pervy guy for taking the photo and publishing it. You live and learn. He's since apologised for it, but it made me wary and a little defensive.

Another time, when I presented an award at the Brit Awards, I felt ridiculous and humiliated when the host said to me, 'Why the wide face?' It's already quite intimidating putting yourself on the red carpet but with the Brits it's so ramped up as you're getting ready to be photographed and scrutinised. Of course, the male presenter wouldn't know I used to hate the way I looked, but I hope that's something we wouldn't experience now. Thankfully, things are changing. I think this unconscious (and conscious) bullying of young women in the public eye has calmed down and I don't really hold anyone personally responsible (except maybe the upskirt photographer/journalist).

The sad thing is, a lot of it made me question myself and think that being able to make someone else happy and satisfied was more important than my own happiness. I wish I could go back and talk to my younger self about that. It's been my goal as a grown-up to be unapologetic. Kind, considerate, but clear with my boundaries. I hope women entering the music industry now feel they have more agency when it comes to outlining their own boundaries and I know I have many women before me to thank for giving me better freedoms too.

Keeping my wits about me in 1997.

5

MEN: The Trickiest Bit to Write – 'Catch You'

16 or 17 here . . . totally unprepared was I, to face a world of men.

I wasn't sure whether I was going to include this in the book, but then this is my little platform to write about whatever I want and the things that have shaped me. This is one of those dark and murky events in my life which I haven't told many people about, but I owe it myself to put it out there, so here goes.

I said to Richard, 'I'm lucky; I've experienced this traumatic thing and I'm OK.'

'I don't think you are OK.'

He's right.

Not in the sense that I feel broken, but I definitely bear the scars from what happened to me when it came to my first experiences with men and sex. And it would take a while to find out what I wanted rather than what I thought was expected of me. The first few experiences I had made me feel as if I was playing catch-up, partly because I felt my first experiences came later than those of my friends, but also because I believed those girls at school who talked about their exciting and adventurous sex lives. I thought if I wasn't doing it too, then I was uptight and the world was going to leave me behind. I could see from the magazines I read and the telly I watched that to be a sorted young woman you had to be amazing in bed, have a twenty-four-inch waist, drink pints and have one-night stands.

I've asked myself why it's important to write about these experiences here, within the pages of my book. Why go over something that wasn't very pleasant? Why make it public? But I think if you experience something you know is wrong then being brave and honest about it helps, and if anyone else has been through something similar it might help us all talk about it . . . who knows?

But that's not all. It's also because I was silent about it for so long. For some, being silent makes sense, but for me it started to feel like being complicit. I wasn't heard when I was seventeen but I think I'll be heard now. If I'm honest, I don't think even I listened to my own feelings all that well back then. I was probably too busy worrying what people thought of me.

When I was a teenager I was conflicted when it came to my relationship with sex. I knew I fancied boys, but I seemed far behind my friends. At fifteen, I felt inexperienced and prudish, while they all seemed to be getting off with boys every weekend and quite a few had lost their virginity. Meanwhile, I couldn't even get a boy to notice me. I remember one night being round at a friend's house and they put on a DVD with a live Take That concert. In one bit (and now I come to think of it, this is a really weird thing to include in the footage if it's true), it looked as if one of the members of Take That had got a bit 'excited' on stage, shall we say. My friends kept rewinding this shot and laughing about it. I was quiet at the back of the room and one girl turned to me and very loudly said, 'Oh, I know you won't like seeing this bit, you're into celibacy, aren't you?' I felt so embarrassed and like everyone knew I was a bit freaked out by the idea of boys. I just wasn't ready.

My first kiss – like for loads of people – was a bit rubbish. It was a boy that a lot of girls quite liked so I was amazed when he turned his attention to me at a party at a friend's house. After snogging on a sofa downstairs he invited me upstairs so we wouldn't have a load of our mates giving us the thumbs up. We found ourselves in the party girl's bedroom where-upon the boy in question locked the door, took the key out of the lock and hid it. I was pretty frightened but after nervously asking him to please unlock the door a few times he finally relented and I was set free. He then dumped me a day or two later. If we'd even been potential boyfriend and girlfriend to begin with, that is.

So far, so normal. I think everyone's early experiences are by and large peppered with these near misses and fancying folk who don't fancy you back and if anyone likes you they will invariably be the one person you are not at all into. It's harsh out there, particularly on a lawless teenage playing field.

By the time I was sixteen, I had only snogged a couple of boys and had never had a boyfriend. One night, I met a boy I liked at an indie club. He was sweet but I was a bit uncomfortable. Sounds weird to say so, but I found him too REAL. I remember sitting next to him on the bus on our way to the tube after our first date ... everything about him freaked me out. He was lovely, but I found seeing the stubble on his face, the way he sat, the whole complete 3-D-ness of him too much. He was so sweet and lovely, but he was just too much of a living person and it made me squeam-ish. I managed three weeks of calling him a boyfriend before I had to break it off. I don't know, I just wasn't ready for any kind of relationship.

Through going to Billy's club night, I met girlfriends outside of school including two sisters who seemed worldly, experienced and well connected. All this seemed very exciting and a chance for me to shrug off my Enid Blyton exterior . . . they didn't see me as a prude but they did see me as a bit of a project. 'Have a one-night stand,' they said, 'it's easy, you just bring a man home with you and then sleep with him.' This seemed so grown up to me. I'd read in *More!* magazine about one-night stands. Clearly, being a grown woman meant being able to do this. But I was still shy and confused . . . how did this all happen? When you asked a guy to come home with you, was it obvious that you were offering sex? The first time I went for a night out with the two out-of-school girlfriends (let's call them Betty and Sue, like it's 1956), I tried to be bold. They brought home a man each. Not boys – even though we were all sixteen, these were men in their mid-twenties that they brought back to their family home. That night I met a man – he was twenty-four – and he seemed to fancy me. I don't even remember checking if I fancied him. Boys hadn't been interested in me throughout my teens so it didn't seem important who I liked. The boys I liked never liked me . . . but here was a fully grown man showing me interest. I asked him if he'd like to come back for a drink; he accepted and sure enough, once we were back at their house (where I'd gone for a sleepover), we started snogging. Soon, we found ourselves lying on the sofa and things were getting serious. I suddenly started to feel completely out of my depth. I didn't want to sleep with this man and I really wasn't into him. I got nervous giggles. He was cross and said, 'You obviously have a problem with your sexuality.'

'Why?' I asked.

'Because you're laughing. This means you have a massive problem.'

I felt humiliated and confused. Was I only doing it right if I had sex, no matter what?

Not too long after, I was out at a gig with a group of friends, including Betty and Sue. By now I was seventeen and I'd had my first boyfriend (the

67

kind indie boy from the club). Anyway, after the gig we found ourselves at a hotel bar for an after-show ... not a party exactly, but probably about forty or so people drinking and talking and hanging out. By now I was in theaudience although we hadn't yet done a gig, just recorded demos and rehearsed. I was such a passionate music fan and was so happy to be hanging out with musicians. At the after-show I found myself talking to a man who was in a band. They were a successful indie band with songs in the top twenty. You'd probably have heard of them although they weren't huge or anything. He was their guitarist and he seemed to like me. I felt flattered. I mentioned I was doing A-level history and he said, 'I did history. Would you like to come back to my flat and see my history books?' Probably the lamest chat-up line in the whole world but under that pretence I left the hotel and went in a taxi with him back to his flat. Let's call him Jim, shall we? Once back at the flat, Jim actually did show me his history books. I found myself putting a book about Napoleon III in my bag. I kept it for a while afterwards but seeing it always made me feel sad and used. You see, Jim and I started kissing and before I knew it we were on his bed and he took off my knickers. I heard myself saying 'No' and 'I don't want to', but it didn't make any difference. He didn't listen to me and he had sex with me and I felt so ashamed I didn't tell anyone. It was how I lost my virginity and I felt stupid. I remember staring at the bookcases and thinking, 'I just have to let this happen now.' The Pulp song 'Do You Remember the First Time?' was playing on the radio and even in this pretty dark moment I thought that was sort of funny in a tragic sort of way.

After it was over, I lay on the bed feeling odd, trying to process what had just happened. He fell asleep and I slept too, not really knowing how to get myself home in the middle of the night. I woke after a short while and I can remember angrily picking up my clothes from the floor saying, 'I said no,' to myself as I got dressed. I went and sat in his kitchen watching TV, feeling dazed. It must have been a Saturday morning as *The Chart Show* was on. I sat there alone, waiting, not really sure what I should do or how I felt. After a while, Jim came into the room. 'Oh I didn't think you'd still be here,' he said. Again I felt stupid. I didn't know I was supposed to have left. I didn't know I was supposed to just go afterwards. I was seventeen and it was my first time and I didn't know how to assert myself or even put myself in the frame. I felt as if I was watching myself from a bird's-eye view.

On the way home I wondered if everyone else on the tube could tell what had happened to me. I felt grubby but also unsure about my own feelings as I had no other experience to compare it to. At the time, the way rape was talked about wasn't to do with consent, it was something you associated with aggression. But no one had pinned me down or shouted at me to make me comply, so why should I feel so violated? What exactly was it that had just happened to me?

I have thought so much about why I wanted to write about this. My life is happy now and I would not say that I felt overly traumatised at the time, and yet I feel as if the culture that surrounded me – the things I saw and read and the way sex was discussed – made me believe I didn't have a case. If you found yourself having sex outside of a relationship then that was casual sex and it should be handled with casual emotion, too. Notch on the bedpost and onto the next. You didn't mean to do it? Well, you shouldn't have gone back to their house then.

My experience was not violent. I was not physically forced into what happened. All that happened was I wasn't listened to. Out of the two people there, one said yes, the other said no, and the yes person did it anyway. The violence of that took longer to register. I also think that it's possible to experience something bad and to know that it could have been worse, and to deal with that in your own way. The older I've become, the more stark that twenty-nine-year-old man ignoring seventeen-year-old me has seemed.

I think most women will, sadly, have a story a bit like this one. Back when this happened to me, consent was not spoken about in the same terms as it is now. We are now far more familiar with the conversation about your right to say what is and isn't OK for you, regardless of what went on before you found yourself on your own with that man in his bedroom. At seventeen, I didn't feel strong in myself, I felt I was supposed to know how to act but I kept getting it wrong.

I think it's telling that, when I came to write this book, this chapter is the one I wrote first. By going back to that room and to that time when I felt I didn't have a voice, I can now give myself that voice. I am not interested in naming and shaming the guy involved – I've googled him and he seems to be happily going about his business and is in what looks like a happy long-term relationship – but I do want to encourage anyone to realise where the line between right and wrong lies. I'm a mother of five young men now and I introduce the concept of consent pretty early. We have words we use when they play, 'Stop' and 'No', and they are powerful. No matter how much fun they've been having up to that point, if one of them – even laughing – says 'No' or 'Stop', then they must stop whatever they are doing. I want to raise considerate, kind people who can take other people's feelings into account. I want them to actively want the other person to be happy, too, rather than just stopping because they have to. Isn't that that best thing? When everyone is having a lovely time?

I hope this next generation of young people has real agency, not only when it comes to not doing what they don't want to do, but also really knowing and responding to what they do want. If I'd had a better sense of that, there's no way I'd have gone back with that man to his flat. I didn't fancy him. But he'd chosen me, and that was what flattered me then and felt like the key ingredient. It wasn't. The key ingredient – and the thing that would have meant I didn't feel the need to write about any of it decades down the line – was whether or not he was what I wanted.

To be honest, I feel each relationship I've had since then has been affected by the one before it. Sometimes it's meant I've felt I didn't deserve any better. In my first serious relationships I didn't know how to assert myself or ask for what made me happy. It wasn't until meeting Richard that I felt my feelings not only had value but were also intrinsic to what would make the relationship really work. With Richard, I had the epiphany that love – real love – is when someone encourages you to be the best version of yourself, but it took that epiphany to break the cycle. For that seventeen-year-old girl, there was still quite a journey to go on before arriving at that.

I never saw Jim again but I did hear from a girlfriend that she'd bumped into him and when my name came up he said we'd dated. We never dated. He didn't even want to see me. He definitely didn't want to listen to me. But now I've found a place for my voice and it feels better. I can completely understand when women are sexually assaulted and don't feel strong enough to talk about it for years, maybe even decades. It takes a lot to voice it because then, on that night, there were only two voices. One was mine, one was his, and I wasn't listened to.

After this experience I went into a four-month relationship with some-one who put me under a lot of pressure to be committed and adventurous and he was a lot older too . . . and was very much in control of how the relationship ran. I wasn't in love, though, which helped. Not like the next boyfriend, which was much more serious. To this day, I wake up relieved I am not in that relationship anymore. But more of that later.

In a roundabout way, those bad initial experiences have helped me feel so grateful for what I have now. My husband is a good man and I could see that in him from the day we met. One of the secrets to a long and happy relationship isn't date nights or romantic time together – although obviously those are lovely too – but the real glue is liking each other. When you're having a normal day at home feeding the kids, sorting a broken loo, organising the chaos and taking the bins out, if you always like each other then you're on the same side and you don't overstep the mark by taking your frustrations out on each other. If I've ever had a sharp tongue with Richard – and it's happened only once or twice – he's good at pulling me up on it and making me feel that I don't want to be that person. There's a fundamental respect and a knowledge that I married someone who is decent. Having spent years with someone that I didn't feel that way about and who definitely didn't feel that way about me, I'd recommend making sure you like each other over everything else. It's easy to overlook it and while it helps that Richard and I fancy each other too, when life is hectic, I know we're always on the same side. So thank you to the bastards that went before. You taught me to be so grateful that there is another way.

6

ME: Hair – 'I Am Not Good at Not Getting What I Want'

Smiling through the dodgy cut and colour.

I wanted to write about my hair because – I'm sure you'd agree – spinning plates is a lot easier when you have good hair. Over the years I've sometimes had good hair but sadly I've spent more time with bad hair than I'd have liked.

When I was a child I kept my hair pretty long. I had the occasional wonky fringe (thanks, Ma) but mainly long hair which was an unexciting shade of light brown or dark blonde, depending on the light.

Going to the hairdresser's as a kid in double figures meant my mum still had the final say in what I was allowed. She liked me with a bob and a fringe, so that was my look for the first few years of secondary. Trips to the salon were largely uneventful, aside from pretending to be comfy when my neck was hurting in those cut-out sinks where they wash your hair, and facing down comments from the hairdresser about having very thick hair said like a compliment but with an underlying tone of impatience.

When I reached teenagehood it was an absolute revelation that I could legitimately, and without too much permission-seeking, do pretty much anything to my hair. In fact, I don't think I've had my hair my natural colour since I was fourteen. I'm not even too sure what colour it would be if I grew it out but I don't think I'd be too into it.

In 1993, all the girls at my school were using a product called 'Sun In'. It was supposed to give your hair golden highlights, as if you'd just returned from a hot little holiday at the beach. Attempting this look in a grey and unbeachy Hammersmith in the mid-nineties didn't always deliver the desired look. Mostly it went a strange kind of orange.

Still, I did contemplate going for the blonde look. The most popular girls were the blonde girls. The ones who tanned. I was not one of those girls. Consistently pale and brunette, I decided to run headlong into my calling and bought from the chemist a hair dye called 'Darkest Natural Brown'. Boy oh boy, it was dark. It was kind of amazing that the black (it was basically black) shade had no other tones in it. I effectively put a big black cloud around my face. And I liked it.

For the majority of my school days, I stayed this colour, either 'Darkest Natural Brown' or a cool colour called 'Blue Black', which added a sheen of navy to the midnight hue.

This suited me fine for a while but then came the day I wanted to push it further. I was bored with just black. What else could I do?

By now I had a record deal and wanted hair that told the world, 'I'm in a band'. Boys are good at this. You'll notice, lots of boys in bands have 'band hair'. I wanted the female equivalent.

By now the year was 1997 and I went for a strong blunt bob with a little bit of a fringe and blonde highlights dyed royal blue in amongst the mainly black barnet. So far, so good, but things were about to go wrong. I got sloppy with my choices. Now living in Camden Town, one day I was out walking and in need of a haircut. I found myself heading down the high road and what did I spy: Mr Toppers! Mr Toppers is a chain of hairdressers – I think primarily a barber's – of which there are a few to be found in London Town. They are well known for their cheap haircuts (at that time only £5 a pop) and their cheery little frog mascot. Mr Topper himself, I presume.

Lord knows why I did it, but I found myself walking in and asking if they could trim my bob. Out of curiosity I had a look back to see who was influencing my hairdos during those dark days of terrible hairstyles. Turns out it seems I wasn't following any hair trends. Maybe if I'd taken in a photo of Alicia Silverstone in *Clueless* I would have avoided the hair hacking humiliation. Then again I'd have given Maria and Helen nothing to cry with laughter over (literally tears down the face crying) in years to come. What can I say? I'm a generous friend that way.

The bob in question wouldn't cost £5, it would be £15, but by then I was committed. I found myself sitting in the hairdresser's chair. Did I only want a bob, they asked? Had I ever thought of going shorter?

Now something weird comes over me when I go to the hairdresser and from the moment I sit in the chair I know that three things will be true:

1) I shall feel compelled to change my hair more radically than I intended. I HAVE LEARNT TO RESIST THIS.
2) I shall think the hair that I walked in with looks better than normal. I AM POWERLESS TO RESIST THIS.
3) I shall find my own reflection more and more unattractive the longer I sit there. AGAIN: POWERLESS.

That day back in 1997 I decided, hey! I've never had a short haircut. Let's go for it! I can only describe the short haircut I was given as exactly the sort of short haircut you'd expect from a barber's which usually charges £5. I can still recall the look of disappointed surprise on my boyfriend's face when he came to meet me at the end of the appointment. I was swivelled round to meet him by the hairdresser in a kind of 'ta-dah!' fashion and his face did not say 'ta-dah!' back. It said, 'What have you done?' I was in such shock I handed over a £20 note and didn't ask for change.

You know it's a crap haircut when the first thing you do when you get home is try putting clips in it, then washing it again in case it dries longer. It doesn't.

Happily for me there was nothing to cement this rubbish hairdo other than the photos for the press and album cover of my first band and two of our videos too. Yay.

As soon as my hair had grown out, I walked straight into bad hairdo number two. Arguably the worst of the bunch. Living in Camden, I sometimes got stopped on the street by Vidal Sassoon trainees looking for people they could give haircuts to. They would use the term 'model' to flatter, but they meant, 'I want to use you as an impartial head of hair, please'.

I'd usually say no, but on this particular day my hair was nicely long and grown-up, but a bit 'nothing'. When my hair gets long it just hangs there like dog ears not doing much. I was twenty, high and dry and wanted a bit of excitement. Cue – new hair. Yes, this would be amazing. Sure, I'll be your model.

I arrived at the Covent Garden branch of the hairdresser's with hope in my heart. The young guy cutting my hair seemed lovely and confident. He was going to do something I would love, he promised.

It was only when he told me, 'It's so nice doing a haircut where it doesn't matter what the client thinks,' about a quarter of the way in, that alarm bells rang.

The client. That's me.

He pinned half my hair up and started cutting away the remaining half at around ear level. He did it in a deliberately uneven way so that in the mirror I could now see what I would look like if I was entering a particularly heartless convent where they wanted to make your hair as ugly as possible. He then let down the rest of my hair (now half the thickness it was) and cut into that. Essentially I'd been given the same hairdo as those brightly coloured wigs you can buy from the joke shop. A mullet.

After the obligatory hair clips and hair wash attempts at home, I settled on bunches for the next few months. This is how I saw in my twenty-first birthday. I had a party in the upstairs room of a local pub. My friends couldn't come as they were at uni; my band couldn't come as I wasn't in a band anymore. It was me, my bad hairdo, my bad boyfriend and a juke-box. Yay.

You'd have thought I'd learn, but my knee-jerk response to this haircut was to go back to the same guy at the same hairdresser's and let him dye my hair blonde.

That's right, he asked me if I'd be happy to be paid tuppence to be his hair model at a hair show in Wembley, but I had to have my hair dyed first. Maybe the mullet would look better blonde? Sure, kid. I went white-blonde but didn't know much about maintenance, so by the time of the show it was yellow. I visited two girlfriends who were at uni in Edinburgh that weekend. I arrived with my hair in the safety bunches. 'My hair is bad,' I told them. 'No, I'm sure it's lovely,' Helen replied.

I undid the bunches and she literally laughed until she cried.

A few months later I had recorded 'Groovejet' and it was video time. I didn't want to have the bad hair in the video so I dyed it back to my favourite dark chocolate brown and was introduced to a man called Sherman who was the go-to guy for extensions. He painstakingly glued in the whole head of hair from another lady, I know not who, but her hair was lovely. Thick, shiny brown hair. 'You'll never go back now,' Sherman told me. But though it was true the hair was lovely, I'm not good at having things I can fiddle with and after a month or two the extensions were growing out. I should have gone back to see him. Instead, I realised I could use my nails to undo the glue and with only a little bit of pain I could slide each extension down off my own hair. So this became my project. Over the next few weeks, whenever I was lying in bed, I'd slide off the extensions and put the other lady's hair in a lovely little hair pile on the floor. One night I stayed over at my mum's, sleeping in my little sister Martha's bed. Thoughtfully, I put the discarded hair into a paper bag for her to discover next to her bed. You're welcome.

For the first solo album I had my own hair (and have done forevermore since then) and a relatively typical brown for me . . . but when you're a new pop star you don't want to stay the same. I decided each single had to have its own aesthetic. For 'Take Me Home', bold eyeshadow and brown hair, for 'Murder', glitter eyeshadow, for 'Get Over You', red hair and blue eyeshadow. The red stuck around for the last single, 'Music Gets the Best of Me', too. To get the right shade of red I would put a bright pink Crazy Color dye over the top of the red permanent shade. This made my hair a colour I think known in fashion circles as 'Ribena'. It was lovely but had to be re-dyed frequently and due to the nature of the dye I had a matching Ribena stain on my pillow and Ribena ears, too.

By the time I was making my second album, I was going through the turmoil of ending a relationship. Take note: when you've been with someone for a long time and things are a little shaky, if they come home one day with radically different hair – it's probably over.

I started out with Mrs Robinson-style dyed colours in my hair . . . brown, caramel and blonde. It was like a gateway drug to what followed – pure platinum blonde for album two. I'm not sure it suited me at all but it provided the break I needed. It was fun to try it on and use several bottles of violet shampoo to keep the blonde that white side of things, but I spent the whole time gazing at brunettes and thinking how lovely brown hair is. It's always felt like 'me', and so halfway through my pregnancy with Sonny, I went back to the brunette bottle. That's pretty much where I've stayed ever since, although I did try and convince my frequent hairdresser Lisa to dye my hair grey at one stage. I think I was about twenty-four and I wanted to be a Prussian-blue grey-head. I think it would have been cool but maybe she was right to say no. I can save it up for when I'm older.

Now I don't do much more than fringes and the occasional bob . . . I've been a gentle red again, but not with the Crazy Color. I love it but I'm a once-a-year-haircut type – sometimes you need to simplify your life. I don't think I was ever someone who spent a lot of time on pampering, but now I'm even less fussed. I feel I've shown my hair a good time, and now we've lived out our wilder days and settled down.

Overall, I would recommend having bad hairdos. Firstly, it's a good idea to try out different versions of yourself to see what makes you happy, but secondly, when you reminisce about the bad hairdos with your friends it'll make you cry with laughter all over again.

7

MEN: First Relationship – 'Heartbreak'

Happy new year . . . I welcomed in 2000 whilst using my hair as the
medium to communicate feeling a little mixed up.

The meaning of life is love. Of this much I am sure.

It's so easy for lessons in love to be a list of 'those who have done me wrong', and as it happens, the first time I started writing this, that's exactly what this was. So in order to balance the books let me write about all the menfolk I dated who were nice and kind to me before I met my husband:

Danny, who I went out with for three weeks when I was sixteen – you were very sweet and thank you for that.

That's it for the list.

When I fell in love with Richard, I had to learn what being in love with someone really meant. How real love lifts you up and when someone really cares for you, you live your life knowing more of who you are because they reflect the good stuff back at you.

Because you see, I now have a lovely husband, but I used to have a terrible boyfriend. One I was with for a long time and even now, I'm glad I managed to get away. This first teenage love was laced with cruelty and I came to believe that that unkindness was what love looked like.

Would I have listened if anyone had told me to stay away from the bad boyfriend? Probably not. I was young when I met him and I wouldn't get away for a number of years. By the end of our relationship I was banned from walking anywhere by myself, singing in the house and I didn't have any say about how and when our time together would be spent. He had a life that was all his own, house parties he'd go to and stay at all night and time at the pub with his mates whenever he wanted it. He didn't want to be with my friends or my family so I would wait to see where he'd invite me to join him and only be there when I was allowed.

But that all came along later and it happened gradually. At the beginning I just saw the good stuff and was swept along by how I felt, letting it paper over any cracks I could see. If you've ever been in a controlling relationship then you'll know how insidious it is. Teeny tiny, almost imperceptible shifts that make you think it's normal to be routinely humiliated in public, or to be told you're a fucking idiot when you make a mistake, or that you're past it and getting wrinkly. Before you know it you're being threatened if you try to show independence. But those days were the thick end of the wedge. Things started at the other end at first.

Credit to my mum: when I told her casually at suppertime – as I was passing her the butter dish – that my new boyfriend was nearly thirty, she didn't freak out. She must have done internally, but she kept it cool on the outside. My mum has always been good at keeping the lines of communication open with us and I think she knew very well that if she'd said anything too negative I just wouldn't have told her any more about it.

This wasn't the first time I'd had an older boyfriend. My previous boyfriend, let's call him Bob, had been twenty-five. He and I had gone out for a few months and it was a slightly scary and intense relationship. Bob was always asking me to tell him I loved him, asking me to promise him I'd one day marry him before saying, 'No, you won't, you'll leave me.' This was the style of our relationship until one day I was dumped. He said he'd call me and then just . . . didn't. I don't mean he spoke to me and broke up with me, I mean he just abruptly stopped all contact. I believe the modern term is 'ghosting'. It was upsetting and confusing but I was young and just assumed I'd done something wrong.

This set the scene perfectly for what came next: my first serious long-term relationship. I didn't want to unwittingly do something wrong again. I'd try my best to get it all right this time.

I was introduced to Mike by Billy, the man who set up the audience. We met at a music venue. Looking back it feels strange that a still-very-young me was introduced to much-older Mike as a potential boyfriend, but I knew a lot of girls going out with older guys and it wasn't seen as particularly unusual. I was so flattered that he was interested. The fact an adult man was into me made me feel better about the boys my own age who would sooner have told me they fancied my mother than me.

I was smitten very quickly. My mum noticed and told me to be careful with how much of myself I gave him, but I don't think anyone could have spoken any sense to me at that time in my life. I was already in a rush for the next part of my story, so when she said, 'Keep some mystery. Don't let him see you brushing your teeth in the morning,' I probably just took this literally and didn't put a toothbrush in my handbag.

When I met him I could see Mike was funny, gregarious and charismatic. He made me laugh and that is always a good start, isn't it? He could sing and dance and, when he was introduced to my family, he was funny with my little brother and sister. His social charm was enough to cloud his laziness and his view that going to work and other mundane activities, like 'being reliable', were for other people. In the early stages of our relationship we had fun. My dad gave me two tickets to New York as a birthday present, and Mike and I went for a week and explored the city. Back in London, we used to go to gigs a lot and watch films together – Mike was a movie buff and loved cinema. He talked to me about philosophy. This was a whole new world to me and it made me feel as if I'd reached adulthood when we sat and talked about Albert Camus while eating pesto pasta in the little council flat where Mike lived.

Mike was out of work for the whole of our first few years aside from one Christmas where he worked for a few weeks in a shop. Looking back, he was probably someone with narcissistic personality disorder. He didn't worry about how to pay the bills; he somehow thought the universe would provide. Having to go to work for a living was beneath him. He had had a fight with bouncers before we got together and this had resulted in a head injury. This left him unable to work, he said, but he could play football for fun with his mates every week and got very drunk whenever he wanted.

When we met, he'd managed to get himself into a flat that a friend of his owned and would coast from one thing to another. He wasn't devoid of talent by any means. He could sing and hold a room with his stories. He had a lot of friends and a few female friends who were a little infatuated with him. Everything confirmed that he was someone special. His mother thought he was the centre of the universe and somehow he was right about the universe providing for him . . . as our relationship evolved I poured all of myself into it. One time, I was out all day promoting for my record deal and Mike – sitting at home all day – asked me to pick up milk or bread or something. I remember panicking about remembering to grab it on the way home, or else he'd be annoyed.

Controlling and coercive relationships are slippery little things. My early memories of our dates were mainly fun. There was the odd thing that should probably have been a warning sign. Tracing a line, the worst of our relationship was its last year, but the roots of unpleasantness had started small and early on.

Being in an unhealthy relationship was like being in a room that was getting smaller. As the floor tilted and the air grew thin, my expectations for what might make our relationship better and more wholesome grew smaller and smaller until it was just kindness and tenderness I wanted, rather than threats and aggression.

But as I said, the weeds started small. There was a time when we must have been together only a matter of months and I wanted to see him while I was doing the first of my A-level exams. I was crying and begging him to come over as my mum wouldn't let me out to visit (it was a school night after all). He refused to come over, despite my pleading.

My wise ma tried to help me get the relationship started on the right track. 'The dynamics of a relationship get established early on . . . within the first six months,' she told me. 'Make sure you're happy with the ways things are.'

Alas, I found a way around his lack of desire to travel from his flat to mine. Warning – if you are the parent of a young girl and hate the idea of her doing stupid things because of boys, do not read this next bit. It will scare you.

I'd book a minicab to meet me in the next road along, then leave the house at midnight, wait for the cab, stay at Mike's flat until about 4 a.m. then head back again, getting only an hour or two's sleep before school or even, on one occasion, my history A-level exam. Not only do I look back and wince at how bold that was on a school night but also at how much my mum would have freaked out if she'd known. I started leaving a note after that . . . resting on top of the pillows piled up Ferris-Bueller-style to look like a sleeping body. I was putting myself in real danger, too . . . loitering in the road in the middle of the night waiting for a cab and then heading to a block of council flats where three women had been murdered.

There were other moments that stood out too, like the time when I was sitting with him in a pub and he began talking about how many wrinkles I had around my eyes. 'You're going to hit your prime in a couple of years, then it'll be downhill from there,' he told me. Sounds so ridiculous now but it's a powerful thing when someone who has your heart tells you your value has a shelf life. He had a little song he'd sing to me which I know is darkly funny but also so cruel:

You're the little c*nt I'll never ever marry
You're the little c*nt I'll never ever love
You're the little c*nt I don't even like
You are a c*ntish girl

I used to laugh it off but looking back, not only is it ugly, it's not even a very good song. Where's the rhyming scheme? I think when you're young and in love, things like this make you try even harder to make your boyfriend happy. I wanted to be the best girlfriend. Uncomplaining, attentive, able to provide support and to know better than to feel jealousy or heartache that they might never love you and might leave you once you're 'old'.

Still, we had our good times too. I believed we were in love – a destructive and angry love but I thought that must be the shape love had to take. If you really loved someone, I thought, jealousy, rage, threats and resentment were all part of the picture. How could you know someone would never leave you unless you threatened to leave them so they begged you to stay? This was so much part of the dynamic that when I got together with Richard, I remember being almost shocked that he'd never been in a fight, he'd never beaten someone up and that violence wasn't something he believed in. I had to relearn the difference between passion and aggression, between brawn and strength of character.

As my relationship with Mike became more serious, I was desperate to leave home and start my grown-up life. My home with my mum and John was a happy one but my life didn't fit that shape any more . . . One day I was sitting downstairs, recovering from a hangover, with my little brother and sister tearing round the kitchen. I was wearing a T-shirt from the newly opened YO! Sushi and as my mum studied my sickly, dirty stop-out face she quipped, 'You don't look very "YO!", darling.' I wanted out of that, to be somewhere of my own where I could stay out late and sleep in later. I was desperate to escape out into the world and so after finishing my exams, Mike and I went to look at some flats and after seeing the tiniest little place above a pub, we put down a deposit, and in July I took two carloads of my possessions and off I went. I was free, I had a boyfriend and was signed to Mercury Records. I was ready for the next bit.

The flat was the size of a postage stamp but I was so proud of it. It was in an area that I associated with music and had the potential of bumping into musicians you loved in the pubs. The music press had always talked about the venues and the bars so it had become folklore. If you were into Britpop, you went there. Now I had a little flat in the heart of it all. If I looked out of the window from the sitting room I could see the tube station, and if I opened my front door I looked out onto the roof of a pub which was a usual meeting point for local folk. Beneath the pub was a club. When I lay in bed at night I could hear the music. Well, not the full song, but I got very good at identifying songs by their basslines. The flat was stuffy and hot and we'd often have the windows open so you'd either hear the pub if you opened the windows in the kitchen or the bustle of the streets if you opened the ones in the bedroom or sitting room. Once you could hear the whole world out there, why would you stay inside your hot little flat?

It was during this time that I began touring with theaudience. I can still remember when I was on the cover of *Melody Maker* with the headline: 'theaudience – Introducing the Best New Band in Britain'. It was exciting . . . incredible really. I'd been poring over *Melody Maker* every week and now I was on the cover. It was officially published on Wednesday but you could get it on a Tuesday in certain newsagents. Mike went out to get it and as I watched him walk back from the tube with the copy, he held it up so I could see my cover from the window.

The most ridiculous thing that happened in that flat was probably the time Jarvis Cocker came back with me from a party. For some reason Mike hadn't come with me but he was home when we got in. At the party I'd got talking to Jarvis who was just finishing Pulp's album *This is Hardcore*. We talked about music and pressure – Jarvis was concerned about how his new album would be received after the success of *Different Class*. We then got onto the topic of Alan Partridge, the brilliant Steve Coogan character whose comedy series had just launched. I said, 'If you want you can come back to mine to watch it. My boyfriend has recorded the new episode so we can see it.' Jarvis seemed quite keen to come back and watch it so we hopped in a taxi. When we got back to the flat, Mike was lying horizontal on the tiny couch. 'Hey Mike,' I said cheerily, 'this is Jarvis. He's come to watch Alan Partridge with us.' Mike was a bit sleepy but sat up and put on the recording. Our flat was so tiny that there wasn't really room for all of us on the sofa so I sat next to Mike while Jarvis was on a little upright wooden chair against the side wall. He didn't look very comfy. We sat in a slightly awkward silence watching the episode before Jarvis made a quick trip to the loo. He then said a very quick goodnight and headed out into the night. 'Was that a bit weird?' I asked Mike. I couldn't put my finger on it but I felt that though Jarvis had come over and done exactly as we had chatted about at the party, for some reason it all felt a bit odd. I promise it wasn't until a good while later that it occurred to me that maybe Jarvis hadn't expected us to literally just watch Alan Partridge. The final punchline happened later that night when I was going to bed. As I went into the bathroom I saw something I'd forgotten about. The previous tenants had stuck band stickers all over the loo seat including one you could only see when you put the seat up, as Jarvis must have had done, to reveal a big sticker with PULP on it. To this day I'm not sure if Jarvis saw that and thought we must be really big fans, or else that we really hated the band.

We stayed in that tiny flat for nine months until my parents convinced me that the best thing for me to do with the income from my record deal was to buy somewhere. I managed to find a little one-bedroom flat that I could just about afford. It was actually fairly cute except for two things – as a basement flat it was on first name terms with damp, and as a basement flat opposite a pub and next door to a kebab shop, sometimes you'd look up out of the bedroom window to see someone throwing up over the railings.

I set about making it home. I painted all the walls, strung up bright plastic flowers from the market, hung beaded curtains . . . made it as jolly as I could. Mike and I were excited to have our own place and it was mainly uneventful except for the odd bit of drama. The controlling aspect of the relationship with Mike was growing legs. He was still out of work and on the dole, promising that if things got desperate he would get a job. Once I lost my record deal a year or so after being there, I can remember counting out the pennies after paying the mortgage and finding just under a pound. This was a cue for me to get a new job while Mike stayed at home, sleeping in until lunchtime then meeting his friends in the pub. I tried a few things to stay motivated and afloat. One day I started writing a book, which was TERRIBLE. I don't mean terrible like this one is terrible, I mean really, really bad. It was going to be about – you guessed it – a girl who had had a record deal as a teenager and found herself dropped by twenty. It was so painfully middle-class that I think I mentioned Designers Guild on the first page. So you see? You can thank 'Groovejet' that that was never finished. I started modelling a bit as I was spotted in Topshop by Models One. At school, my friends and I had idolised models. They seemed impossibly glamorous and as it was the nineties, there was a group of supermodels we all knew by name. The real deal of modelling was far removed from that image. The strangest thing of all to me – coming at it with the experience of having had a record deal – was that modelling agencies took on zero risk when they put a new girl on their books. From the moment I signed I was paying for my own travel to casting appointments and from the moment I did a test shoot (so that I could build up my portfolio) the cost of the shoot was held on my account, ready to be recouped as soon as I made any money. I was only a model for four months and if I see any photos of myself from any shoot I did around then, I have the saddest eyes ever. Looking back, I think I was quite depressed. I had lost my deal and my band, I was being incredibly careful with my diet and had got too thin, and I was unsure of what would happen to me next. And every night after trudging around town and making no money, my lowlife man would be waiting for me. Expectant for supper and for me to stay at home while he went on pub crawls.

I remember one night we had a curry and I dropped the jar of mango chutney. It shattered and I fainted after cutting my foot on the glass. The flat was stiflingly hot as we had two massive industrial humidifiers on to combat the damp problem. Mike panicked and called an ambulance. I was OK, but my wound needed looking at. Mike went with me to A&E but you don't get treated quickly when all you need is a couple of stitches, so although we arrived around 8.30 p.m., by 2.30 a.m. we were still waiting. The next day Mike had promised his pals he'd meet them in the park to play football so he . . . left. He left me in A&E on my own at 2.30 a.m. because he was bored. I was modelling at the time and had castings from 9 a.m., meaning I had to leave by 8 a.m. I finally got seen at 4.30 a.m. and made my way home alone. It was the first properly concrete thing that happened which made me see our love was not balanced.

Anyway, I got on with it, trying to make ends meet and find a new beginning for my work, my music. Mike was talking about us starting a new band together. I was hesitant. He'd ended up having fisticuffs with the drummer from my old band and his volatile side was coming to the forefront more apparently. Fisticuffs happened pretty frequently, in fact. He'd often come home from the pub having had a physical fight with someone and around this time he was being more abusive with me. It sounds absurd, but I didn't quite see how dangerous it all was. Being scared of him became part of our fabric, and I had fooled myself into thinking grown-up men, real men, were physically demonstrative and dominating.

The other thing that happened in that small, damp flat is that my dad and Mike had a fight. Looking back it was inevitable and whilst I didn't like how he went about it, it must have been very hard for my dad to see the dynamic of the relationship and how I had diminished myself. 'I just see you working so hard and being so unsupported . . . I don't like it, Soph,' my dad said in the aftermath. But I didn't get it. I loved Mike, he said he loved me and I thought all love must be good love.

Thinking back to the darker moments, I remember a lot of heavy drinking which would lead to big shouty arguments. Sometimes at home, sometimes in the street. On one occasion Mike grabbed me by the wrist and painfully squeezed and twisted my arm. A passer-by saw this and walked on quickly to get away from us. This was significant for me. When you get mistreated in front of someone and they do nothing, you start to think it's not that bad. The next day my wrist was so swollen I couldn't put my watch on.

There was one moment of magic in that place though. Actually, life-changing magic. It was in that bedroom, on a little ghetto blaster I had by the bed, that I first heard the instrumental of 'Groovejet'. That little acorn grew a tree that would become my solo career, which would introduce me to my future husband and lift me out of that sadness. Funny how things turn out sometimes.

When 'Groovejet' was out it was to and from that little flat I would go. I would leave on a Friday or Saturday night and drive with my tour manager JP to clubs up and down the country, sing 'Groovejet' once or twice, then back in the car . . . sometimes two clubs in a night. It was exhausting but also exhilarating. I signed to Polydor and began to put my album together. At home, Mike was increasingly verbally aggressive and ugly. He wouldn't let me sing anything at home, telling me, 'You're singing out of tune,' whenever I opened my mouth. We moved into a new flat. It was a beautiful little flat and the atmosphere was happier as we were so busy.

Suddenly I was travelling to Asia, Australia and around Europe. The album came out and I was trying as hard as I could to make our relationship a happy one. The controlling side of Mike was coming out in certain ways. He would be very strict about the people I was allowed to interact with and I feel really bad that I didn't stand up to him more . . . One time we were at a radio roadshow and one of the fellow singers on the bill was someone who'd done *X Factor*. He knocked on my dressing room for a photo and Mike said no, it wasn't cool to be photographed with him. My dad was there too and he felt so bad that he went outside to where that singer was waiting and they chatted for a while. Another time I sang and Katie Price was there. Again, she asked to come and say hello and Mike said no. I felt bad but to be honest sometimes when the world is going fast and someone else is steering the ship, it feels reassuring that someone seems to know what they think is best for you. I do know he can't have been all bad . . . but also I have had people come forward after we broke up to say they wished they'd stepped in when they'd seen how unhealthy the relationship was. Even one of his family members reached out to say they'd always felt his behaviour was appalling but that they were too scared to say anything. I think I always knew about the demons in his psyche but I thought I could fix it. I thought if I could create a warm and loving home around him, he'd change.

I stuck it out, always, except for one night when he came home drunk and kept shouting at me I was a 'f*cking c*nt,' so I packed my bags and called my mum, arriving home at about 2.30 in the morning. I think my mum just thought it was a dramatic tiff and I would have definitely said anything I could to have convinced her of that. I was still 100% committed.

Looking back, it's hard for me to remember proper times we shared. I spent a lot of time away promoting my album and Mike hardly ever came with me. Australia, South East Asia, Europe . . . he wasn't there and I spent my time away working and having fun with Lisa who was my hair and make-up artist, but more importantly was and is one of my best friends. Mike would be at home – or rather, he would stay in the UK and party a lot. I think I had begun to feel like I was plan B to Mike – I was what he would do if his plan A fell through. He was getting more and more into partying and I was working flat out, missing so much that if I had an evening spare I would see my family or friends. He made excuses not to. One time my mum and family were going to Barcelona for the weekend. Mike was supposed to come but at the last minute he didn't. What was worse – I didn't miss him. I think Mike was just making it easier for me to leave. If you don't have shared memories and friends and plans, what's left?

Things were complicated. Having always previously bought homes in my own name, when I was able to buy a house I bought it in both our names. I only lived there for a short time, a very sad time. We'd bought in a new area and we were totally cut off. No one was ever 'just passing through', the house had a sad atmosphere and by now Mike was forbidding me to go anywhere without him or even to look out of the car window as we drove anywhere. He was threatened by any contact I had with people outside of our normal circle. My self-esteem was very low and I didn't think I was worth much. Mike was now going to big house parties in his spare time and experimenting with harder partying. I felt lonely and alone. Even now, if I'm anxious or stressed I have a recurring dream rooted in that time of my life. It's never the same house, but I dream I've just moved into a new home – but it's dilapidated, or haunted, or both. There's always a sense of impending doom and I wander round the strangely shaped rooms thinking, 'How do I create a home out of this?'

The house we had bought was 1970s era and needed compete modernisation. The previous occupants had painted everything red, white or black. The man selling it was grieving – his wife had died in the house not long before – and the place felt heavy with sadness. At one point on our first viewing of the property Mike hit his head on a light and the homeowner said, 'That's probably my wife's ghost.'

I did my best to make it feel cosy and happy but I felt the house could take as much as I could throw at it and nothing changed its fundamental sadness. I made weird choices with the decor, painting our bedroom a cold, loveless grey. That was the room where I remember trying to hide from Mike when he was in one of his rages, but he burst in and pinned me down on the bed, pushing down my bare legs with one of his arms and holding his clenched fist above my thighs threatening, 'Say that one more time and I swear I'll fucking punch you as hard as I can.' He didn't act on this threat, but I was terrified.

I remember one of our last conversations before we split . . . he was making his usual 'joke' of pretending he was going to run off with someone.

'I went out for drinks with Max last night. The waitress was really flirting with me. I think I might take her out one night.'

The old me would have felt jealous and reacted to this prod, but now I hoped it was true.

I could suddenly see that Mike and I were not a good thing. My constant optimism that one day we were going to be happy, truly happy, started to crumble and I could see that I needed to get myself far, far away. The enormity of that realisation was heavy with the weight of all that I knew I had to do to shake myself free, but it was also framed with the lightness of hope. Whatever was on the other side was where I needed to be and it would be better for me. My head acted before my heart and I knew I had to get myself out of that place as soon as I could.

I first left in the spring. I went to my mum's for the week, telling Mike I needed time to work out how I felt, but something in me had shifted. He was pretty open, not angry. It was all puppy-dog eyes and romantic statements. He begged for another chance and we had a weekend away to see if there was anything that could be done. We had a strange and gloomy little trip to Birdworld to give ourselves time to work it out. It's not an inherently sad place, but looking at birds in cages is probably not the best visual metaphor for salvaging a sinking relationship. I felt hollow. By now Mike was promising me engagement rings and a better future, but emotionally I'd already gone.

I felt exhausted by my first attempt to leave and settled back into our old routine again for a few more weeks before Mike confronted me. What was wrong? Did I feel the same as I used to? I had to be honest. It was over.

*

I finally left and moved back in with my ma for a while as I figured out what to do next. Mike went from remorse to anger. He said he was going to kill himself and that it would be my fault. I knew better than to believe him and I stood my ground, but I was scared of him.

What followed was a lot of legal wrangling to get him to agree to sell the house. It was an intense period. I was just starting to get to know Richard and was falling in love with him, while releasing music from my album. I met with Mike one day, much later, to sort out some ongoing financial stuff at the management office. It would be the last time I saw him. I told him I was seeing Richard and he was surprisingly calm. I remember feeling relieved it was out in the open and headed home. That night the rage kicked in and he called. He hoped I'd get cancer and burn in hell. Everything he'd done previously to make me feel small and to make me stay with him had worked so well, but now . . . none of it did. I wasn't going to stay and take it anymore. I wasn't going to settle and be so sad and so alone. Once his usual tricks failed, I saw him as a small mean man. I feel grateful I have since been taught how love can lift you up and I feel relieved even now that I got away. I could have been living a very different life.

I asked my mum later, 'Did you notice I was unhappy?' I think at first she just thought it was an immature romance But I think the murkier corners of my life with him were kept away from my parents. Mike enjoyed being liked by them and was his most charming when my mother was around. I hid the hurt and the shame of the ugly dynamic. My parents were both in relationships that didn't echo mine, but I always hoped I could get mine to be more like theirs. I really thought I could. I know what I'm describing is the same trajectory of many relationships that don't work, but they don't all involve physical threats and the routine wearing down of someone's morale. It's possible to grow out of love without destroying each other in the process. It's not the norm to be held down with your boyfriend's fist aimed at you. I can't remember now what would provoke him, but I do remember the fear.

Mike's bad behaviour towards me was more obvious to other people. When Richard first met me, he met Mike the same day. He later told me that he was shocked at how rude Mike was to me. He would undermine what I said and casually humiliate me. Richard thought to himself, 'One day someone will come along and make her realise she doesn't have to be with that guy.' He never dreamed it could be him.

The thing is, what Richard noticed about how Mike spoke to me was something I'd become so used to. When we first started going out I remember him saying something mean to make a joke of me in front of his friends, but when they laugh along, you think it must be normal, that you're being over-sensitive. And then it just becomes how it is. Who's going to remark on it after that? I've been with couples who have a weird dynamic like that. You think that must just be what makes them tick.

Meanwhile I often felt ashamed of how things were and so my parents were unaware of the darker sides of my home life. I felt that if I kept doing my best, I'd make the whole picture rosier over time and things would really improve. It's hard to admit to yourself when something isn't right.

Towards the end I wasn't allowed to look out of the car window. Looking back I can't understand why, but it was as if Mike thought I might communicate my unhappiness to others. Maybe he thought they might recognise me and interfere if they thought things weren't going so well on the other side of the glass?

'Don't look out the window . . . I told you, don't look at the other drivers! And don't walk on your own anywhere. You'll get your legs broken. Don't come crying to me if someone hurts you.'

At the time I broke up with him, so much of the way he'd encouraged me to see myself stuck. I felt old and haggard . . . like I'd given myself away. The practicalities of the split were tiring but through the fog I was making my way to a new beginning. During the house sale I gave Mike so many things just to make him go away . . . my home recording studio equipment, a brand-new car I had been gifted after an endorsement. Nothing mattered; I just wanted to be free. The legalities lasted a very long time . . . I remember when my baby Sonny was in hospital after his early birth, I was pacing the hospital corridors outside the neonatal unit talking to Mike, trying to sort it all. In our last conversation, I walked back and forth again in the sitting room of the new house Richard and I had together. Mike wanted more from me. I said, 'I've given you the car, isn't that enough?' He said, 'To be honest, I'm not exactly dancing in the street about it.' 'You disgust me!' I shouted, then hung up and threw the phone across the room. When I looked down, my pacing up and down had sent my tiny son to sleep in my arms.

Some years later, I heard Mike had been jailed after committing a hit-and-run, with his child in the back of a car he wasn't insured to drive. He hit the man so hard it cracked his windscreen. He only got caught when he handed the car in two weeks later for repairs. The victim had so many bones broken from the impact of the car that he had been left a quadriplegic and had traumatic brain injuries.

What an awful, heartbreaking thing to happen.

It's strange that when the chance to write this book came up, my first instinct was, 'I want to tell this story. That I was in a dark relationship that I felt stuck in and ashamed of – but I got out.'

Then I had a last-minute wobble.

I was worried that once I wrote it all down, maybe I'd be questioned. I'm the one who might have to prove what I'm saying went on is true, and maybe time has warped some facts? I found it hard to remember detail and to articulate the subtle boundaries between what could be called bad behaviour and something more significant. But what I do remember is the emotion. I remember the unhappiness, the desperation to put it right, the tension of trying and the fear that came when I got things wrong. Not too long ago, Richard and I were doing some boxing training at the All Stars Boxing Gym in Kensal Rise. Our instructor asked Richard and me to spar, and having Richard face me with his fists up made me, in the middle of this old-school boxing club, suddenly burst into tears. It took me completely by surprise. I was too shocked to even feel particularly embarrassed. The sparring had reminded me of something I'd put in a hidden corner of my memories. So whatever nuances I do or don't recall, I do know that my last relationship wasn't right. I do know other people find themselves in similar situations. I do know that when you're in it, you feel in over your head and you have to build yourself up again, and I do know you can make it better. It took every strength I had to do it, but I got out and I know how precious the life I have now is because of it.

8

MUSIC: Why Does it Feel so Good?
– 'Groovejet (If This Ain't Love)'

Cristiano Spiller and I, Groovejet's mum and dad.

There is a song which changed my life and it's the song that most people associate with me. 'Groovejet' was busy being a club hit at the time theaudience was releasing its first album. Funny idea, that. I was totally monogamous with indie music but somewhere out there was a kernel of a song that would steal me away from all that and open my eyes to the wider world.

When I first heard the track it was the instrumental club version working its magic in the clubs. It had started its trajectory over in Miami where it was played in the club with the same name. With the song building in popularity, the DJ behind it – Spiller – was now under pressure to give it a top line (a melody sung by a vocalist) and release it commercially. He signed the track to EMI's dance imprint Positiva, who I now know are famous for their success with massive dance tracks, and they started the process. I was oblivious to all this. The dance music world at that time played no part in my life.

At this point and throughout the whole of theaudience's existence, I had written nothing. I wasn't really interested. I'd never tried to write a song (outside of some terrible songs when I was about ten. Sample lyrics: 'I was standing outside the school gates when a boy came along I could sure appreciate – his eyes were blue and his hair was brown, he was the hunkiest boy all around town').

Anyway, by May 2000 when the instrumental of 'Groovejet' was sent my way, I had been an unemployed musician for six months (following a year when theaudience were trying to make a second album and nothing was going right) and I was pretty miserable. 'Grooovejet' arrived at my little basement flat in an envelope, sent from my publishers. Credit to Mark from Rondor, the guy who suggested to Spiller and Positiva that they add my name to the list of potential singers and whose decision would change my life.

Anyhoo, there was this little shimmery CD arriving at my flat and I put it in the ghetto blaster next to my bed and when I heard it I was . . . insulted. What were they thinking?! How could my publishers send me a bloody dance record when I was an indie singer? I turned the CD off midway through, took it out and chucked it on the floor. What a waste of time, yet another company who just didn't understand me.

Two weeks later I was tidying up my flat and I found the CD. I couldn't remember what the song called 'Groovejet' – scrawled on the CD's surface in black marker – sounded like. What was it again? I put it back in the player and this time I was obviously in a less petulant mood. I quite liked it. There was something in the feel of the music that made me think, 'Maybe this is actually all right.' Positiva had emailed me looking for a top line and I decided I would have a go.

At the time, Martin Hall managed theaudience; he was a well-known and respected band manager. He was on holiday when I emailed EMI to say I was interested. They invited me along for a meeting about 'Groovejet' and I went on my own. It wasn't until Martin got back from his trip that I told him about it. 'I've decided to have a go at writing and singing a dance song. It seems like it could be fun.'

I had many reasons for doing the track but really I think the main motivation was needing a change. I'd been so burned by my experience with theaudience – the snide remarks in the music press, the sadness that it hadn't really been a proper band at all, feeling lost and aimless . . . I didn't have a clue what to do next.

Like a lot of folk, I like to be busy and I'm a simple soul. Just a tiny little plan can be enough to keep my mind occupied. But I didn't have any employable skills. I didn't have a plan B. I was miserable. Well actually, I was depressed. I felt very down and whenever I saw friends I felt I was only pretending to laugh or smile. It never reached my eyes and I remember being shocked that no one seemed to notice. It's actually pretty easy to fool people that you're fine.

I had started to try and kick-start some other projects. I made little bags, all brightly coloured fabrics with glittery thread and sometimes words sewn on. It sounds ridiculous now. Still, a little craft project was enough to soothe the old lady side of me and kept me feeling as if the days had a purpose.

The other thing that kept me getting out of bed in the morning was modelling. I had been excited at the idea of having a job in something that potentially complemented my singing career, but I absolutely hated modelling. Maybe if I'd got more jobs I would have felt differently, but as it was, I found it lonely and weird. I didn't want to be doing it. It made me feel acutely aware of how I'd failed already and I missed music so much. I'd put some theaudience photos at the back of my book and sometimes people would notice and be positive, but sometimes they'd be dismissive. I felt pretty lost.

At the agency were a couple of nice people working the desks, but there was one woman who was one of the biggest cows I've ever met. She had honed being bitchy to an art. She called to tell me I had the cover of a magazine. I was elated. Finally! A decent job! I called my mum and told her. When I turned up the next day I was shown a load of support tights and was told I'd be done in an hour. 'I thought it was a cover?' I said. 'Oh no, we won't even see your head. We just need you to model the different support tights.' I did the pictures then cried in the loos and went home. The cow must have high-fived herself with that one.

I also felt unprotected. When you sign your deal you have a checklist of stuff you're happy to do and stuff that you're not. I had said no to topless stuff and anything with real fur. This didn't stop me from being asked to do it when I turned up at shoots. Usually, at that point the client was annoyed. 'Well why won't you wear the fur?' shouted the stylist to me at a shoot where the rails were full of fur and fur alone. 'I'm sorry – it's on my list at the agency that I don't.' At another shoot I was asked to go topless. The photos were for a naff hairdressers to put on their wall. I was talked into going half-topless. Embarrassingly, they put a necklace of sequins on my bare chest and then stuck the sequins in place to cover my nipples with eyelash glue. Years later those photos – me with sequins barely covering my modesty and the saddest eyes ever – were sold by the slimy hairdresser boss to *Heat* magazine.

So by the time of the 'Groovejet' meeting, any opportunity to flee my reality was welcome. The idea of doing a dance record which said 'screw you' to the indie music press was incredible. It felt liberating to be outside of that radar. It was an adventure and out of my comfort zone. I knew nothing about the world of dance music. I think that's why, at the meeting, I didn't get the significance of some of the details about how the song was doing. Looking back, the label were pretty confident about the track doing well commercially, but I thought that was just talk.

After I had sat in the meeting in one of EMI's glass-walled conference rooms and told my manager Martin of my plans to have a go at singing the song, I went home to write my first ever top line. I hadn't written any songs in theaudience. It hadn't been important to me. But now I had a bit of an epiphany. Up until then I'd been able to explain away anything that had gone wrong for me without taking too much responsibility. But now I could see that this was not the most grown-up way of dealing with things. If I really wanted to sing I would have to put in the legwork and not blame anyone else if it didn't happen. I was prepared to be a bit vulnerable and put myself out there. The fact of the matter is, if you're a solo artist or the lead singer in a band, no one cares if, when the single flops, it was the drummer who chose the song. You're the figurehead and you must be accountable – or at least folk will forever associate you with the outcome no matter what.

With that in mind I wrote a top line on 'Groovejet' and recorded it in EMI's demo studios in their basement. It was the first bit of songwriting since the two songs I'd written on my Casio keyboard, aged eleven. The verses and middle eight were used but my original chorus (which was, admittedly, pretty pale in comparison to the fantastic one Rob Davis wrote) went 'And so it goes, and I told you so. Shows that I love you, shows that I know what is true.' I'll sing it for you one day if you like.

The label chose the bits they liked, spliced them with Rob's chorus and sent it back to me. At first I was pretty annoyed. I didn't want to sing 'ain't' as I felt it wasn't a real word and I was pernickety about such things.

The label put their foot down and I went along to a proper studio to record the vocals, where I also met Spiller for the first time. He was a seven-foot Italian man with a kind face and next to no English (but still more than my Italian). We communicated with smiles and thumbs up and translated production notes through his manager. I don't remember much about the day and went home oblivious to the fact I'd just recorded a song which would change everything. Pretty exciting to think of that, even now all these years on. Isn't it crazy to have the sort of job where a song can change your life? I love it and I still get that little bit of excitement when I write now.

Next, it was time to film the video. I went back to EMI to meet with the video commissioner Trudy and decide on a video treatment – basically a little pitch from video directors about what kind of video they would make if they were chosen to do it.

The one we ended up doing seemed to be based mainly on the fact that DJ Spiller is very tall and that people in Thailand are generally not. The video was made with a German crew in Bangkok and we'd be there for a week. I'd met Spiller once before and knew Trudy from the label but everyone else was new to me. I travelled to Bangkok on an overnight flight with Trudy. When I met her at the airport it transpired she was afraid of flying so we had some wine before the flight. I wasn't a big wine drinker but I matched her drink for drink. As we boarded the flight I could see I wasn't handling it as well as Trudy. We sat down the middle of a line of four in economy and drunkenly chatted for hours as the plane put itself into night-time mode and darkened the cabin. I remember the air hostess coming over to tell us to stop talking as they were getting complaints. Eventually Trudy slept (rather sweetly, on the shoulder of the stranger to her right) and I sat uncomfortably and tipsily all the way to Thailand.

If you've ever been to Bangkok, you'll know what an incredible assault on the senses it is. I had never been anywhere like that before. It was a proper culture shock. I emerged (hungover) from the airport and headed to the centre of the city where I found myself in the heart of this crazy, busy, noisy, colourful place. Everything was new. I remember the smells of the place, the dangerous roads, the cacophony of life everywhere you looked. I felt far from home and completely out of my depth.

We filmed for maybe four days of that week and it was a heady mixture of fun and feeling homesick. After early morning starts I would get ready with the kind make-up artist Carol, who kept an eye on me while I was away.

The initial treatment hadn't really featured me much and so I wasn't too sure exactly what my role was. In fact, with the original treatment I was only written into the video idea in the last two sentences. I think it was along the lines of, 'We sometimes see Sophie looking for Spiller. Maybe waiting by a bus stop or arriving somewhere he's just left.' I think the main steer I had when we were shooting was to look a bit bored and be vaguely looking for Spiller. Spiller's role meanwhile was to be having lots of fun being famous and tall – trying to use things designed for smaller people in Bangkok. We see him bending down to look into a mirror at the wrong height, being big on a little chair, Thai fans standing on chairs to be the same size as him . . . that kind of thing.

One notable thing for me in the video was that at one point I travelled in a tuk-tuk. It was the first time I'd ever been in one and years later, when Richard and I were in India, we thought it might be fun to own a tuk-tuk at home in London, to use it for the school run, that kind of thing. She's a real cutie and gets a lot of attention. Our postman once asked if my tuk-tuk was 'the one from the video'. I like the idea that I might have hunted down the one from Thailand twenty years later and had it shipped over. Slightly more eccentric than the reality of buying it from tuktuk.co,uk and having it shipped from Manchester.

Even though the treatment was a little bit slapstick and oddly comedic for a song that wasn't about being tall or lonely in Thailand, I think filming it in Bangkok was kind of genius as it lends a strange mood to the whole thing. It's shot in a way that captures a sort of *Lost in Translation* sense of displacement and also is directed with a languid intensity that conveys how you feel when you try to do anything in an extremely hot and crowded city.

At the end of every shoot day we'd sit down for supper and the table was full of Thai people speaking Thai, Germans speaking German and Italians speaking Italian, while Trudy, Carol and I chatted to each other. Thank goodness they were there. One night a big group of us went to a 'ping pong' show. Seeing that poor girl on stage lighting cigarettes using a lighter she'd put inside her doodah was horrible. She had the saddest eyes I've ever seen.

Once the video was made, my job was done for the time being except for a bit of promotion. I found myself talking to all sorts of different dance music publications and I was often honest to a fault. I would talk about the fact that I didn't like dance music, to the point where the guy doing press for the track told me I had to stop saying that. I had thought I was complimenting 'Groovejet' . . . kind of saying, 'I don't like dance music but I do like this track!'

Things then started to happen quickly. Two months before the song was due to be released, the song was A-listed on Radio 1. This meant it was immediately getting around thirty plays a week. Then, six weeks before release, the song was used for an advert by the BBC for their 'Sounds of the Summer' campaign. It was also around that time that somewhere in an Apple office in Silicon Valley, a new bit of tech called an iPod was having its first prototype tested with a song called 'Groovejet'. I'm tempted to write this again in case you missed it as, to be honest, it's probably the only one of my achievements that my kids have reacted positively to. So, yeah, mine was the first voice to come out an iPod. Ta-dah!

But while the momentum was growing with the single, something was pushing back on the song from a different place. Victoria Beckham was about to release a song with Dane Bowers and the True Steppers. It was a garage song and so was seen in terms of genre as a bit of a rival to house. There was immense pressure on that song to be a number one – all the other Spice Girls' songs had gone to number one and Victoria was already an incredibly famous and successful woman.

At first, I was a bit confused about the conversation that the press and the label were having. We were weeks away from release when they found out that both songs were being released on the same day. Why were they talking as if 'Groovejet' might be a number one? I had no idea that the song was predicted to do that. It was a crazy position to be in. There I was, a previously very unemployed singer from a dropped indie band who had sung on a dance record as a bit of an adventure and now it was assumed that the song would top, or nearly top, the charts. I had no idea everyone was so confident about the track. But to make it weirder still, a song that was about to be the biggest success of my career so far was now being talked about as if it was number one or bust. For me, anything in the top ten was incredible. I didn't want to feel as if I'd failed if the song wasn't number one. But still, Positiva were sure that we had a big shot and so the wheels in both EMI and the True Steppers' label began to turn.

As I began promotion for the song – almost always on my own as Spiller was in Italy for all but one week – I felt as if I could feel the heat from the Beckham/Bowers camp. Whatever TV I did, they were about to do or already had. Every radio station, magazine and newspaper was speaking to both of us. They put Victoria and me up against each other like boxers about to head into a ring. The press spoke to my family, tried to ramp up some weirdness about who was posher – Posh Spice or double-barrelled me? In amongst it all I tried to keep my feet on the ground. I knew it was cartoony and not long lasting. I made jokes to keep the humour in it but looking back, some of them probably didn't land too well. I remember being asked if I was going to marry a footballer too and I said, 'I did consider saying my boyfriend plays for Man City and we have a kid called Chiswick.' I was trying to make a joke of the comparisons but it probably looked bitchy. Truth be told, it was all a little intimidating and distracting. I felt a bit freaked out and wanted to focus on the song.

The two weeks leading up to release were really intense. Spiller arrived in London so we got to do bits of promo together but essentially I was pulled in every direction possible by the label. The press officer was trying every angle he could think of to get coverage. Aside from a slightly dodgy shoot for the red-topped newspapers where they put me in the red dress from the video and then backlit it so you could see the outline of my whole body, Matt also suggested to me we do a photoshoot with one of the contestants from Big Brother where a paparazzo would take it in such a way it looked as if I was dating the contestant. I said no, but it showed how far everyone was prepared to take things to try and get 'Groovejet' to number one. Even my mum was doing interviews about the release.

During that promotional craziness, I got to one TV studio where Victoria and Dane had left me a note. It said, 'Good luck on Sunday', and they'd both signed it. It reassured me that behind all the daftness in the press, they were just two people who hadn't lost sight of the intensity. Still, it ramped up and up. The week of the release was pretty ridiculous. I felt so much weight on my shoulders and I thought, 'I can't fight the might of this.' I didn't blame the Victoria camp at all. It must have been so horrid for them that they felt so much pressure to be at the top of the charts. Genuinely, that's full on. Plus it's a bit of a game, isn't it? And the press were obsessed by the whole thing. The chart battle was on the national TV news, in the papers and the *Sun* even ran a nasty front page with a photo of the Beckhams at a signing at Woolworths and the headline 'DESPERATE'.

Still, that chart week was fun in a way. I was running on adrenaline and the two singles were so closely pipped, it was really gripping. We received numbers on sales – called the midweeks – every day from Tuesday to Friday. On the Tuesday, the True Steppers were 2,000 sales ahead. By Wednesday it was down to 1,800, then 1,200 by Thursday and finally just 500 sales ahead by Friday. Then it all went quiet until the final chart was revealed on Sunday.

That Saturday I'd been working, doing yet more promotion. As I sat at the bus stop, waiting to head home to my little basement flat, I noticed it was nearly 6 p.m., and I knew Woolworths on the high road was open until then. I had about fifteen minutes. What if I quickly ran in there and bought 'Groovejet'? 'What if that's the sale that makes all the difference?' I thought. 'What if tomorrow they are number one by only one sale?' I shrugged it off, 'Nah. I'm not going to do it. Que sera sera.' And with that I boarded the bus and got myself home.

The next day wasn't the way I'd have planned it if I'd known I was going to get good news. I had a Radio 1 roadshow to get to in Plymouth. I went with a tour manager and didn't take any friends. I do have family in Plymouth – my lovely Uncle Duncan and Auntie Elaine are there – but typically they weren't home that day. To perform the track, the label had hired a band to mime. Money well spent there.

We'd just arrived when Jason Ellis from Positiva called me. The connection wasn't great but I could make out, 'You're number one. You outsold number two by 20,000 copies yesterday.' Seems I was right not to have bought my own copy the day before.

I felt a mixture of things. I was happy, of course. It was an amazing achievement and I was so proud of the song. But also, I had literally no one there to celebrate with. It was a really odd sensation.

As I sang on stage, I wasn't allowed to let anyone know the chart position yet but I probably performed it with uncharacteristic (for that time) jolliness.

As I was going home, with all my make-up off and a stupid T-shirt I'd bought from Topshop that made me laugh (it was a red top with PECKHAM on it), I climbed wearily into the car to go home. A photographer ran over. 'Can I get a photo?' I reluctantly climbed out of the car and posed, fresh faced and wearing the silly top, putting my arm out in front of me with one finger raised in a '1' sign. Then I said 'Bye' and got myself back, where I met my boyfriend in a pub. By then it was evening and I was so tired. 'Champagne, please,' I said to the barman. 'We don't have any,' he replied. 'Erm, OK . . . a pint?'

I took my pint to the table, drank maybe half then started to fall asleep. That's the way to celebrate, eh? Plymouth with no friends followed by a little kip in a pub with a pint you didn't want. Rock and roll.

The weeks that followed are a bit of a blur. I was invited to my first film premiere – the Guy Ritchie movie, *Snatch*, and I didn't understand that usually you get a fancy car that drives down the red carpet and drops you where all the photographers are at the cinema door. I went on the tube and walked along the red carpet by myself as limos drove past me on one side and the autograph-hunters stood over the other side of the rope. One of the limos slowed down as it reached me and the window in the back went down. Inside was a smiley Spice Girl, Melanie C. She shook my hand: 'I wanted to congratulate you on your number one! It's a great song.'

Soon after that I was invited to go to Ibiza for the first time. I'd been asked to sing at a big club night called Renaissance in a venue called Privilege. It was a whole new world. I travelled to the island with my boyfriend's sister Sara and no tour manager. I have made this mistake a few times in my life and it's daft not to take anyone with you in your camp who can look after you if things go wrong. When we got to the hotel it was evening and Sara and I took a disco nap as I wasn't singing until 4 a.m. We arrived at the club around 2 a.m. and I was wide-eyed . . . the club was huge with an amazing sound system and real palm trees in the middle. The place was packed with thousands of people. It's possible Sara and I were the only sober ones in there. There was a DJ called Sander Kleinenberg playing and his set single-handedly changed my view of DJs. Up until then I had not really understood the cult of the DJ. To me it was always some bloke (I know there are female DJs but I don't think I'd ever seen one at that point in my life) playing one song after another, usually taking requests as he went. But in this club, Sander was playing house music and I could see he was creating a real journey with the sound. It was brilliant and Sara and I danced until it was time for me to sing. I realised that really good DJs do that – they create a story with the music they play and can keep you on your feet for hours.

The next few months saw me singing in many, many more clubs although none as impressive as that one in Ibiza. When Martin had resigned as manager, he offered me one bit of advice. 'Just don't go singing "Groovejet" in all the clubs in the land. It's a bit of a cul-de-sac – you'll end up in that club world and won't get out.'

Martin was a kind and lovely man with good advice, but I completely and knowingly ignored him on this occasion.

I had been royally broke and, having not had any options in the music world for so long, I seized this chance to sing with both hands. I honestly didn't think too hard about it. The success of 'Groovejet' translated into bookings at every dance club up and down the country and I think I said yes to every booking. I had a tour manager called JP and he'd turn up at my flat every Friday at about 8 p.m. ready to transport me to a house night at a club in Manchester, or Birmingham maybe, and off we'd go. We never stayed overnight so I would just snooze a little in the back of the car while JP downed Red Bull after Red Bull. We'd pull up outside places called things like Equinox at around 1 a.m. and I'd be woken up by the car stopping. I'd be shown in through the back of the club to a waiting area, which was rarely an actual dressing room, more likely the manager's office. I'd wait in the brightly lit office staring at the pinboards with staff rotation notes written on the Page 3 girls calendar on the wall until it was time to go onstage. As 'Groovejet' had been released under Spiller's name (I had my name on the single artwork but it was promoted as a track by Spiller) most clubs didn't have a clue how to introduce me. My name – often misspelt and mispronounced at the best of times – was read out in all manner of ways as I walked on stage. My all-time favourite – because Bexter and Baxter, although wrong, get boring pretty quickly – was one nightclub bringing me out (literally through glitter curtains) as 'Sarah Alabaster'. Usually, though, I was introduced as 'Spiller'. In fact, because of the publicity the single had received on its release, I was now getting recognised around the place and it was usually accompanied with the heckle, 'Oi! Spiller!'

I found my new fame part amazing (I couldn't believe how things had turned around after being dropped just the year before), part intimidating (once your face is on telly people don't always think you're a real person. I'd be talked about while I was standing right near people and it freaked me out) and part amusing. Fame is a funny little beast. If people recognise you because you sing a song they love, then that's fame with context and that feels pretty good actually. But fame where they just know your face is like being a walking cardboard cut-out. Vacuous but pretty harmless. Still, I tried to evade being recognised when I was on my own and if someone did say something to me, I'd quite likely put on a French accent and pretend they'd got the wrong girl.

Those club gigs were a bit of a revelation. Finally – some money in my bank account! The main gigs paid fairly well but to top it up my tour manager would sometimes arrange secret cash-in-hand gigs on the side. He knew loads of smaller clubs so he'd make a phone call to the clubs when we were near and I'd get maybe £200 cash in hand after hopping up and singing one song, because obviously I only had the one song. Sometimes I had to sing it twice. My all-time record for turning up at a club, singing, then being back in the car was eleven minutes in total. The little cash-in-hand gigs, which became known as 'shoe gigs' as I told JP I'd use the money to buy more shoes, might take a bit longer as JP might want to catch up with whoever he knew there while we stopped by. Occasionally I'd have two club shows booked and if I got a shoe gig too, well then I'd be out all night singing. I must have done somewhere in the region of seventy gigs like this in total. Although I could see why Martin had tried to put me off, I was so happy to be booked for work. I'd sometimes meet other singers waiting backstage in those club office rooms. It might be two or three in the morning and I'd get chatting to singers like me who had put their vocals on dance tracks. They were often uncredited and so their ability to build on the success of the songs was much harder. Even though they might be the voice of that big hit song, it was the DJ's name which people would remember. This meant the clubs and getting those bookings became crucial, and maybe they'd sing at every one and then go around again until the bookings dried up. I didn't fancy being stuck in that world but at the same time I knew my place in the food chain so I felt lucky to be busy at all. A lot of the clubs were grimy and lairy, filled with very straight crowds and a slightly fractious atmosphere. The full-on house club scene was still not my thing and those clubs put me on edge. I didn't feel I'd found my home.

Still, aside from the money in my bank account, the little kernel of my love of disco was beginning to blossom. Not from the playlist in these clubs, but as JP and I travelled up and down the country to each of these gigs, he would put on various CDs in the car to keep us happy. One of them was a great album of seventies DJ Larry Levan DJing at a New York club called the Paradise Garage. The music was incredible and I'd often ask JP to play that album as we drove. One of the tracks in particular really stood out to me. It was a seven-minute-long version of Cher singing 'Take Me Home'. Little did I know how that song and I would have a very long, very happy relationship together.

Around that time Polydor had begun courting me. They were keen to sign me for a solo deal. The MD at Polydor at the time, Lucian Grainge, had seen me singing on a TV programme and decided he wanted to have me on the label.

And so with that I embarked on the next chapter of my career – from band to featured artist to solo artist, and beyond.

9

ME: Rent-a-Quote – 'Me and My Imagination'

Giving it some 'tude back in '88.

Martin, the manager of theaudience, gave me one bit of advice that changed the course of my life a little. This was the piece of advice from Martin that I did listen to. He told me, 'Don't be rent-a-quote. If you always come out with bald, bold statements, the press are going to come looking for you every time they need someone to deliver a contentious quote. Do you want that to be you?'

I didn't. So over time I modified myself a little. Not to the point of being beige or having no public opinion at all, but I learned what I now tell my kids all the time – to think before I speak.

But not before I'd made a few mistakes.

In the early days of my band's journey we began doing interviews. Lots of them. Print, radio, TV . . . we were a new band signed to a major label and so we were wheeled out to wherever would have us. I was happy to be asked questions. I was an eighteen-year-old girl with a ton of ideas on how the world should work and what was cool and what wasn't. How brilliant that I had this opportunity! Finally, the world would be put to rights.

Only – when I opened my mouth I'd quite often come out with utter rubbish.

I hadn't yet learnt the golden rule. When you are in the public eye and you are asked questions, you don't ACTUALLY tell the truth. You skew it a little. Even saying 'I hate cowboy boots' (me, *Melody Maker*, 1998) looks harsh when it's written down.

For this book, I have reread tons of old articles and it's painful stuff. I came out with whatever was on my mind without any filter and I sound so flipping pleased with it all.

However, I do know that some of my spiky little lines came from pure insecurity. I felt the world of the music press was very hard to please and I didn't know how to assert myself. And that wasn't just in interviews. At the record company the big boss man didn't seem too interested in asking me – an actual teenage girl – what other teenagers liked to listen to. When I offered my thoughts on music he told me, 'You're a very opinionated young woman.'

Then there was the issue of my double-barrelled name, which made people assume certain things about me. And there was the fact that a lot of the journalists knew who my mum was. Now, I'm super proud of my mum, but I felt like my *Blue Peter*-coloured childhood was being used to ridicule me and make it impossible for me to have any of my own mystery.

Speaking my own mind and getting into this kind of trouble started young. My first mortifying 'Whoops I said that out loud' was when I was eight. I was away with my dad and my granny on holiday visiting relatives in Winnipeg, Canada. My great-aunt and uncle live there. It's funny, I haven't been to many Canadian places and if I meet someone who is from Canada they always tell me how boring Winnipeg is. This may be true, but aged eight, I was pretty excited to travel. My great-uncle had worked for Heinz and had a phone that looked like a ketchup bottle. Winnipeg could never be dull with that in its world.

My great-aunt Sylvia scared me a bit. She was of the mind that children should be seen and not heard and I felt a bit on edge. I remember early on in the trip being taken to a restaurant. I wanted to order a drink for myself but I got confused and asked the waiter for a 'stiff drink' when I meant to say 'soft drink'. Oh my god, now Sylvia thought her eight-year-old great-niece was a hardened drinker. But more embarrassing was yet to come. One night we were driving in the car with Sylvia and Uncle Bob up front while I sat sandwiched in between my dad and granny in the back. Bob was telling a story about being stopped by a policeman for speeding. I'm not sure why, but in the brief silence following the tale about the cop pulling him over, I decided to pipe up with what I would have done if I'd have been pulled over.

'I'd have told him to bugger off,' I said.

Stunned silence in the car.

'What?' said my dad.

'The policeman, I'd have told him to bugger off.'

Embarrassment flooded through me and I spent the rest of the silent drive home with my face buried in my dad's arm.

Another classic 'Why the hell did I come out with that?' moment was when I was eleven. Again, in front of my dad . . .

This time it was my eleventh birthday party and at that time, 1990, every kid I knew watched *Whose Line is it Anyway?*. For those who haven't seen it, it was a TV programme with two teams of stand-up comics who had to improvise scenes and they won points for the funniest improv. For my birthday party I had friends over to my dad's house to play our own game of *Whose Line?*. For one of the rounds, each team had a prop which they'd use to improvise as many things as possible. For example, if you had a remote control you could make it a phone, a battery pack . . . whatever you could think of on the spot.

In front of all my friends and my stepmum Polly and her sister Sally, my dad gave each team a prop. My team were given a large Chinese painting brush which Polly kept on the mantelpiece. It had its bristles still stuck together – they wouldn't come loose unless the brush was dipped in water.

'Don't get the brush wet,' said my dad as he handed it to me.

'How would I get it wet?' I said sassily, hands on hip and then – thinking my friends would find this an amazingly funny line, 'Perform oral sex on it?'

Silence.

Sally gave an awkward howl of a laugh.

Then more silence.

This joke had not landed as I'd hoped. Embarrassment started to pile in. My dad and I never spoke of this again.

You'd think that these memorable and mortifying early experiences of blurting out whatever was in my head would have steered me towards a kind of caution, but no. Sometimes my brain just thought, 'This is funny,' before saying it aloud and then realising it wasn't.

As I got older, I just got more confident with saying whatever was in my head and sometimes it landed me in trouble.

I'd always thought of myself as a singer with quite a low register (it's weirdly got higher since I had bubbas), which led me to describe myself to Neil Hannon from The Divine Comedy when I met him at a music show and was a bit nervous as 'a bit deep-throated.'

Great.

In 1998, the audience were offered a support slot for Robbie Williams' headline show at the Royal Albert Hall. My view was that any band or artist supporting another band or artist was not about economics but about a big thumbs up from one to the other. I imagined that whoever supported whoever on tour meant that backstage they were big buddies . . . hanging out, playing ping-pong together . . . all of that. I was not a Take That fan and nor was I a Robbie Williams fan. He did not represent my musical feelings at the time (I find it quite funny now that I have supported Take That on tour – and I had a lovely time doing it), so for me it was an obvious 'no' about doing the support date.

However, my band and management felt differently. It was a huge opportunity. A great chance to reach a new demographic. We should definitely do it.

I felt just as strongly against. The more we argued, the more polarised the positions became. I suppose at heart it was an old-fashioned power struggle. Most things in the band were decided by committee but ultimately I did hold the trump card with whether we actually turned up and did stuff. Meanwhile the band was booked to do more press and TV promo for our third single release, 'A Pessimist is Never Disappointed'. Foolishly, we began talking about the Robbie Williams support date in the press. I thought I was being so flipping clever when I went on Jo Whiley's TV programme to be interviewed, and I spouted my thoughts about why Robbie Williams wasn't my cup of tea.

Alas, he was watching at home and obviously what I'd said wasn't very well received. He started saying stuff about me in the press, too. Looking back, a lot of it was pretty petty and daft, but still I'm not someone that likes bad blood. For twenty years I felt really crummy about it all. I know internet trolls will know this feeling well, but I really didn't think that someone so famous would actually take any notice of what I said. I finally got an address for him last year and wrote him an email apologising. He was very gracious about it. He seems really lovely, actually.

I suppose the moral of this story is to be careful what you say.

Took a while for me to learn that, though.

When I signed to Polydor they enrolled me in a media day to help me steer my way through interviews without so many mishaps. I found it a little patronising, but to be honest it probably did me some good. One of my favourite bits of advice was to answer the question I wished I'd been asked, rather than the one I'd actually been asked. Watch and you'll see politicians do this all the time. Or you can gently move the topic to something you prefer . . . for example when people asked me, 'What does your mum think about what you're doing?' I learnt to say, 'My parents both think I'm great,' or whatever. I have never actually said, 'My parents both think I'm great,' though. Mum? Dad? You do, right?

10

MUSIC: Read My Lips – 'Take Me Home (A Girl Like Me)'

Performing songs from Read My Lips, wearing a dress
I still love from the Take Me Home video

After the success of 'Groovejet', Universal offered me a solo deal with Polydor. If this had happened to me any sooner I wouldn't have felt ready but after the crash course in having an international hit with 'Groovejet', I was excited and focused about getting started on my own two feet. I was ambitious and now, after the failure of my first band, I felt a little more fearless, too. I decided to make the most out of every chance I had. I know I have a slightly Pollyanna streak (a gift from my equally pragmatic and positive mother) and so I genuinely have felt, ever since 'Groovejet', that I am very, very lucky to have been given the opportunities I've had since then. Even now when I release new songs I know I'm fortunate. There are so many singers, so many songs, why should anyone still give me the time of day? So there I was . . . ready to be heckled by my own name, not 'Oi! Spiller!'

I felt as if I had a pretty good handle on the sort of pop singer I wanted to be. Most of it was a little reactionary. I have said this to my kids many times, but the stuff that used to feel made me different in a bad way was now the stuff I sought to accentuate to differentiate me from the pack. This was the early 2000s and pop was a dirty word. On the radio there were, by and large, two types of pop star – either flirty and extra-polished like Britney, or smiley, high-fiving pals like S Club 7 or Hear'Say. I knew I was neither. I felt like the odd kid. My name wasn't a pop star's name, I wasn't blonde or tanned or good at dancing or particularly popular, but through music I was beginning to find my tribe and this was the time to celebrate all that. I wasn't Teflon-coated at all, but I think I'd had enough thrown at me to have made myself a small suit of armour.

I remember meeting the MD of Polydor at that time, Lucian Grainge. He told me he wanted to give me a record deal. I then didn't see him again until the paperwork had all gone through. The people I dealt with in the meantime were A&R men called Paul Adams and Simon Gavin. They nurtured the deal and set to work on getting an idea of what my first solo album would be like. As that took shape, I had my first meeting with Lucian as one of his signed artists. Simon, Paul and I were ushered into Lucian's office, a long rectangular room with Lucian sitting at a huge desk at one end and a small sofa at the other end, which the three of us squished onto. There was a bit of an awkward silence then Simon asked me to tell Lucian all about a video idea I'd had. I rattled on – probably for too long – about a video I wanted to make which, to be honest, I still think would be kinda cool now although maybe not for me but for someone young and cool who can dance. If anyone wants the idea, here it is: the pop star is on the tube with headphones in. Whenever we cut to the pop star we can hear what she hears – an energetic, seductive and irresistible dance track. We then cut to the rest of the passengers as they travel in glum silence. Back to the girl. She can't help herself. She dances along the tube carriage, sometimes sitting on a passenger's lap, sometimes playfully grabbing a stranger's newspaper or hat, until finally she gets to the middle of the tube carriage where she launches herself round the pole and pole-dances for her life. We then cut to the stunned, silent tube audience. At the next stop, the pop star smiles and gets off the tube.

Ta-dah!

You can have that.

Anyway, I finished my tale, told with slightly nervous loud enthusiasm, to a silent Lucian. I felt Simon and Paul shift nervously next to me.

'So,' boomed Lucian, 'we have a problem. And it's a big problem. And it involves you, and me.'

Oh god, I thought. They didn't mean to sign me.

'The problem is this: I wanna make you a star. How do you feel about that? And to do it, we're going to be spinning a lot of plates. None of that Woolworth's crap.'

Relieved that Polydor had meant to sign me after all, I got on with the business of making my first album. Musically, I worked with a lot of different people. Early on I suggested the cover of Cher's brilliant seventies song 'Take Me Home', having heard it so many times on the road with JP as I went from club to club singing 'Groovejet'. Happily, my main A&R man for the album, Simon, loved the idea. I wasn't so keen on Cher's very grown-up and slinky, sexy lyrics (they are fab but very boudoir: 'Wrapped in your arms tonight, just making love') and I wanted something a bit flirtier, so I rewrote the words in the verse. This song was earmarked as a possible single.

Other songs were written with some session writers/producers who my record company introduced me to like TommyD, Steve Osborne and Damian LeGassick (who I went on to make my second album with). I also personally asked to write with some people like Alex James (the bassist from Blur) as I'd always been a huge fan. I met with him first for a cup of tea at the Groucho Club in Soho (a members' club so notorious for being a place to find the movers and shakers that once, about five years before this, my friend Becca and I had gatecrashed one night. We walked in to find Keith Allen playing piano but then the receptionist at the door told us, 'You two have been very naughty. You have to leave.'). Now I was sitting two seats away from the same piano, having a meeting. It all felt quite surreal. Even at that first meeting Alex gave me a golden piece of advice: 'You have to accept that your journey as a singer will have highs and lows. No one's career is a straight upward trajectory.' He's 100 per cent right about that and it's a comfort to have known it for the last couple of decades. Along with producer Ben Hillier, we wrote one of my favourite songs on the album, 'Move This Mountain'. On the day we recorded my vocals, Alex was up in Liverpool so I'd gone up to a studio there to sing. As the day drew to a close, Alex asked me how I was getting home.

'I've got a train ticket,' I said.

'Would you rather fly home?'

This was literally the coolest thing that had happened to me at that point.

We went to the little airfield and Alex and I flew in his little plane with his instructor Tony, the same man who around ten years later would teach Richard to fly when I bought him flying lessons for his thirtieth birthday.

The other notable writing session I had was with Moby. He'd approached me, getting in touch through the label. I flew alone to New York to spend a week writing with him. On arriving at his apartment, he asked me, 'So is Mike your boyfriend?' 'Yes,' I replied, and with a funny little smile Moby said, 'Hmm . . .'

The rest of the week felt a little odd. I worked as hard as I could on the instrumental music Moby had given me but I felt he regretted bringing me over. We had an evening when I went for dinner with him and a friend, an artist called Damian Loeb who made huge and amazing photo-realistic paintings. Being totally inexperienced about the art world, I breathlessly told him they were incredible and how I'd love one for my home. 'How much are they?' I asked. 'Oh, they go for around $25,000.'

I shut up a bit after that. We then went to a macrobiotic sushi restaurant for supper, which was hands down one of the most disappointing meals I've ever had. How did they manage to take all the fun out of sushi?

I spent a lot of time wandering round New York by myself. Luckily for me it wasn't the first time I'd been there and I found it a very easy city to walk around solo. I loved discovering the little shops and parks and liked feeling independent. I don't get a lot of time in my own company and, truth be told, I love it.

I'd gone to New York twice before as a child and had found it so glamorous. This trip with Moby, however, was rather lonely and the feeling of homesickness was spun into the lyrics of the song I wrote ('Is It Any Wonder') while I was there. I had a little hotel room overlooking the rooftops and I could imagine somewhere out there was a mother with her baby in one of those tiny loft rooms . . . that's what I was thinking about. I'm not sure Moby was that into anything I'd done and confusingly when I got back to Blighty, although he was happy for me to use the song we'd done together, he wanted it released under his own name, Richard Hall, so no one knew we'd worked together.

The final songwriting collaboration was more successful. I'd heard from the label about a song that they thought could be a hit but it wasn't finished and was just a very loose demo on cassette. In a swanky recording studio where I was finishing another track, Simon Gavin walked in and played the first version of 'Murder on the Dancefloor'. It was a very rough recording which I think Gregg Alexander – the guy who wrote it

– had sung in his car. I'm pretty sure he told me he'd written it one night when we wanted to go out and his car wouldn't start so he'd just chucked down the idea with just a melody and acoustic guitar. The lyrics were half done but some of it was just smudgy singing to get the melody across. Simon told me that Gregg was the singer from the New Radicals who I knew from their hit 'You Get What You Give' (I still think that's a great record) and I knew that Gregg had written 'Life is a Rollercoaster' for Ronan Keating. 'You can have a go at finishing the lyrics but I think the song could be a hit.' I don't remember if I agreed but I knew I liked it. My radar for working out what's going to be a hit and what isn't is actually pretty bad. I've always just gone on how it makes me feel. This is a good barometer for enjoying the work you do and for sleeping well at night, but it means that when a song doesn't do what you expect in the chart, it can be confusing – I love it, why doesn't everyone else? I'm used to it now.

I took the demo of 'Murder' home and wrote the missing lyrics. I imagined the song was about that moment when you're out dancing and the night is peaking. I wanted it to be a bit playful and fun. At that point I hadn't met Gregg so I was a bit alarmed when he rang me. He didn't even say hello, just: 'Sophie? You better not steal the moves, Sophie.' I thought maybe he hated what I'd done but actually he thought it was cool.

The label put in some writing sessions with Gregg and Matt Rowe. Matt arrived off the back of huge success working with Richard 'Biff' Stannard to write most of the Spice Girls' music. Matt sometimes played the chords to '2 Become 1' when we were working. I always thought it was such a gorgeous song. I found Matt and Gregg easy to write with and we did 'Music Gets the Best of Me' for the album together.

At the opposite end of the scale, I had a very tricky session when it came to the song 'Get Over You'. It had been sent as a pitch to Polydor for me and at that point was called 'Don't Step On My Groove'. Having had 'Groovejet' and knowing 'Murder on the Dancefloor' also had me singing about not killing the groove, I was worried people might start thinking I was groove-obsessed. I'm not groove-obsessed, I'm just groovy. It was decided I would work on the track with the original writers and pull it more in my direction. The production team behind the song were called Merlin and they were based in Stockholm. In the year 2000, Swedish pop writers and producers were dominating the pop charts both in Europe and America, and the pressure was on to a) make this song a hit, and b) make lots of money from it.

I was sent to Stockholm for three days to rewrite and record the song. Simon Gavin travelled with me but he was only due to stay for the first day to settle me in before heading back to London for work. When we arrived, the Swedish writers – Henrik and Mathias – were in good spirits. They seemed super friendly and keen to make it work. I worked with them there to finish the song and after the first day they seemed really happy. The next day I trotted back to the studio – alone this time as Simon had gone home.

'The work you did yesterday . . . we really liked it, but we played it to the rest of the company and no one else likes what you've done.'

I felt a chill. Had they just waited until my A&R had gone home before saying this to me? I felt as if they were hiding behind the team. I spent the day painstakingly rewriting the song and also justifying every change. The chorus was now 'Get Over You' and I was happier with the lyrics overall but the experience had been painful. Every word change was vetted by the rest of the Merlin group (faceless to me – I never saw the committee, I'd just get the feedback) and then it was given the thumbs up or down. Everything was decided on whether or not it would increase the song's hit potential.

When I came to record my singing, every vowel, breath and tone was assessed. In the end I started inventing reasons to leave the room just so I could get a break. It was pretty soul-destroying. Years later when I was making my second album they asked to write with me again. I sent an email back to them: 'I wish you all the best, but I can't work how you work. Making music isn't supposed to be clinical, it's instinctive and you took all the fun out of it for me.' They didn't reply.

With twelve songs recorded, the album was now done. I obviously wanted to put 'Groovejet' on there but slightly surprisingly, Spiller said no. After the song had been on over 600 compilations already (that's 600, folks), I thought he might be happy for me to release it too, but he was adamant that I wouldn't have it on my record. The version on the album is a live one from my tour . . . that's Richard on bass, there. It ends with something I said as a dare, which is quite funny. There's a song on the Ferris Bueller soundtrack by a band called Yellow which has no lyrics aside from 'Oh yeah' and a sort of 'chick . . . chick-chick-ah!' noise. I was dared to say that in the gig, so right at the end of the Shepherd's Bush concert I shouted 'chick-chick-ah!' and then, as luck would have it, that was the version they cut for the record and you can hear my shout-out as the last thing on the album.

The artwork was done with photographers Mert and Marcus. They were brilliant and used the slightly unusual technique of taking turns to take the pictures, so that when they got the contact sheet no one knew who had done what. I loved the pictures . . . Richard Avedon-esque with red lips and black flick eyeliner. The make-up artist with me that day was Charlotte Tilbury. She was already a big name and I loved what she did. I had a piece of blue chiffon which we blew about in a wind machine while Mert and Marcus snapped away. The design team Michael Nash Associates – who I have worked with ever since – were so fabulous with the concept for the *Read My Lips* cover, with designer Stephanie using lipstick to write my name over the images of me. I loved its boldness and its clarity. I knew her idea wouldn't ever look dated. That's why real creative talent stands the test of time . . . those people are aware of fashions but use their good taste to create something that will always look good.

The same goes for the video director I ended up working with for the majority of my videos. It was decided that 'Take Me Home' would be the first release in the UK. There was a brilliant video director called Sophie Muller who was interested and the label were all really excited as she was their first choice for the project. 'She needs to speak to you first, to see if she wants to do it,' my A&R man told me. Happily, Sophie spoke to me as if she was already on board. 'What do you want to do in the video?' she asked. 'I want to wear amazing vintage dresses and dance like I'm in an old Technicolor movie . . . I want to be held up and twirled around by dancing men in suits.'

That's basically what we did.

The video budget was crazily high – I think it was £110,000. Mind-blowing and very much the norm for a priority act on a major label back in 2000. It was a two-day shoot with a whole set made to look like a street scene complete with shopfronts and street lights – even a working fountain! A huge poster sat on top of the roofs with a painted close-up of my face. It was all pretty heady and extreme. I loved every minute of it. I've always loved making videos – all that industry, just to make a little film to go along with my song! Bloody brilliant.

Turns out I fell on my feet in more ways than one with that first solo video. Not only did it mark the beginning of my working relationship with the incredibly talented Sophie but I also met Lisa Laudat and Louise Constad that day. They were doing my hair and make-up and were so funny, clever and outspoken that I knew I loved them both early on. All three of those women have extraordinary vision. Louise's make-up is beautiful and distinctive. So innovative, too. She is the one who created the shimmering gorgeousness of the glitter emerald eyeshadow in 'Murder on the Dancefloor'. Lisa is a master of hair and also make-up, too (Louise was her mentor).

Director Sophie Muller was instrumental in helping me gain confidence in being the sort of pop star I wanted to be and I'm so incredibly lucky that I met her at that point in my career. The landscape for female pop stars at that time was by and large either a 'super-poised, triple-threat dancer/performer/slick lady' pop star or a 'best friend super-smiley sister you never had' type. I didn't feel I could pull either of those off. I didn't have any dance lessons until I was thirty-four (thanks, *Strictly*) so option one was out and my default setting for this new world of fame was slightly guarded, so option two was out as well. I have always been someone that will run towards the strengths rather than be disappointed I can't succeed with the weaknesses, so rather than being full-on smiley 'please like me and we'll be BFFs', I decided to go with all the things I've always loved, like the palette of fifties and sixties emerald colours and a little bit of mystery. The choreographer for the shoot was Michael Rooney – Mickey Rooney's son – and he created such beauty with the routine the male dancers did around the fountain. I've just watched the video again and maybe what I said about playing to my strengths was a little hasty! I was so rubbish at the dancing in the routine, but with twelve costume changes, I definitely knew how to distract folk a little!

It's hard to pinpoint exactly what makes Sophie my favourite director but I think it's a combination of the fact she has very good taste, a clear vision, a good sense of humour and I trust her completely. I'm not writing this to flatter her, but it's important because when you're starting out, these people in your life help guide you. She was very firm that the record label would not be able to film any backstage videos or invite any camera crews along. Nothing to ruin the magic. That's quite unusual.

We are encouraged to think that content and information has to be on tap to keep people interested. It takes confidence to just present something at the end. It's always resonated with me that Sophie felt the same way about mystique. For me, it was also a way to protect myself. With 'Murder on the Dancefloor', people were already sure about who I was. They thought I was snooty, stuck-up, aloof . . . I didn't hugely mind. Having had my fingers burned by my experience in my first band, I wasn't overly keen to give everything of myself in case that was rejected, too. This version of me that was being criticised in the press wasn't exactly me, so I felt removed. I don't feel like this now, but back then it overwhelmed me a little that my name wasn't my own anymore. 'Sophie Ellis-Bextor' was an artist and a brand, but it was still just me, too. I felt as if that could get lost a bit so rather than try and show my true colours I had a little bit of fun with the character people thought I was. Hell, some folks were even a bit scared of me and that 'head teacher' vibe isn't all bad.

With the video for 'Murder', I went for it. I had an idea to base the video on a sixties movie starring Jane Fonda called *They Shoot Horses, Don't They?* in which there's a dance competition and they all dance until they collapse.

In the video for 'Murder', my character was horrible. A conniving, nasty person hell-bent on winning. If you've never done it, may I recommend playing the baddie. I got to poison, trip up and break the legs of my fellow contestants. Sophie and I had the best time with the auditions for the video. Couple after couple came and danced in the tiny production office. Sophie and I laughed, clapped and cheered through the audition tape. So many amazing people and they were all so fantastically up for the video premise. They threw themselves into the roles and pretended to be caught cheating, slipping on butter or choking on their poisoned orange squash. Obviously, my character wins, teaching you that crime does pay.

Over the years we've had so many adventures and we have a core little team for making the videos. I've now done maybe fifteen videos with Sophie, working with Lisa Laudat and Robbie the director of photography too. From 'Wild Forever', which we shot in Mexico, to 'Today the Sun's On Us', shot in Iceland (I play another criminal there . . . it's a theme), 'Catch You' in Venice (where I'm a stalker in red, based on one of my favourite films *Don't Look Now*) to 'Love is a Camera' in Florence (where I'm another evil woman . . . this time a witch), we've had a ball.

Often we'll think where we'd like to go and then build a video around it.

The video for another single, 'Get Over You', was made with a video-directing team called Max and Dania. Unlike the two-day shoots for 'Murder' and 'Take Me Home', this was all done in a day. Again, I'd had an idea, this time inspired by the mannequins I'd seen in a shop window. I imagined them breaking free. Good news – it's fun to break out of a window and film a video with eight sets of identical twins also playing shop mannequins.

The album came out in September and thanks to the success of 'Take Me Home' (it went to number two in the UK), the album was off to a good start. I'm not going to lie, it felt good that I had moved past the 'one-hit wonder' comments that were swarming around after 'Groovejet'. But when it came to the album, it was 'Murder on the Dancefloor' that made it fly. For most countries that was my first single and it was given brilliant radio support. I found myself following it all over the world. For the first time I visited Australia, New Zealand, South America . . . it was incredible. Having had the first deal go so wrong I really could see how lucky I was to be having the success I was having. Some of it was insane – like doing breakfast TV in Mexico with a guy dressed as a clown, or dancing live on Italian TV with the whole crowd doing the dance routine from the video, or sitting next to John Travolta on Australian telly. (John had just flown in with his own Qantas jet. I gave him one of my CDs as I grew up on *Grease*, and I told him how big a fan I was. He looked perplexed, but I'm sure he loved the record.*)

As the album was being released, Universal Records held their big annual conference. This was a Big Deal in the land of Universal. All the heads of all the labels in one place. A chance to showcase new signings. I was a priority act (this is a real term) which meant I was on the mantelpiece as one of their new signings to promote internationally, and so it

---

* He's never listened to it, has he?

was that I found myself landing in Mallorca first thing in the morning on the 11 September 2001 to sing 'Murder' in front of the Universal massive, accompanied by four dancers.

I was due to sing at 8 p.m. on an outside stage in front of all the executives. As I'd had an early start, when I had some quiet time in the afternoon I dozed on the hotel bed. I was woken just before 4 p.m. by my phone ringing over and over. When I didn't answer, my friend Sarah sent me a text: 'Are you OK? Just checking you're not in New York.'

I was a bit confused . . . why did she think I might be there? What would be the problem if I was?

I message her back . . . 'No, I'm not there. What's up?'

She told me to put the TV on.

I turned on the news just as the second plane hit the World Trade Centre.

Like billions of people, I then watched, hypnotised with horror, as the buildings collapsed in a huge plume of dust. It was shocking then and as I replay it in my mind, it's still so shocking now.

I think because it was such an enormous shock, the conference still went ahead as planned even though, as the ramifications of what we'd all witnessed unfolded over the forthcoming weeks and months, so many other things were cancelled. But that evening, everyone went about their business on autopilot. It was almost too big a deal to comprehend. I knew singing a song with a title like 'Murder on the Dancefloor' was jarring but it was decided I would still sing it and so I did.

The atmosphere was so strange, with everyone having the same conversations over and over about what had just happened and what it might mean.

This wasn't my only meeting with the head honchos. As I went around the world promoting the record I was wined and dined in most cities I visited. The head of Universal in Jakarta took us to a very posh Chinese restaurant where the lack of communal language meant most of my jokes didn't land (once you've told a joke then explained the joke, it's rarely funny anyway – conversation was a little strained). My main memory is of a live prawn throwing itself out of a pot and onto the carpet in a bid to escape when the chef flamboyantly cooked in front of us.

In Germany, the boss man had two tables for supper. Lisa, JP and I arrived early and all sat together but once the big guy arrived they were made to move to the 'B' table. At the 'A' table, boss man looked at me and all the other signed artists sitting around him as he exclaimed, 'How nice to be surrounded by all my golden eggs!'

Yuck.

I know you don't need this pointing out, but I do think the most precious thing in life is to surround yourself with good people. Good counsel will always see you right. While my star was in the ascendancy with the album, it wasn't how fame affected me that was significant (after my early rise and fall with theaudience I knew better than to buy into any of it. The fame side is fun but it's sort of nothingy at its core.) What was more pressing was that fame didn't affect anyone around me. No one in my family and no one I'm friends with has ever been starstruck by anything I've got up to. They've been happy for me, surprised, support-ive and wise, but never starstruck. It's helped so much.

I'd say it's a survival instinct in me that whenever I've started any new project – be it my new life as a solo artist, or *Strictly* – anything where I find myself in a new group, I quickly find my 'people' and cling to them. The steady people who have a life outside of the silliness and are having the most fun as they know how brilliant our job is. Lisa was my partner in crime for the first album – she kept me level, talked about real-life things like missing her kids or how she'd grown up. She taught me a lot and we had so much fun. One day I had a complimentary fruit basket in my hotel room and it had a lovely pink net as a base so we used it in my hairdo for the promo that day. If we had free time we'd go out and explore. Now, my person for all of that is Richard. He'd never let me get caught up in myself too much and we know to grab it all because it's so flipping awesome to travel and perform and write. Unsteady, cruel sometimes, hard graft and deeply uncertain, but addictive and bonkers and fun, too.

Meanwhile, along the way my old flame acting would occasionally come and poke its head round the door with the odd audition for things. The biggest and closest I came was when I was approached to audition for a Bond girl. After a few early auditions, I got down to the final three and was invited to screen-test at Pinewood. Embarrassingly, I had to do a slightly sexy scene where I needed to be in my underwear. More embarrassingly, the chap playing Bond in the audition was an actor called Colin Salmon who I would later meet properly and come to know as a good friend of Dan's (from The Feeling). Colin and I filmed this ever-so-slightly out-of-my-comfort-zone scene where we had to be a little smoochy and sexy. I didn't get the part and I thought no more about it until years later when I was reintroduced to Colin in a social setting. On realising we'd done this film test together, Colin leaned over to me and said, 'Just so you know . . . I didn't say those things.' 'What things?' I replied. 'Oh, nothing,' he hastily replied before changing the subject. Reader, I will never know what he didn't say.

*

As the album continued its journey I occasionally felt a bit lost in the middle. Conversations with the label about 'units' and 'breaking territories' turned me off. There was talk about trying to break America but it would have meant so much time away, correcting folk on how to say 'Ellis-Bextor' and hoping they played my record . . . I suppose you learn early on that the whole thing is like Jacob's ladder. You never reach the top, the rungs just keep going up and up above you. There's always a next bit.

Overall, I remember that first album's momentum with fondness. It's a lovely thing to feel strapped to a rocket that's headed where you want to go. I felt I had a tenacity of spirit which would mean I'd be a singer in whatever sense it presented – with or without success. I knew after the lessons I'd learned with my first record deal that getting this chance again was incredibly lucky and having the solo career was something I seized with both hands. Whilst I had spent a lot of my formative years with some older man (record exec, songwriter or boyfriend) telling me how and where I should place my next step, when I sang I felt autonomous. I felt empowered. The success of the first album gave me the space to grow up and gain independence but also it gave me the chance to have fun and be young, too. I met amazing people who helped me work out what mattered and they are still close to me now. In fact, I married one of them.

*

The whole adventure with the first album took about a year and a half before attention turned properly to album number two, *Shoot from the Hip*. By now I knew no matter what that I had to try and get out of my relationship with Mike. I find it hard to listen to *Shoot from the Hip*. It's so raw in places. A lot of the songs are about new love beginning ('Nowhere Without You') and old love dying ('You Get Yours') and the weirdness in the middle ('The Walls Keep Saying Your Name'). It's not that I don't like the record – I do – but I was going through so much when I wrote it. I wasn't thinking commercially, I just wanted to write what I was feeling, and that confusion is so apparent. Each album I've done is a diary entry, and this entry was painful . . . I wrote it in the anguish of finding my way out of a relationship. Still, aren't I lucky that my day job means I can explore that stuff rather than ignoring it? It's very cathartic, even if it's a little close to the bone.

11

ME: Panic Attacks – 'Mixed Up World'

Little nurse me. All the gear and no idea.

I think I had my first panic attack filming a TV show. I say 'I think' because the panicky, anxious feeling had been brewing for a while, building up and waiting for the right moment to tip me over the edge.

'Murder on the Dancefloor' was about to be released as the second single from the album *Read My Lips*, after 'Take Me Home' had come out. Then the album was to be released. I remember arriving at the TV studio and my TV plugger Sarah sitting down with me and excitedly showing me my diary, which was completely packed for weeks. I stared at it and immediately felt a wave of panic. Sarah was smiling at me. 'Isn't it great? You haven't got a day off for . . . four weeks!'

You see, for a record company, the only diary that looks good is a busy one.

I couldn't match her enthusiasm but I nodded my head and then walked in a bit of a daze onto the set. I was starting to feel anxious and claustrophobic. As the sound man put on my radio mic I started to feel more and more shaky . . . if I'd wanted to leave the set, I couldn't have. I couldn't find any legitimate way of escaping. The room was windowless and the set was too bright with TV lights. I can't remember all the guests but Jo Whiley was the host and one of the other guests was Jay Kay from Jamiroquai. I was feeling really uncomfortable by this point. Everything seemed hyperreal and I couldn't work out if people were talking too fast or I was talking too slow. As we sat down I thought, 'I can't do this'. I said, 'Sorry I've just got to go to the loo,' and Jay Kay said, 'Yeah, I've just got to go and do a shit,' as I scuttled away out of the studio. I ended up on the street outside where I took deep breaths and tried to calm myself. To his credit, my manager told me we could just leave if I wanted but I managed to get back in and finish the filming.

Afterwards, I felt elated. As anyone who has had a panic attack knows, the only upside of the nightmarish 'am I actually going mad' midst of the attack itself is that once it subsides it can give way to an almost euphoric high. I suppose the old-fashioned fight-or-flight version of that high would have been 'Hooray! The mammoth didn't eat me!' Which is a bit more fundamental than 'Hooray! I managed to plug my new album on telly without letting on I felt like I wanted to run away screaming!'

These panic attacks became regular visitors in my life. They were probably brought on by the combination of feeling out of control when it came to my personal life, hectic work plans being made on my behalf, and me burning the candle at both ends. My boyfriend was partying whenever he could and I was often along for the ride, but I then had work the next day and had to be pulled together and talk on camera. I'm not sure it was endlessly sustainable and it definitely wasn't much fun.

If you've never had a panic attack I will try and explain it. It starts for me like a general feeling of anxiety. My breathing gets shallow and more rapid and as I look around I feel as if everything around me is moving at slightly the wrong speed. I feel out of sync with the pace of reality. I feel as if anyone who can see me must notice I am not acting normally, that I look panicked, as if I'm struggling to keep up. If I don't escape the situation and lock myself away somewhere private then the next stage of the panic is a sense of falling into a hole of madness. When it first started happening I didn't know what it was. I thought I was going mad and that I might fall deep into the feeling and not emerge. I'd be lost to the insanity forever and my friends and family would be tiny figures peering over the edge of the cliff, looking down to where I'd fallen and their shouts for me to come back would be useless.

I might be in any situation – on Oxford Street in amongst shoppers or out with my mum and sister for lunch – and suddenly I can feel that familiar slip of reality. I look around to see everything slowing down or speeding up and my heart starts to race. I feel as if I will be like that forever and never find my way out.

Some of the paranoia might have been the result of a one-time acid trip. Yep, you read that right. Don't worry – I've already told my dad about it. I'd gone to meet Mike at the pub. It was just before closing time and he and his friend were already pretty drunk. Mike had struck up a conversation with a large group of Brazilians on a nearby table and they invited us back to their communal house where they had acid. I'm a Londoner who works in the music industry so, you know, it wasn't exactly, 'Hello drugs, nice to meet you,' but I hadn't been introduced to Mr Hallucinogenic before. I was intrigued. My dad has spoken about his experiences in the seventies. Maybe it was something I was supposed to try once? We went with them and took a tab. My brain went all *Doors of*

Perception very fast . . . Blimey acid is full on. It must have been mind-blowing back in the sixties when no one knew what the hell it all meant. Even knowing a little bit about what the drug was doing to my mind still made for a very extreme experience. Turns out I don't like feeling out of control. I felt as if my mind had different layers of reality and I couldn't hold onto which was the 'right' one. Whenever I started to wobble, I'd wander to the garden of the house and stare at the flowers and plants, watching the psychedelic colours radiating out and the way the plants seemed to weave and grow before my eyes. Meanwhile, Mike had got himself into a fight with one of the Brazilians in the kitchen. To make up, they'd both taken more acid. Great job.

We headed home the next morning, London still pulsating before us as we looked out the taxi windows. Once home, I watched *Teletubbies* while the drug wore off. I then fell asleep and when I woke, Mike was still tripping. He'd been awake for over twenty-four hours by then and was spinning out. He'd had to call a friend to sit with him because he felt so awful.

I never did anything like that again but when I started getting the panic attacks, one memorable attack began while I was on a busy street and a woman in a fur coat passed by. It looked as if her coat came to life and moved to face me. Pretty sure that was a flashback, which contributed to my anxiety.

After a month or two of these episodes it was my mother who diagnosed me (and this was before the days of what she and I now call Dr Google). I was at home with her and she said she'd read an article about panic attacks and thought that was probably what was going on with me. It was actually such a relief to know I wasn't crazy or alone . . . but then, what to do about it?

I spoke about it with a few friends and one of them – part of my work team – recommend beta blockers. They work by slowing down your heart, which I thought sounded terrifying. For someone already struggling with feeling out of control I didn't want to take anything that would change my heartbeat.

That being said, I was caught up in wave after wave of promotion and hard work. I was hardly home, rarely saw friends and family and was feeling quite lonely in the middle of it all. One day when we had a live TV performance, I could feel the familiar sensation of the onset of panic. The triggers seemed to be any situation I felt I couldn't walk away from without being conspicuous. Tube carriages when the tube suddenly ground to a halt in a tunnel caused immediate panic. I would feel as if everyone could see I was having an attack. This paranoia increased the panic and I'd be sent spiralling into a shortness of breath, the craziness in my head and an inability to get a proper grasp on the passing of time. Other panic-inducing situations included things like meetings with my label where we'd sit in a boardroom with the door shut. I couldn't get out and would sit there feeling claustrophobic and hideously passive. Or watching a play with a seat in the middle of the row so I couldn't get up and walk out without everyone seeing. Or sitting on my own waiting for someone in a busy place. Anywhere where I felt powerless to change my surroundings without everyone guessing that I couldn't cope.

But the biggest and baddest of these situations was live TV. When you sing on telly, telly is in charge. They want to know where you are at all times when you are in the building and once you are there, you have to be ready for your moment ahead of time so I'd often be camera-ready half an hour before my performance. This meant half an hour to get nervous and panicky. Nerves alone are not the same feeling, they feel justified and more focused, whereas anxiety is wild and careless and ruins your chances of acting how you want to act. Anxiety makes you feel as if you might cry, shake, run away or collapse in on yourself and acknowledging it, for me, made it worse. Once I'd said it out loud or the inner shakiness had found its way to the surface, I felt lost.

Pre-recorded telly wasn't quite so bad. You could sing twice and have a chance to regulate your breathing. Everyone was more relaxed and if there was a last-minute delay, there was time for that. But not so in the live TV world. I'd be brought to set – too bright, too far from reality – and I'd stand in position waiting. The floor manager would tell me, 'Two minutes before we come to you,' with a hushed voice so as not to be heard over whatever was being broadcast and then they'd walk away leaving me on my own feeling as if two minutes was the longest time in the world.

I remember wondering what was going to happen to me. Was I going to combust? Fall to the ground? Run away or sob? It was silently terrifying and all-consuming.

On this particular day of the live performance, a person working with me offered me a beta blocker. I decided to take it and it did . . . nothing. It didn't even offer the placebo effect. Zilch. Nada.

I thought to myself, 'Enough of this . . . I need to sort this out.'

The most popular route to help with panic attacks seemed to be hypnotherapy and this was what my mum suggested. This was the first therapy I'd ever tried – for anything – and I was a bit wary. The first session – with a very well-meaning practitioner – did nothing for me at all. She put on calming music and told me to just lie still and relax, which sent me straight into the beginnings of an attack, so I made my excuses and left.

After that a friend told me about someone who had been treated by Paul McKenna. He was a massive household name at that time and I had no idea he helped treat people privately too. He'd become a regular fixture on TV and claimed that, through his hypnosis, he could change your life. I wasn't sure whether he could really help me but I got in touch and trotted along to his place in Kensington. He asked if I wanted music while we did the session and I said no, and so we began chatting. We spoke about the triggers of my anxiety and then talked about other situations in my past when I'd felt that way. He said to imagine that I was standing in a room and in the corner of that room there was a television with a black and white image on it. The image should be an image of me from when I first remembered feeling out of control. I thought back to when I was little and my mum and dad had split up. As I explained in Chapter 2, my parents worked out a custody arrangement where I spent every week and every other weekend with my mum but school holidays were split equally between the houses. When it came to the school holidays over Christmas there was an uneven number of nights. This became a bone of contention for my two households, who would fight over whether that extra night would be spent at my mum's or my dad's. I remember being at my dad's house and being asked by my stepmum, Polly, and my dad whether I would rather be at my mum's or dad's for that extra night. In truth I wanted to be at my mum's. I love my dad but my instinct was to be at my mum's house where I spent most of my time and it was the place I thought of when someone said 'home'. I was about six years old and that was what my heart was telling me but obviously this wouldn't go down too well if I said it out loud. It was this scene I saw on the TV when Paul asked me to picture my earliest memory of feeling anxious. The image I saw was me standing there while my stepmum explained how my dad was feeling about not seeing me as much as he'd like. While she spoke, I felt incredibly guilty and out of control. The pressure was too much and I didn't want to hurt anyone or upset anyone but how could I avoid saying my true answer? Paul listened and told me to get closer to the screen and then let the image turn from black and white to colour. 'Now step inside the image. Climb into the scene and speak to that little version of yourself. Tell her you're now an adult, that it's OK she didn't know what to do and that you've grown into a happy grown-up so she doesn't need to worry. It's all going to be OK and you can tell her that.'

I did what he said and shortly after that the session ended and I walked out of Paul's house in a daze. To my mind, hypnosis is not some crazy voodoo thing or a party trick, but it's a medium, a way of speaking to a deeper level of your own consciousness to try and change the associations of your thoughts. I was completely awake and aware throughout my session, but boy was it powerful. For the next two or three days, I could remember so many details from the time I was around the age of six or seven, things I had long forgotten . . . I could remember the toys I'd had and the way they smelt, theme tunes for the cartoons I loved, the way my bed felt when I lay down in it in my little bedroom. It was all at the front of my mind – crystal clear and visceral. I felt very emotional and raw, as if I'd peeled back layers of myself to unveil the little six-year-old me again. It was bizarre but it really worked.

Since that time I've had the inklings of the panic attack – the occasional little tug – but never again has it bloomed into a full-blown thing. Whatever Paul McKenna said to me that day, in only one session, was really incredibly effective in giving the power back to me. I have spoken to people whose anxiety caused them to make different decisions in their life and it could very easily have been me. Feeling that grip of fear is paralysing and I honestly think I would have had to avoid so many things in my life if they'd continued. I'm so grateful to Paul McKenna. Especially amazing was the fact he never charged me. He told me to make a contribution to charity instead, which I did of course. Pretty cool, that. Impressive all round, Mr McKenna. Now, hypnotise me to think I am the world's best breakdancer, just for fun.

12

MEN: R – 'Wild Forever'

R and I. Always happy to have a quick snog in a photo booth.

How do you sum up on paper someone who you share your life with? Richard – I call him R usually – is much better than me at talking about romantic stuff.

When we met, we were both twenty-two. It was in a studio at John Henry's rehearsal rooms in the January of 2002 and I had come along for Richard's second callback audition for my band. My first album was out and doing well so it was decided I would head out on my first solo tour.

My early impressions of Richard were that he was boyishly handsome and had a ready smile. Even on that first meeting, I remember he had a kind face and was easy to be around. He found lots of things funny and was often laughing. His eyes are big and brown and there's always been a reassuring, calm clarity to how he sees the world.

On that first day, he played a song or two with Paul Stewart on drums (Paul was an old friend of Richard's and they had already played a lot together in various bands). I arrived at the studio in a floor-length black wool Zara coat, which I still have. It cuts quite a strong silhouette so I must have looked fairly dramatic in that rehearsal room. I watched Richard and Paul play through a couple of things and then walked over to say hi.

The first thing I ever said to Richard was a slightly surprising, 'Nice amp.' It was a lovely blue amplifier and worthy of a nod, but it was surprising in that it is the only time in my life I've either a) really looked at an amp or b) complimented anyone on one. We now have a neon sign in Richard's home studio which blazes NICE AMP from the studio to the kitchen through the window whenever it's turned on.

My first tour was pretty long – covering all of the UK and Europe – but lots of fun. I was still getting mixed reviews but I was having a good time on the road and I got on really well with the rest of the band. They were the same age as me, which I liked too as it meant all our reference points were the same. Angie on keys was gorgeous company and we always had a giggle together and guitarist Martin was a sweetheart, too. We were a happy little bunch of campers.

Richard and I had known each other for a good while before the idea of anything romantic occurred to us. It's funny, up until then I'd always been fairly cynical about relationships that had sprung from friendships. Surely there had to be some clue, some spark from day one? But for me it was only when we had our first kiss that all the dots joined up.

For that first year, we toured and played festivals and spent lots of time together. I remember thinking Richard was kind and warm and funny. He was always very good at listening. It sounds awful, but when I was introduced to his girlfriend at the time she really wasn't how I'd imagined his girlfriend to be and it caused me to think, 'Maybe I've misjudged him a bit?' She seemed nice but not very exciting. I also remember Richard telling me that before her, he'd gone out with a different girl for years and there had been no break in between and I thought, 'Uh-oh, serial monogamist – stay away.'

Meanwhile, I was still with Mike and things were getting increasingly controlling at home. He did leave me to my own devices with the touring and the work, though, preferring to stay behind. This gave me time to think and whilst I wasn't yet thinking of leaving him, I did find it wonderful to be on the road in a happy touring party with people my age just doing the sort of fun and silly things we should be doing. Staying out dancing, late-night drinking, stopping the tour bus at 2 a.m. by the sea to go swimming in our underwear . . . just being twenty-three and daft. As a 'priority act' with the label I didn't have much time to myself. I hardly saw my old friends, missed countless parties and get-togethers.

During the tour, my confidence in my stage persona was growing and I think all this set the scene nicely for being open to the idea of shaking things up with my love life, too. For years I had tried to make Mike happy. I thought that I could make it work and turn it into a wholesome, supportive relationship but the fractures were growing. In contrast to the freedom I felt when I was away, the framework at home was getting tighter. Mike and I had just bought our first place with both our names on the paperwork and the house was far away from any of my family or friends. I was cut off and lonely. The house was too big and too sad. These were the days of not being allowed to walk anywhere alone and not being able to look out of the car window and Mike being increasingly experimental with his nights out away from me, like doing hard drugs at house parties with his mates while I worked or sat at home alone.

I embarked on my solo tour, which started in the UK and finished in Europe. Everything had been going as normal until we got to Europe where the band and I got up to mischief and danced the night away whenever we could. One night in Frankfurt we found ourselves in a gay club where they played everything from Abba to Kate Bush ... it was awesome, I laughed till I cried with Angie, dancing to 'Bad Girls' by Donna Summer and pretending to beep our boobs whenever they sang 'Toot-toot ... ahh ... beep-beep!' Then when 'Wuthering Heights' came on Richard and I ran around the dance floor performing interpretive dance. It was great. There was a pole for pole-dancing too, so of course I had a go. We didn't leave until 2 or 3 a.m. but we weren't ready to crash. As the bus moved on to the next German tour date location, we all sat in the back lounge drinking vodka Red Bulls (to the extent where I can never drink it now. It turned the whites of my eyes yellow. I kid you not). We were laughing and joking around into the small hours and slowly everyone went to bed until it was just Richard and me in the back lounge of the tour bus. As the bus travelled along the German motorway we found ourselves sitting close together until our hands were touching and then – we kissed.

It knocked me for six. I honestly did not see it coming ... it was like a lightning bolt. Straight away. A connection I'd never experienced before and did not anticipate. I knew I was doing something I shouldn't, as I was in a relationship, but I think my feelings were so tangled I couldn't see the wood for the trees. It was pretty magical but also felt like it turned everything upside down. We were both seeing other people, so that was pretty bad, but also I needed to think straight and try to unravel why I'd got myself in this situation if I was committed to my boyfriend? It scared me to think maybe I'd put so much of myself into something I was starting to pull away from.

But with Richard, even with all the craziness and the intensity, it fundamentally felt right. I knew he was a good man. I knew he was thoughtful and talented and had a gentle humour. It was like a movie montage in my head where suddenly I could see a playback of every time he'd made me feel good, or made me laugh, or heard something I'd said then reminded me of it a few days later to show he'd really listened, or said something smart and insightful and perceptive, and was never conceited or mean. Before we started dating he had a mobile phone which had died. I gave him an old handset to replace it. He sent me a thank you gift of two mugs that looked white but when you poured hot water into them, a photo appeared. The pictures that were revealed were of a quirky doll called Blythe. Blythe is a doll that was only produced in 1976 by a company in America. She's a funny-looking broad. Head the size of a satsuma, and eyes that change colour when you pull a string at the back of her head. I loved her from the first time I saw her in a photography book and, through her, discovered eBay in the late nineties, where I spent hours searching for my own Blythe doll. The significance of all this is that when I told Richard about this strange doll I wanted, he remembered it and then personalised the mugs. No one had ever done anything like that for me before. It was so thoughtful that when I first saw the photos, I nearly cried.

While I was breaking up with Mike I stopped all contact with Richard. It had become clear that no matter what would happen with R, my relationship with Mike had come to an end. I was pretty heartbroken about it but not because I wanted to be with Mike. It was more that I felt I had put so much of myself into that relationship and I felt as if I'd failed.

I moved back into my mum's house and then a while later I finally went on my first date with Richard, who was now single too. After all that build-up, things could have felt different now that we were 'allowed' to see each other, but no, our feelings were just as strong. We kept everything very hush-hush. We didn't want anyone who knew us being too judgemental about our new relationship and we needed time to see how it would feel to bring it out into the daylight, but it was all . . . easy. Just to be in a relationship with someone who listened and who was kind. I don't need grand sweeping gestures of romance but little things, like remembering how I like my toast or making a tea without asking, I'm a sucker for. I think everyday kindness is the number one glue for long-term relationships . . . You have to have boundaries you don't cross so you don't fall into casual bad behaviour.

I'm sure we all know couples who almost play-act their squabbling, but when it's routine to undermine or humiliate your other half, you start forgetting why you're even with them in the first place. My mum (again with the wisdom) said she knew John was right for her as he made her want to be a better person and she always felt that he was a better person than her. I completely get that now but I didn't before Richard.

Still, as our relationship grew stronger, I had to relearn how to really love someone. I'd been taught that taking chunks out of each other equalled passion, which I thought was part of love, but it isn't. Slowly, slowly, this was unlearnt and better ways were shown to me.

Richard jokes that Mike set the bar low, but it's not true. I would have known Richard was right for me no matter what. Our first proper date was a restaurant miles from the flat I was renting in Notting Hill. I'd moved to that part of London as it was near my family but also a new little pocket of London for me. Or at least new to live in. I had wanted an easy area where there were nice shops to potter in and places to buy coffee. I craved simplicity and a bit of soft focus. I moved in with my best friend Maria and although Richard and I were newly dating, I still antici-pated a fun and stress-free year with Maria in that flat. No need to rush.

Richard arrived to pick me up with flowers. He drove us to a little restaurant in North London. He was worried about paparazzi as we'd had photographers snooping around, so that's why we went somewhere so out of the way. We had a lovely meal and then sat looking out at the view from Richard's car in Alexandra Palace car park. It was beautiful but then comical – an event at Alexandra Palace finished and suddenly the car park was full of people in black tie. Spotting us snogging in the car, one chap gave Richard the thumbs up. I was, of course, mortified.

During our early courtship, the paparazzi would often hide behind lamp posts in Portobello Road waiting to spy on us. At this time, Richard used to style his hair in the way a lot of guys did in that early noughties era – he'd put gel in and shape his chestnut hair into a little spike. It was funny how the papers had to cut round this shape to put the secret photos of us in their pages. Later, Richard started wearing his hair in the way he still tends to, with the fridge low over his eyes. This is an easier shape to cut around, I'd imagine, but not the inspiration for the change.

I think it was in the same week of our first 'proper' date that Richard told me he and his friends had formed a new band. They didn't have a name yet but he gave me a CD of their stuff. I was, if I'm honest, a bit apprehensive about pressing 'play'. What if it was rubbish? That would be awkward. As the music played I was so relieved to hear that, not only was it not rubbish, it was actually really good. Even that early CD had songs on it like 'Fill My Little World', 'Sewn' and 'Love It When You Call'. It's cute really because I feel as if the first The Feeling album, which went on to be huge and sell over a million copies, was the soundtrack to Richard and me getting together, and to Sonny's early years too – I used to sing 'I'll love it when you crawl' as alternative lyrics.

My family loved the music too and it's never stopped impressing me when I go to see Richard do a gig and see him being really good at what he does. It's sexy to see your other half being brilliant at what they do. At the first gigs I was always right down the front, standing in front of the Richard. I loved seeing the band grow and being there from the very beginning was special.

We had hardly been dating any time (and by this I mean the very early days of seeing each other) when we found out I was pregnant. I remember that while I watched the pregnancy test turn positive, Richard was on the phone to Dan, the singer of The Feeling. Dan was struggling with a computer problem and Richard was helping him to fix it. As he told Dan what buttons to press and leads to unplug, I showed him the positive result. In a distracted daze, Richard put his thumbs up to me and nodded. After he hung up the phone we made an oven-ready supper – fish fingers and chips, I think – in a robotic way, occasionally interrupted with a nervous laugh or a kind of 'Well, there it is then' sort of sigh. It was . . . fine. The pregnancy news was like an awkwardly shaped wrapped present between us on the dinner table. We both knew it was there, we knew we'd have to unwrap it, but for now we could just take a minute to silently acknowledge it while we ate our supper.

To be honest, I think we unwrapped the baby-shaped present over months and months . . . we still tried to pretend we were a normal new couple and went on dates in the usual way, even though the growing bump was a sign that soon we would be a tiny family. Richard didn't even move in until two weeks before he became a dad. Looking back, it was the best way to handle it as it meant we gave our own relationship a little space, independent of the fact that soon, two would become three.

Also living in the flat at that time (and no doubt aware that the bump was a sign she'd have to move out sooner than planned) was my best friend Maria. She was a solid person for me to talk to about everything. Whilst I was mainly happy to be having a baby, there were some initial wobbles and Maria was one of the only voices around to take me out when I was about five or six weeks along, put a glass of red wine in my hand and tell me, 'You don't have to have this baby if you don't want to.' I loved her for that as she could see that life was running on its own momentum and I appreciated being given a moment to 'own' the decision that had been presented to me. That is a good friend.

Looking back, I think the drama of the baby news played to our strengths. I am someone who deals better with emotional drama. I don't freak out when someone close to me is struggling or going through something tricky. Richard is better with immediate-physical-danger drama. For the record, I'm kind of crap at that. I freak out about my children being near: fire, bodies of water, hinges, sharp things, glass . . . it's exhausting. Richard is calm about these things. With an unexpected pregnancy, I think you have a little of both. It's emotional but it's also logistical. We both felt kind of . . . OK. Excited. Optimistic. And we were right to. Sonny made us a family, and family was good.

*

Richard and I were spending lots of time together by then, but only a handful of people knew about the baby. I was in my lovely flat with Maria, our plan of a fun-filled, carefree year together gone, but it was comical and almost predictable really. I wasn't planning a baby but getting pregnant really didn't shock me as much as it maybe might have done. On some level it did feel like 'oh, of course'. At that point R and I still hadn't said 'I love you' or made any plans for the future. We tried to continue our dating and getting to know each other as if we were any other new couple – not two people about to be parents. I used to joke it was like the bit in the movie *Green Card* when Andie MacDowell and Gerard Depardieu had to fake their relationship's longevity with pretend photo shoots to make it look as if they've been on skiing and beach holidays. Richard and I went to New York when I was ten weeks gone and we came home with lots of pictures of us in a wintery world – we even ice skated at the Rockefeller ice rink.

Still, the fact that our relationship was very new showed itself pretty starkly sometimes, like a panicked and stupid present I bought Richard for our first Christmas together. I obviously wanted to get him something a bit big and special, but I didn't really know what he was into. Lord knows what made me think the answer of the question was 'a large inflatable room'. I know, what even is that? It was essentially a room you could blow up by filling up joined hexagons of plastic. A blow-up igloo. It came in three sizes, and to show my love I bought the biggest one. I have spent the last seventeen Christmases making up for it. We never even blew it up to its full glory. I'd offer it to you but after spending a decade in my mum's shed it went to a car boot sale. Farewell, inflatable room.

Crap presents aside, in those early months I had a few moments of 'Who is this man who is the father of my child?' In New York, Richard had been browsing in a record shop. I came to meet him and as we left he turned to the record shop owner, pointed at him and said, 'Keep it real.' I think Richard was still pretty nervous around me and sometimes it would make him say funny stuff by accident. I actually (luckily) found it endearing.

Our next trip away before parenthood followed in February, this time to the Sicilian town of Taormina. We strolled around quiet beaches, ruins and little Italian coastal towns with the slightly chilly end-of-winter sun on our faces.

I knew I had fallen for Richard but I was still waiting for him to say 'I love you' first. One night, I fell asleep beside him and when I woke I had dreamy memories of him talking to me and saying how strong his feelings were. A couple of days later we were sitting on the sofa and he told me his feelings again. I know you don't have to hear 'I love you' to feel loved, and I know it's not for everyone, but for me, with the baby in my tummy and a little uncertainty in the air, it felt wonderful. And right.

Richard took the stress in his stride. The fallout of my break-up, the financial pressure I was under, the album release, impending fatherhood . . . if he was freaking out, it didn't show. I think it helped that we didn't know any other way.

Richard did a good job early on of pretending he wasn't into the idea of getting married. He would always show complete disinterest if I mentioned it or anyone else did. After Sonny was born, and so we were already committed to each other, I still liked the idea of making it official. One weekend we had gone on a trip away to Barcelona with my mum, stepdad, little sister Martha and a friend of hers. Sonny was with us and he was about eight or nine months old. We were only gone for three nights but Richard had brought with him – as well as his actual luggage – this fairly large grey record bag which he had slung about him for the whole trip. I did wonder what on earth he had it for. On the Saturday night my mum took Sonny so Richard and I could have a night out together. As I passed the baby to my mum, she said in a singsong way, 'Have fun!', beaming at us. As I shut the hotel door I turned to Richard and said, 'She's acting weird.'

Turns out she knew what was about to happen. R and I wandered down to the little part of Barcelona known as Barcelonetta where there are bars and restaurants right on the water. As we sat drinking a beer, Richard started talking about our trip to Taormina. He said that he'd realised something on that trip . . . that if he had a whole lifetime with me, it wouldn't be long enough. Richard then reached into that big record bag to find the ring. The only thing in the bag. He went down on one knee and I suddenly wanted to reassure him.

'Yes!' I shouted.

'Let me ask first!' he said. 'Will you marry me?'

Turns out he'd already taken my dad out and asked him. Now I didn't personally need that, but I'm sure it meant a lot to my dad.

I'm definitely not one of those people who had big ideas about how my wedding should be – I did know that if I was going to tie the knot, the only person I would want to be married to was Richard. But I knew that I liked the idea of going away.

Our wedding was pretty dinky. Just sixty of us in Italy. If you're hoping for a small wedding with only your nearest and dearest, then may I recommend a foreign wedding. It really weeds out the guests pretty sharpish and you end up with only those you love around you. Sonny was fourteen months old and so I didn't want to wear just white, so my dress had a bright pink underskirt made from netting fabric from a shop on Portobello Road. My three little sisters were bridesmaids and because I'd been a bridesmaid as a kid many times and worn some questionable outfits (sorry Dad and Polly, but putting me in a floral frock edged with bells that actually rang as I walked was traumatic for ten-year-old me), I wanted to make sure that my sisters wore what they wanted.

Our friends and family flew over to stay either in the palazzo where the ceremony was or the little hotel in the local town. It was so much fun because we all went a bit crazy. The bar bill alone was over £7,000. We had a relaxed pizza supper on the Friday night. Richard and I spent the night before our wedding together with Sonny in our room with us too. It didn't feel right to spend it apart from him. Then the next morning, the day of the wedding, just after we'd had our breakfast, Richard and I slipped off into the local town and did the official paperwork for our marriage. We only took a couple of people from the palazzo with us as witnesses, and it was lovely to have the town hall bit just for us. Richard was wearing a Metallica T-shirt and shorts, I was wearing a bikini with a little sundress thrown over the top, and my plastic 'bride' tiara from my hen night. It felt just like us and just for us. Then it was time to go back to our wedding party and get ready for the next bit.

Louise and Lisa got me ready in my big white frock. Martha, Dulce and Maisy, my three little sisters, all had party outfits with little sashes I'd made with 'Bridesmaid' written in sequins. My dad walked me down the little aisle under the heat of the June Italian sun while an accordion played 'True Love' from *High Society*. Our priest conducted a lovely ceremony in Italian of which I understood not a word (except for the occasional times he gestured to Sonny and said 'famiglia'), but it did all sound lovely. After the 'I do' bit and Richard kissing the bride, the instrumental of 'Bernadette' played with James Jamerson's bass guitar ringing out.

The speeches probably went on a bit – we had seven – but some were short and sweet: my sister Martha thanked me for marrying someone whose band was popular at school and said how much she adored Sonny; my mum's speech was eloquent and funny and sincere; Richard's was lovely . . . my dad really was the one who caused the video tape he was filming on to run out. He spoke for forty-five minutes! On one hand it was adorable . . . he's a natural raconteur and very funny . . . but he was nervous and, as the father of the bride, this was the big moment. And it was kind of bizarre in places (sorry Dad), like the bit where he handed out tokens to a pretend coffee shop near his house called the Tardis Café, 'the little shop with the big taste', and the jokes made about being married to my mum first (Polly took it well), and one about nearly marrying a woman from the petrol station who then called it off 'and now I can't drive past without filling up'. The true scene-stealers though were the two jokes he made about me. One: 'I was walking past Sophie and Richard's bedroom earlier and all I could hear was "Uh . . . uh . . . uh," then the door swung open a little and there was Sonny trying to take his first steps.'

The final joke took about seven minutes to set up, but I'll cut to the punchline for you. 'The people at the palazzo worked so hard to get the place ready for today . . . moving furniture, hanging lights . . . they also tried to lay a new carpet. I saw two workmen trying to hammer it down but nail after nail bent. At last one turned to the other and said, 'It's murder on this dense floor.'

Ba-dum-tish!

Finally I got up. I had secretly been rehearsing with Dan and Ciaran from The Feeling. As I stood up, Dan fetched his acoustic guitar and Ciaran picked up a little melodica. As the sun started to go down I sang 'God Only Knows' by the Beach Boys. I'd started crying by verse two. We had a lot of singers in the congregation so they joined in with the harmonies. It sounded gorgeous, the sun was setting on this beautiful Umbrian hilltop, the swallows were flying overhead and soon the fireflies would be out. But what made me emotional was Richard's face. I can still remember his expression now. He looked so touched and that was really special.

After we'd eaten as much as possible (I'm not daft . . . Italy was our first choice as not only is it beautiful and the red tape for marriage is straightforward, you can also then eat bucketloads of amazing food and drink incredible local wine), we danced the night away (first dance – 'All Night Long' by Lionel Ritchie) before R and I snuck off around 2 a.m.

The next day we had a long brunch with everyone before Richard and I headed off to Rome for our tiny three-night honeymoon. I didn't want too long away from Sonny. Now whenever we manage a night or two away I always think we are adding a little more onto our honeymoon.

My mum gave me three bits of advice over that weekend. The night before our wedding she told me, 'I'll now say to you what my mum said to me: it's not too late to change your mind.' (Pretty sure she was joking about that.)

And then, 'Be selfish about your marriage. If you have to sometimes choose between the kids and your husband, choose your husband.'

The third: 'Don't expect to be happy all the time. Of course you should hope to be happily married, but happiness every day shouldn't be expected. Sometimes you're just getting by and that's part and parcel.'

All pretty solid things I think. Someone told me that the first year of marriage is the hardest. At first I thought that sounded really depressing but then I realised that it wasn't until after I got married that I really thought about how I felt about marriage itself. Obviously I've seen my mum and dad both have happy marriages after their unhappy one, but it's still a big deal to make that commitment. I love it though. It made me feel as if a lot of the petty grievances disappear because you've already decided wholeheartedly that you're on the same side.

*

Leading up to the wedding were the final negotiations for the record deal for Richard and the band. They signed the deal the week before we tied the knot. There was a lot of heat around the band by now based on the songs they'd written and their strength as a live band. They'd played together since they were sixteen or seventeen so it was second nature to them . . .

plus they'd done a couple of seasons as a covers band in the French alps. Musicians who play in those function bands have to do two-hour long sets maybe ten times a week. That is the training you need to get really good.

As the band took off, the landscape around Richard, Sonny and me changed. We were already used to change and drama and it all felt kind of right that something exciting was happening in a different direction. Richard was now being whisked away to perform all over the place and I was happy for him. It made things more balanced too as I know it meant a lot to him to have his own space to be creative and be part of his own band. Some session musicians aren't chasing that – I can think of hundreds – but I think Richard always wanted to be able to write and produce and have his own thing and we both support that drive in each other.

*

As the years have gone on and our family has grown, I sometimes wonder how much of our life Richard would choose of his own free will . . . I think we'd have fewer kids and probably live out of London. Our home is bright and colourful and noisy and I sometimes picture one of those videos where Richard is sitting fairly still on a sofa as the rest of us run around, hyper sped up, kids . . . bunting . . . art on the walls . . . babies crawling. But underneath his 'go with the flow' nature I know he's as invested as me in the world we've made around us. In lots of ways we are different sides of the same coin. We feel the same way about the broad brushstroke stuff like religion, politics, work, play . . . but we are not the same person. On stage, Richard is happy to be part of the band and has no desire for the main focus to be on him, whereas on stage I am happy to be the frontperson. At home it's the opposite. If we have a party to go to, it's likely Richard's script for the night has way more lines than mine. He's much more gregarious and social.

I have learnt a lot from him when it comes to being more confident. At any big social event I would normally just find a cosy little corner and pretty much stay there all night. If I saw someone across the room I vaguely knew then I would shy away from saying hello. Richard is the opposite and I realised if we wanted to have a shared experience of the same night out, I'd have to keep up and be bolder about chatting to people. It's helped me to be braver, as I'm fundamentally quite shy.

A combination of years of that and the podcast I now do have massively helped remind me that so much of confidence is actually a trick. With the podcast I've had to approach all sorts of people I've never met before to ask them if they might want to be involved. The worst they can say is no, and when they say yes, it's amazing. In tandem with all this of course is just growing up and shaking off your inhibitions. My job on stage is to reassure the crowd that they are in safe hands with me, even if I'm feeling wobbly on the inside. This gets easier and it's the same with social interaction.

Richard is generally calm in a crisis, it's probably why he's so good at flying. I can proudly tell you that I am the one who helped make that part of his life. Richard has held a pilot's licence for over a decade now and it's all because of his boyhood dream . . . and a stupid phase when he played a lot of golf. I don't know your opinion on it but for me, golf is deeply unsexy. Richard got into it when we were in our mid to late twenties and he was making his second album with The Feeling. At the same time, Richard started wearing monogrammed slippers, a monogrammed dressing gown, grew a long beard and started smoking a pipe. I was not having it. Every time he went to play golf he took forever, he wanted to do it all the time, plus the gear is ugly. What I needed to do, I realised, was distract him and swap one hobby for a sexier and ultimately more useful one. As our thirtieth birthdays swung into view (Richard is four days older than me) I bought Richard ten hours of flying lessons. My plan worked! He was hooked! He's good at it, co-owns a tiny plane with Nick Mason from Pink Floyd, sometimes flies me around . . . success! I put the golf clubs in the attic myself.

Now, I've painted a pretty rosy picture of things round here but, of course, sometimes Richard drives me mental. We've also had times when new babies have been in the house and we've lost sight of each other a bit. It's important to take stock and I can't think of any relationships that can rest on their laurels. But it's important to check in with yourself too. That sounds obvious, I know, but at one point Richard asked me what I wanted to do and I realised I didn't actually know what I wanted because usually I went with what made everyone else happy. It's vital to keep an eye on that stuff. I think the trickiest bits for Richard and me have not been the big dramas like premature babies or financial strain, but the slightly difficult times when one or other of us has felt a bit unlovable. I know that can be part of a bigger issue but talking about it is a good place to start.

We don't always feel exactly the same way about things with the kids but it's never insurmountable. We tend to make the big decisions together and then the smaller things I get on with given that I am more of a control freak when it comes to the smalls. I have sometimes overheard Richard forget what school year the kids are in or even possibly their ages. That's not to say he's not fully engaged with all the most important things – he is, and his way sometimes helps me see where I could change tack or delegate here and there, too. I love the fact Richard has been supportive of giving the kids the best bits of my childhood as well as his. His parents stayed together and honestly his folks have had to deal with a lot of ups and downs so I'm so impressed with their togetherness. They still seem to like each other, which we all know isn't a given. My childhood home is ten minutes away from us now and I adore having my ma so close. In spirit, our home is a lot more like the house I grew up in than Richard's (brightly coloured happy tat everywhere) and obviously our jobs are closer to my ma and pa's than Richard's. I'm a real family girl so I love the fact R has welcomed that so readily.

It's also nice that we are the same age. I do appreciate having the same reference points – it means we can both sing the *ThunderCats* theme tune with the same enthusiasm and remember watching the same terrible late-night TV shows like *Get Stuffed*. Having known each other since we were twenty-two and having been a couple since twenty-four, we've grown up together. We still love the same things and luckily they are perennials . . . our fun is not about success or failure, but eating nice food, making cocktails (he makes the best margaritas), taking the kids to the park, listening to music and dancing . . . we're very happy when we have time alone and can happily do not very much together. Our best days aren't planned and our future is open. We both like knowing that, so long as we're in it together, *que sera sera*.

2005 when we said 'I do'. I'd say it again now.

13

MOTHERHOOD: The Beginning – 'Love Is Here'

Puffy with pre-eclampsia and the night before I became someone's Mama.

Motherhood – the biggest, spinniest plate of them all. So big and heavy that actually it isn't one plate at all, it's a collection of plates spinning on top of a large plate, and those plates have plates on them, too. It's a full-on dinner service drawn by Dr Seuss and I had no idea what I was getting into when I had my first. Then again, who does?

And as my babies grow, the plates grow too. My teenager is beautiful and complex and needs me so much, yet he's naturally pulling away and gaining independence. None of this is unique, but I honestly don't think folk talk as much about the parental needs of the bigger kids. Or at least, there's a lot of fixation on new parenthood and having a baby. When I had my eldest, Sonny, he made sure I had an inkling of the scope of our relationship when I first laid eyes on him. Two weeks after my twenty-fifth birthday I gave birth, on the morning of 23 April 2004, and on that afternoon I was taken in a wheelchair to visit my brand-new baby. He was born early so he'd been whisked away as soon as I had him. Now, an hour or two later, I was finally able to meet him properly and the two emotions that struck me the most were: 1) Sonny was a whole, complete person who just happened to be a baby when I met him; and 2) even if I had twelve babies I would still always wonder about having a thirteenth. (Don't freak out, Richard . . . if there's ever been an effective contraceptive then it's a year in and out of lockdown with all our offspring. I'm knackered.)

Some days I compare raising my kids to running and managing a business. I feel as if I have a box file in my head for each and it's filled with admin. The 'Ray' box might be full of notes like current shoe size, when to book a haircut (usually overdue), bring down the next size up of clothes from the attic, email the school to see if Ray's guitar has shown up, book the playdate he keeps asking for, etc.

That's day-to-day life, but the other analogy that I feel works for the more emotional side of mothering is that having five kids feels like being a spaceman tasked with nurturing life on five planets. I have to regularly visit each planet to check how the plants are growing, provide shade for any areas burning in the heat, water what needs watering, check the overall ecosystem and adjust accordingly. My spaceman job is pretty twenty-four-hour because all my planets need little tweaks all the time. They all respond individually to things and all flourish and bloom under different conditions. I am not exactly the same mother to each of them and if my usual techniques don't work then I have to rethink things and try and learn a new skill.

It's funny, because when babies turn into toddlers people talk a lot about their character coming out, but I think the same can be applied to parents. To keep a baby safe and sound is by and large something anyone can do: keep them warm, let them sleep enough and feed them well. To keep that same child happy and supported when they are older calls for something different and I think that is when your character as a parent emerges. You have more options and you have to try and work in tandem with what works for your family as it grows. And grow it does . . . when I had my last baby, Mickey, my eldest was fourteen. It changed the pregnancy because I felt very much that I was having a whole person-who-would-soon-be-grown, rather than just a chubby baby. It shifted the emphasis for me which meant I felt I went into it with my eyes a bit more open than before.

I always wanted to be a mother. My closest sibling, Jackson, was born when I was eight and I adored him. He symbolised the 'happy ever after' after my parents' fairly fiery divorce. Thanks to how the cards fell, ever since Jack came along there has always been a baby in the family with a gap of no more than six years. New babies always brought happiness and optimism as far as I was concerned. In my mum and stepdad John's case, my mum had found herself pregnant when they had been together only three months. There was a bit of controversy over her pregnancy at the time. My mum had been presenting *Blue Peter* for four years by then. After announcing she was having a baby, they didn't renew her contract. My ma has always maintained that that was always their plan at the BBC and that the 'unmarried new mum' aspect of her life had nothing to do with it. I think that's a better rhetoric than being fired for being knocked up, so I'm happy with that.

Although I knew I wanted to have children one day, when I was in my early twenties I wasn't thinking too much about it. I was busy with my solo career and motherhood still felt a little out of reach. I do remember feeling a bit of a pinch when I went past twenty-three without having a baby. My mum had had me at twenty-three, and my grandma had had my mum at the same age, so a part of me thought that could be my time too.

As it turned out, when my baby did come along it kind of gave roots to a very new relationship, but – and I know how peculiar this sounds – I wasn't surprised. I wasn't planning to get pregnant – but on some level it made complete sense to both of us that we were soon to be three. We were far from trying to have a baby – we were a new couple and just getting to know each other romantically, and if I'm completely honest I wasn't sure at first whether it was a good idea. It wasn't a hasty 'let's not use anything' kind of a situation. Not to go into too much detail but suffice to say I am not too good at always remembering to take pills. I'm now on daily medication for an underactive thyroid and I frequently look at the pack of pills – by the sink to jog my memory – and think, 'When on earth did I last take those?' If you're reading, Mum, this hardly ever happens. Honest.

Anyway, my occasional slip-ups in taking my contraceptive pill were nothing too out of the ordinary but nothing had ever happened so I assumed it was kind of OK so long as you usually did the right thing. When Richard and I got together it felt very real, very quickly. We used to make jokes about having a baby. Around that time, Katie Price and Peter Andre had a baby which had a name fashioned out of their mothers' names fused together. Richard and I tried putting Sophie and Richard together to make 'Sori'. I remember Richard once saying to my tummy, 'Sori? Are you in there?'

As it happens, someone probably was. Only it was Sonny and there was nothing sorry about that. I did have a couple of wobbles early on – was having a baby now a very smart thing? But none of the arguments against motherhood spoke to me louder than having the baby.

It was honestly the best of times and the worst of times. I had just finished recording my second album which was about to be released. My relationship with Mike had finished but the fallout was ongoing and I had moved into a little flat with my best friend, Maria.

I remember quite clearly going on *Top of the Pops* singing my song 'Mixed Up World' and thinking that if the record company – or anyone

– had any idea about the predicament I was in at that moment, they would truly think my world was mixed up. Richard and I hadn't told anyone we were dating. We wanted a chance to see if our relationship would work without anyone giving us their opinion on my bass player now being my date. And now we were expecting a baby. How was that going to factor into our relationship?

Also – was I sure I wanted this baby anyway?

I spoke to my mum about it. She sounded disappointed but she was supportive. She gave the number of a doctor I could speak to. I still remember my chat with that doctor because she was so lovely and said something that really stayed with me: most women don't know what they should do, they just wish they weren't in that situation at all.

I have had many friends who have had abortions and every time, I think they have done exactly what is right for them. For me, though, I couldn't quite get to that headspace. Yes, Richard and I were new and the timing was crazy, but my mum spoke some wisdom to me the moment I had told her I was pregnant and I believed in the words she said. 'It might not be the right time, it might not be the right man, but it's the right baby.'

And how right she was. As my tummy grew, so did the love that Richard and I felt for each other. I felt deep down that Richard would be a good daddy and I felt so supported that he hadn't run a mile when he found out I was having his baby.

The reactions from folk around us when we told them our news was mainly positive, with varying quantities of shock. The shock came not just from the speed of the new relationship and our impending parent-hood, but also from the fact that none of my friends had ever really spoken about becoming mums at that point. As it turned out, my close friends only started having babies when I had my third. Not many had even held a baby – Richard included. But my girlfriends were happy for me. They had supported me so much in leaving my old relationship and joined me in nervous anticipation of this new generation of small people.

One even cried when I told her, saying, 'You've managed to turn your life around, I'm so happy for you.'

My poor dad, who had struggled so much with my turning into an actual woman who could date – and maybe sleep with (the horror) – actual real men, now had more emotional challenges ahead. He came to visit Richard and me at my little rented flat and I told him, 'Dad, I'm pregnant.' His reaction would go on to be a story all my friends know. The first thing he said was, 'So, you've had sex then!' He then began to do what I can only describe as self-soothing – stroking his hair over and over as he took in the news. 'So, I'm going to be the youngest grandad ever . . . Richard, where did you say you went to school again?' It was honestly like watching someone go a tiny bit mad. He then decided Richard and I should perform a little ceremony where my little six- and seven-year-old siblings 'could be flower children so they can understand what is going on'. He then literally backed out of the flat whilst waving in a daze. Poor Dad, If he could have imposed some kind of lockdown like the one we have seen this year for when I was between the ages of sixteen and thirty, I think he would have done.

Meanwhile, the rest of my family was starting to get into the idea. My little sister Martha was over the moon. A naturally maternal person and a huge fan of all things baby-shaped, Martha has always been a wonderful auntie. She's been the first family member to cuddle a few of my offspring and the love from the uncles and aunties all round is a gorgeous thing.

Around this time, Richard and I went for our first appointments at the hospital. I had done a little bit of research and decided I liked the idea of going to a hospital where I could have what's called an 'active birth', which I think was essentially being able to wander about while you're in labour and do whatever you felt like. I thought that sounded nicer than a medicalised birth with your feet in stirrups. A few folk had told me about a private hospital called St John and St Elizabeth where the labour ward looked more like a local birthing centre than a big hospital with strip lighting. That sounded more my vibe. As I arrived at my first appointment there were tasteful black and white photos all over the walls of the birthing wing showing beautiful couples giving birth by candlelight. It all looked a lot less intimidating to me.

Richard and I weren't living together. He was in a shared house in Wembley and it wasn't until I was about three months gone before we decided he should probably live with me, seeing as we were about to have a baby. But all that came later and so for our first appointment with the midwives we arrived from different addresses. I was on time and went into the doctor's office to start going through the paperwork while we waited for Richard. The office door was left open so I could see very clearly when Richard, red-faced and running, ran straight past the room looking for where to go. He then came running back and threw himself into the seat next to me. I looked on with amusement but also slight panic. If you've seen the movie *Knocked Up* then you'll know the dynamic. Richard was visibly nervous. He was chewing gum and a bit shifty in his chair.

If you've ever been to one of those early appointments then you'll know that it's mainly questions fired at the mother-to-be and the dad, if he's there, gets the odd question at the end. Richard must have been really nervous because after I'd detailed my medical history, my family's medical history, my current medical and emotional state, Richard was asked the first of his two questions. 'How many siblings?' asked the midwife. Richard, still chewing gum, one arm casually slung over the side of the chair, held up a finger and answered, 'Uno'. Instead of thinking, 'Oh great, he speaks Spanish,' my mind was reeling. 'Exactly how well do you know this guy you're having a baby with?!'

But if it's a little unnerving seeing the father of your baby behaving in an odd way in the doctor's room, it's way more unnerving meeting your baby's grandparents when you're already four months gone. Richard's parents had come along to gigs before but I'd never exchanged much more than a 'hello' backstage. Now I was going for lunch with them with a big bump of grandbaby along for the ride. Richard's folks – Daphne and Tony Jones – are very sweet and the lunch went pretty smoothly, although it was quite funny how my nearly mother-in-law spent a lot of time giving me the hard sell about her son when my tummy was a pretty big clue I had already decided I was into him. She also informed me that Richard was very flexible, thanks to the yoga she'd done when she was pregnant with him.

With work, I didn't want to tell anyone until I'd reached twelve weeks and I was nervous about the reaction. I was fairly sure the record company wouldn't be jumping up and down with glee. I remember filming the video for the second single of the second album, a song called 'Won't Change You', and I was about ten weeks pregnant. I felt as if I was going through the motions and whilst I was still enjoying myself, my eye was not on the ball at all. Although I was obviously not drinking, the emotions I felt most of the time were not unlike being tipsy and that is the only defence I have for co-writing the terrible lyrics in the verse of that song 'I tried to change my accent, my diet too . . . I'll still change my under-wear if that's OK with you.'

Around that time, my PR, Sundraj, had phoned me a couple of times to ask if I was pregnant. There were rumours and journalists were asking the question. I was still very early in my pregnancy and protective of myself. What if I miscarried? So I told him, 'No, I'm not pregnant.' Then as I approached my eleventh week of pregnancy he changed from 'The papers are asking if . . .' to 'The tabloids know you are pregnant. You can provide a comment if you like, but they are going to run the story tomorrow no matter what.'

It didn't occur to me that the reason the press knew was because my phone was being hacked. Well, my phone, Richard's phone and my mum's phone. At that time I'd only been in the public eye for a very short time. 'Groovejet' had propelled me into a place where I was more known and with it came a level of fame that for me was not always welcome. I'd never had the paparazzi follow me before but I found being followed and photographed while I went about my usual day sinister and odd. How many photos of someone carrying shopping along a street do you need? I also started getting phone calls from people I didn't know. Sometimes in the middle of the night someone would call drunk from a party and sometimes a radio show would cold-call me live on air.

What was most common was when someone would call and then abruptly hang up when I answered. I now know this was a sign of hacking as they want to click through to your voicemail, not to you. At the time I thought I had a phone stalker and this went on for a long time.

I did not put two and two together about the fact that new information in my life – potential work offers, dating Richard and finding out I was pregnant – all got to the press with lightning speed. I thought that was just what happened to famous people and so I better get used to it. I became more careful with who I talked to but it always seemed that the walls had ears and the information would get out there no matter what I did.

Now that the press knew I was pregnant, I had to quickly phone round my friends and let them know before they read about it. Their reactions were largely comical. Lots of high-pitched screams down the phone from my girlfriends, some stunned silences, too . . . but overall they took their lead from me – it was unexpected but it was going to be fine. I really did think that, even in the madness of the new relationship and the Speedy Gonzales pregnancy, it all made some kind of sense.

I found mixing my public image with my pregnancy pretty jarring. Up until then I'd kept my private life well away from the public gaze but now there was a slightly bitchy curiosity about my new situation. I guess if you have a young pop star who is usually in a world where it's all about how you look in your videos and seeming young and free, suddenly having to navigate pregnancy is not the easiest. I struggled with how to dress and how to carry myself. I think things have changed a bit now, but this was nearly twenty years ago and having a baby was seen as an awkward accessory to pop star life.

I suppose the image of motherhood has had massive shifts over the generations. After all, it was only in my grandma's day that once women had babies they were expected to stop focusing on their own work. My paternal granny gave up the possibility of university and further education in order to get married and raise my dad and uncle. My maternal grandma was a teacher but being a working mother was still a quiet thing you got on with. Pregnancy was private and being a visible working mother was not to be celebrated. For my mum's generation things had moved on a bit in that eighties women were encouraged to 'have it all' – be a powerhouse in the boardroom and a domestic goddess at home, but still with traditional morals. It seems absurd now that my own mother drew so much controversy when she got pregnant with my brother Jackson out of wedlock. Now, that would seem ridiculous.

In 2003, I was newly pregnant with a man who wasn't my husband and there were a lot of snarky comments in the way it was reported, not to mention the fact that the subtext running through it all was that motherhood was unsexy and frumpy so – watch out, pop star! You're about to get swollen ankles and that won't look good on *Top of the Pops*! A report from the *Sun* shows a photo of me six months pregnant with the words: 'Here's Sophie Ellis-Bextor finding out how high heels can be Murder on the Dancefloor when you're six months gone . . . her set was . . . more bump than grind. Her next performance will be in the labour wing where she'll be wailing not singing.' I felt kind of ridiculous for a lot of the pregnancy.

Once Polydor found out about the baby, just after the second single 'Won't Change You' was released, they decided to stop pushing the album and leave it at that. The second album was released and it did OK in the charts but nothing like the splash the first one had had. But still, I was doing the odd performance and promotion for the album throughout the first six months of my pregnancy and I felt as if I had no clue how to dress my new shape. At twenty-four, I was opposed to buying maternity clothes as I felt that would be like admitting fashion defeat. With each subsequent pregnancy, maternity clothes have gone from strength to strength, but back then it wasn't so easy to find fun, youthful maternity wear and I just didn't see any options that made me feel like me. I wore clothes I liked a size or two bigger than normal and made do. I had the most awful blonde hair for the majority of the pregnancy and quickly started to get quite puffy as the baby grew. In short, aside from the way Richard made me feel, I felt very unattractive and like I'd lost myself.

I thought I'd love pregnancy but the further on I got, the worse I felt. My face swelled as well as my hands, my feet, my ankles. By five or six months I had to buy shoes a size up just to have something to wear. I was getting headaches and felt more and more antisocial the bigger I got. Everyone around me was being sweetly supportive and up until the end kept telling me I was blooming. I knew that I wasn't though. I felt awful and frustrated. Maybe I was just rubbish at being pregnant? Maybe the stress of the ongoing financial wrangles with my ex was making me ill? Throughout my pregnancy I was dealing with settling into my new rental while also looking for a home to buy for Richard, the baby and me. Richard only moved into my rental flat two weeks before Sonny was born, as it turned out. The whole while I was trying to get the rest of my belongings from the house I'd bought with Mike and also releasing a new record. It was all pretty stressful.

It genuinely never occurred to me that the puffy hands and feet and the headaches might be a sign of something more sinister. For the whole pregnancy I'd had minimal interactions with the hospital. At twenty-four and in good health, I was very low risk. I think I'd had a twenty-week check and then wasn't expected back at the hospital until twenty-eight weeks, but in those two months my symptoms had been escalating. By the time I took myself for my twenty-eight week check-up, I was really feeling pretty rubbish. At the appointment they went through all the usual stuff, but when they checked my urine and blood pressure, the readings weren't great. I had protein in my wee and my blood pressure was too high. They gave me some pills to help my blood pressure and told me to come back on Monday to see how it was going. 'You don't need to make an appointment, just come in and we'll check you when you get here on Monday morning.'

With that, I went home to start taking the pills. The next day, the Saturday, I had the christening of my goddaughter. I didn't want to go. I felt pretty miserable. I looked terrible. I put on this brightly coloured, ill-fitting party dress and tried to make myself look nice but I knew I looked anything but. I wasn't glowing like I was supposed to. I was puffy all over and my eyes looked sunken. I squashed my feet into my shoes and off I went. At the christening most people said the usual 'Oh, you're blooming!' which I think is probably taken by most pregnant women as being the acceptable way of telling us we look less than great. It wasn't until we were back at my friend's flat after the ceremony and having tea that the baby's grandma – a nurse – looked at me and said, 'You don't look well. You need to get checked out.' Honestly, I could have hugged her. Finally someone was telling me what I was thinking.

The next day I remember hearing Richard practising his bass through the walls for a gig he had that week. He had now moved in and was in the room which had been Maria's room. We'd been officially living together for ten days and it felt just right.

As he played I was lying on my bed surrounded by my pregnancy books. I used to love reading about each stage. How big the baby was by now, what you should expect . . . although the books are so focused on pregnancy that I used to have to keep reminding myself that pregnancy is just the bit that happens before things really go wild and the baby arrives. Also sometimes things happen that you haven't read about and it can really throw you. I once woke up around six months pregnant to find my boobs had made wet patches on my nightie as I slept. No one warned me about that! Looking back, there were quite a lot of surprises with that first baby. It's hard to know what's normal and what isn't. Plus the pregnancy books focus on the typical. Sometimes they will have a little subheading about something that might happen off grid, and then the book continues talking about the more normal flow of things. For me, that's what happened that night. One little subheading talked about pre-eclampsia. It described the symptoms and what might happen. I sat bolt upright. I knew in my heart that that was me. I started crying but also felt a tinge of relief at the possibility that how I'd been feeling wasn't just me being crap at having a baby.

The next morning, Richard drove me to the hospital for my check-up. When I arrived he was struggling to find a parking space so he dropped me at the door and told me to just ring when I was done. I went up to the reception and told them what I'd been told: I just needed to have my blood pressure checked to see if the medicine was working. It should only take a minute.

I can still remember sitting in the room as the midwife took my blood pressure and told me that no, I would not be going home. I needed to be transferred to a hospital with a neonatal unit straight away. I was introduced to a consultant called Gubby who phoned ahead to another hospital to see if there was a bed. I rang Richard. 'I'm not allowed to leave. They say I have to be taken to another hospital straight away. I have pre-eclampsia.'

To save you googling it, pre-eclampsia is a pregnancy condition in which the body tries to reject the placenta. It can vary from mild to so severe that the mother can go into a coma (the word 'eclampsia' comes from the Greek for lightning, as the coma can come on very quickly) and die. In the olden days it was often how first-time mothers died. The only 'cure' is delivering the baby. I've been told it's more common with black mothers, with overweight mothers and/or with mothers over forty. As a twenty-five-year-old white first-time mother, I was a bit of an anomaly. My theory is that the stress of the whole situation over the previous few months may have contributed.

As soon as Richard came to join me, we travelled together to Chelsea. I didn't have time to think about the fact that I was waving goodbye to my candlelit birth at that point and I definitely hadn't taken on board that the bed they were checking was available wasn't for me, but for the baby. I was thirty-one weeks pregnant, I hadn't yet had antenatal classes, I hadn't yet bought the house for us to bring the baby home to and I hadn't bought any clothes for the baby. I felt completely unprepared.

Richard and I phoned our parents to let them know what was going on but we didn't want to panic anyone. We were given a tour of the neonatal unit so we could see what lay ahead for us and the baby, but even then I think I was in shock. My baby wasn't due for another two months. I remember looking at all these tiny little premature babies and they really didn't look like typical chubby newborns. In their incubators, surrounded by wires and bleeping sounds, they looked more like wise alien creatures.

For the rest of the week I was closely monitored and the baby checked. Kind friends brought me what I hadn't had time to pack, pyjamas and toothpaste and fairy lights to cheer up my hospital room. I was given steroid injections to boost the baby's lung growth. I wasn't feeling too worried about the baby at that point. Although I was shocked at the speed at which things were happening, I was also relieved I was now being treated when I'd felt rough for so long, and reassured by my only previous experience of a premature baby, my little sister Martha, who had been born ten weeks early.

Martha was a tiny baby, 3lb 2oz, when she was born, but she was gorgeous and strong and came home after six weeks. After that I wasn't aware of her prematurity having any lasting impact on her – certainly my memories of her childhood had been happy and healthy – so I carried this positivity with me as I waited and watched to see how long I could stay pregnant with my own baby.

Each day was seen by the medical staff as a positive – when your baby is coming early, every extra hour in the womb is a chance for them to grow stronger and have a better chance at thriving once they are in the world. I managed to get to the end of the week. On Friday, Gubby came to tell me that she didn't think it was safe for the pregnancy to keep going and that I'd be taken first thing the next day to the theatre to have a caesarean. I think right up to the last minute I was processing the idea that I would not have a natural birth and I would not go through labour. Even now, I've never experienced it and I think I have a real fascination with the whole thing. I'd like to have given it a go. Especially with the first couple of pregnancies, I was so geared up for the birth. I wanted to see how I'd fare at going for a natural birth and I'd almost looked forward to the adventure, although I have had many friends tell me that it's not really something I should feel sad I've avoided.

I had a friend, Helen, come to visit the day before the birth. 'Can I bring anything?' she asked. This was in the era before mobile phones had such amazing cameras so we asked for a disposable camera and some CDs to play while I gave birth. She turned up with both, so Sonny was born to Michael Jackson's *Off the Wall*. I remember asking the nurses to please skip track seven as I didn't want to have a baby to the saddest song on the album, 'She's Out of My Life'.

The morning of Sonny's birthday, I woke with shooting pains going up from my liver and all along my arm. I now know that was the sign of my liver packing up. I really was going to be delivered of my baby as close to the wire as possible.

The operation just felt . . . weird. I'd spent so much of the pregnancy thinking about the labour and the natural birth, so missing both was like skipping important punctuation. It was a pretty abrupt ending to pregnancy, although I did appreciate how lucky I was to have such an amazing level of care. I don't remember being scared. I think it all happened too fast to think like that. I was just going with whatever the professionals had decided and I was too inexperienced to know any other way. Gubby performed the operation herself. She was one of those doctors who, when you find yourself in choppy waters, you cling to like a rock. Whenever I've found myself in any kind of turbulence I always look around and find the person – in my experience it's often a woman – who is keeping calm and talking sense. Gubby was that woman for me and I'm sure for a lot of other women who have found themselves in similar situations. It's crazy that for me I'll always remember her name, but for her I'm just one of the many women she helped on one day.

I was feeling unwell and a little wobbly about the delivery so I asked Richard if he would promise to stay with me and not go off with the baby, no matter what. Meanwhile, my mum and dad and Richard's folks arrived at the hospital to wait in the ward until I was out the other side and their grandbaby was born. What I didn't realise before about caesareans is that the first bit is pretty quick – under ten minutes until the baby is let loose on the world. As you're awake up top and numb below the chest, you can feel the tugging and pulling. People have described it like someone doing the washing up in your tummy but I'm quite a literal gal and no, it felt like someone opening me up and pulling the baby out, only without any pain. As the baby was pulled out and 'It's a boy' was proclaimed, Sonny cried. I don't know why, but I wasn't expecting that. I thought an early baby like that would be silent. His cry filled me with hope.

Typically, about five minutes after Sonny was born (it was always going to be Sonny, figuratively and literally, I knew Sonny for a boy, but once he was born I felt an overwhelming sense of 'Of course it's Sonny, it was always going to be him') a nurse put his head round the door and said, 'Grandma wants to know if it's a boy or a girl.' He then set off to inform the new grandparents about who was new to the family.

As Sonny was assessed I was put back together on the table. Richard, in his new father joy, stood up to go and have a look as his new baby. This caused me to have a panic attack. I don't blame R at all, but I was probably already only just holding it together with having our baby so soon and in such a different way to the birth I'd planned.

Anyway, I was now full-on freaking out on the table and the anaesthetist, with a glint in his eye, asked me if I wanted something to help me calm down. I don't know if you've seen the bit in *Bridesmaids* where Kristen Wiig's character has medication on a plane to help with nerves, which she washes down with a large whisky, but that was me. I was GAWN. Out of it.

I don't remember being wheeled back to my room, or Sonny going in a different direction to the special baby care unit, but by the time I was back with my mum and dad (as I entered the room my dad was filming with a little video camera – more footage I never want to see), I was asking the nurses if I could have champagne (no, apparently). I also kept pulling off my oxygen mask. Apart from that, I was tickety-boo.

I didn't see Sonny until later that afternoon. By now I was in a wheelchair and so I was taken to his part of the neonatal intensive care unit. I can still remember seeing him properly for the first time in his little incubator with wires and machines all around . . . but all I really saw was him. My tiny baby boy. No chub, no hair, but so perfect. The rush of hormones was amazing. Intoxicating. I knew then that Sonny was his own person and I realised that my job was to help him become his whole 360-degree self. That I hadn't had a baby, I'd had Sonny.

That night I slept on an open ward with a morphine drip for company. All around me were women who were either having tricky pregnancies and needed bed rest, or new mums out of surgery.

There was a surreal moment early the next morning when a nurse came to see me. In hospital you get very used to having to fill in each and every medical practitioner who comes your way. When this nurse asked how I was, I told her about how I'd found my night. She smiled sympathetically before asking me to please sign two autographs for her kids.

I stayed in for a week before I went home. It felt so peculiar leaving Sonny behind but I reassured myself that there was no alternate reality where he was with us at home. I'd either be still pregnant, or he had to be in hospital. Still, it's a weird bubble you're in when you have a new baby and you're new parents, but no buggy to show for it. I do feel so massively for anyone who has a sick bubba where their trajectory isn't upward. Touch wood, but until now with my babies, at least if they've been patients it's been with a view to their coming home one day.

Sonny was in hospital for nearly six weeks. In that time Richard and I visited twice a day. Early babies have no sucking reflex until thirty-four weeks, so I had to express my milk with a pump. To get my milk to come in without a baby, I had to manually express . . . and even after much pumping, you'd only get a drop or two of colostrum (the pre-milk goodness your body makes for a newborn). Now I have no judgement at all on whether or not babies are breastfed or bottle-fed, but for me, a new mum to a premature baby who I couldn't easily hold, the milk was the only thing I felt I could give that the doctors couldn't. It was my role and it was a way of keeping the bond between Sonny and me while he was in hospital. This led me to the weird and wonderful subculture that is breast-pumping mums. For a long time with my newborns, the pump was all I knew.

I would express my milk day and night and then freeze the little tiny bottles of milk to take to Sonny. Sometimes I'd be running low and would sit in the passenger seat willing the traffic to be kind so my milk could get to my baby. Sometimes I wouldn't make it and Sonny had donor milk. I was grateful and felt a strange bond with these other mummies in the same boat as me. That being said, sometimes when I'd arrive at the hospital and see hundreds of full frozen bottles all with the same baby name sticker on them, I'd feel a bit of a failure.

With a premature baby there are three milestones to hit before you can take them home: eating well, regulating their temperature and regulating their oxygen. Happily, Sonny had no bleeds on the brain when he was born (something they check straight away) and he only had one partially collapsed lung (very common as babies develop their lungs at the end of pregnancy . . . makes sense really). Other than that, Sonny did well and by the time he was ready to come home I couldn't wait for the next chapter of our lives to begin.

While Sonny was still in the hospital, Richard and I had found a new home together, a lovely house on Chesterton Road in Portobello. We only got the keys three days before Sonny came home and Dan's brother Jim and his girlfriend Daisy did such a brilliant job of painting all weekend so that when Sonny came out of hospital, the house looked like our home. I remember there were boxes everywhere and only a mattress and radio in our room with his little basket.

I felt as if we could finally begin to really enjoy being parents. It felt lovely to be in the early summer months and walk around with the pram and my own gorgeous baby lying safely inside. Richard was around a lot, but as he was finishing his album I also spent a lot of time on my own. I was surprised to find I still felt quite isolated sometimes. I found aspects of new motherhood incredibly lonely. I didn't have any friends with babies so I felt a bit in limbo. I was also nervous to be alone with a baby who had spent the first two months of his life being so closely monitored.

I slept with Sonny in the bed with us. I've never actually told anyone before, but I've had all my newborns sleep with me. It's often frowned upon, but I think it helps massively with getting a bit more sleep when they feed a lot and I also think it's helped get my kids sleeping better sooner (not that they are all great at that – Mickey, I'm looking at you). Finally, I'd argue that in my case, it might have saved Sonny's life.

Despite the scare of the illness in pregnancy, no antenatal classes, the new small baby, and Richard and me and buying a new home while

Sonny was only days old, it was what happened when Sonny had been home with us for two months that has stayed in my mind as the most traumatic. Two months of happy days spent with our small baby ... wandering round Portobello Market, having my mum over, time with the grandparents, aunts, uncles ... Richard recording his album in and around the house (the room with my shoes and clothes in became the unofficial drum studio for Paul. He even had a pile of my shoes fall on him mid-take once. Sadly they didn't fall in the same tempo as the song he was recording). We had made plans to go to Cornwall over the bank holiday weekend. It was Notting Hill Carnival and the streets all round us were cordoned off. We were planning on being home on the Saturday to enjoy a bit of Carnival then set off on Sunday to go and see my mum and John in a place they'd rented for the week. I woke early on the Saturday morning, Sonny in my arms, and was surprised to see it was 6 a.m. Usually, Sonny would have had a feed around 4 a.m. (I'm not a routine person but he was naturally falling into a little pattern ... trying to follow Gina Ford's *Contented Baby* book was easily the most miserable of my first weeks as a new mum. I smiled as I put it in the bin). I kissed his little forehead and it was boiling hot. I thought I must have overheated him and quickly checked he wasn't under the cover but no, not only was he not covered he also had feet like ice blocks. In a panic I woke Richard and tried to find the little thermometer the hospital had recommended we get. It was just an ordinary under-the-tongue one, but the nurses had shown me how to hold it under the baby's arm to get a good reading. They'd also warned me to add a degree or two to get a more accurate idea of the temperature.

Sonny's temperature was soaring ... well over 106°F.

While Richard phoned NHS Direct, I tried to get Sonny to feed. He was moaning and his eyes looked far away. The heat coming off him was scaring me.

'They are asking if we want an ambulance?'

I nodded and went downstairs to pack a bag for us. As I waited for the ambulance in our kitchen, just Sonny and me, I rocked him and looked into his eyes and told him not to worry. That we would get him to the doctors and they would make him better, but the worst thing is, I was lying. I knew there was a chance he was beyond help as I could tell he was seriously ill.

The ambulance arrived in two minutes and took us to St Mary's in Paddington. I later found out this is the number-one hospital in the country for dealing with meningitis. The ambulance staff were upbeat and chatty. I know we talked a lot about the Carnival as the ambulance weaved its way through road closure signs.

When we arrived at the hospital, Sonny was given a big dose of Calpol and was taken to a room next door to the one we were waiting in. We could hear him crying through the walls as they did a lumbar puncture. It was awful and heart-wrenching, I felt totally useless but relieved that everyone at the hospital had such a clear plan of how they would treat him. I think Richard and I were in shock but also, when we are under pressure, we focus on the now and not on what might happen. The main headline was that the doctors thought he should make a full recovery so that was where we focused ourselves. And even in the most stressful of situations come the mundane moments and we could still make the odd lame joke to break the tension a little. We didn't want to alarm the rest of the family, so you tell yourself you're feeling more OK than you are so as not to pass on the panic. When we spoke to the grandparents later it was to reassure them that everything was fine now but yes, Sonny had meningitis, but it was under control.

To a certain extent it was all true – we didn't get the official diagnosis until the afternoon by which time Sonny's temperature was under control and he was coming back into himself – but I think the jolt of fear and adrenaline took a while to process. For years after I would freak out if any of the kids had a high fever. For all Sonny's early days in hospital I had been completely optimistic. Having had a premature baby sister, I had seen the happy ending with her and felt Sonny would be fine too . . . but I knew instinctively that he was on a downward slope with the meningitis and it took a while to be honest with myself about how much that had scared me. I used to brush it off very quickly . . . I never wanted any of my babies to be defined by the things they'd experienced and I take most things in my stride, but that day is definitely up there in my top five scariest moments of my life. The Paso Doble on *Strictly* is probably number six.

I found the early years with Sonny pretty joyful. He was a happy, smiley and very loved little boy. That's a good way to start a life. I was surprised by how personal the journey into motherhood was. By that I mean of course it's a universal thing and for ever after, when you're responsible for a child, it opens conversations with anyone else in the same boat. Once you have a child in your life, every news story about a child transports you to the heart of the story. That child is your child.

But it's also personal: only your baby has you and only you have your baby. People talk a lot about the way kids grow and get their own personality, but I could feel it happening in reverse, too. As Sonny got older, I was faced with more options for what kind of mum I wanted to be.

Sometimes, of course, I did feel lost in amongst it all. I think this feeling began in pregnancy, when I started to be treated differently from the moment I was visibly pregnant. Yes, I was having a baby, but I wasn't defined by it, and so people congratulating me for making it out the house to watch one of The Feeling's early gigs really grated on me. I felt as if my independence was already starting to be questioned. It made me feel I'd been taken over by something and then you start worrying if you'll ever find your whole self again on the other side.

I know once Sonny was born and Richard and his band were riding high, I felt a little invisible in any role other than being Sonny's main person. In 2005, The Feeling were the most played band on British radio

– something I was incredibly proud of and they really deserved it – but I'd go to their gigs and the record company people wouldn't ask me if I was up to anything because it was assumed I was now a mum and that was it.

They were right, in a way. I hadn't found my feet with my new music at all – that took months – and I did feel like the corners of who I was had been rubbed away. I hadn't done National Childbirth Trust classes and so hadn't met any new local parents, and none of my mates had kids. It was isolating and lonely. Plus, if I'm honest, a little bit boring. I adored my little boy but playing with baby stuff all day wasn't wholly satisfying. I needed to find myself again and have things that were just mine – not Richard's, not Sonny's, but mine. I felt I didn't know who I was anymore, as if everything I'd achieved up to that point was old news. I needed to start again and I used that to fuel my ambition. Time spent working away from my little one had to count for double now. It helped me focus but it wasn't overnight. For about two years I felt I didn't know who I was anymore. I didn't know how to introduce the post-baby me to the old pre-baby me. It can be crystallised by the way I felt at the soft play centre. Sonny would be jumping in and out of ball pits having a whale of a time and I'd be feeling grey . . . sitting on a plastic seat looking after his shoes. It rubbed the edges off me and I felt homogenised. Just a chaperone, then home again. Richard was away on tour for a lot for that time, from when Sonny was two to maybe four. I was trying to write my third album and I knew it was the most important one.

As someone with no qualifications, I was going to cling on to the day job with both hands. I always have a little image in my head of me using heels as crampons and getting myself up the hillside. There have been so many times in my life where I've felt I could just hang up my microphone and everyone would just move on with their lives, but I'm fairly tenacious at my core. You're not getting rid of me that easily, and now I had a toddler in tow. With the third album, I was determined to earn my right to keep singing and releasing new music and I really took my time. I didn't release the album until Sonny was three, but it was like a layer of inhibition had gone. If I was going to perform, knowing I had family safe and sound at home made me feel less concerned about the haters. This didn't happen overnight . . . you can't rush how you're feeling and I couldn't speed up getting back to myself again. I was very lucky I could take my time and I think the fact that I spent the longest getting back to work after my first child speaks volumes. With my later kids I definitely got better at shifting gears and combining my life with being a new mum. Blimey – nothing knocks you for six like that first baby.

Sonny was born early and tiny, but we adored him
from the get-go. He made us a family.

14

MOTHERHOOD: Second Baby –
'What Have We Started?'

Hello, Kit! Welcome to the world.

After I had Sonny, I felt quite blindsided by how much being a mum changed everything. I enjoyed having a little boy and was as obsessed and impressed as any new mum. Sonny just brought me a lot of joy. Parenting was full-on and when it came to my work I was going to have to find myself again, but being a mother – well, being Sonny's mother – was a role I adored. As none of my friends had had any babies, Sonny was like the communal bubba and that was great too. By the time I had my third, most people were having kids of their own so it was lovely that Sonny has been able to have proper 360 relationships with the favourite people in my life before they got rightly distracted by their own or other friends' offspring.

By the time Sonny was four he was mentioning a baby, a fictional baby, a lot. We'd see toys in a shop window and Sonny would pipe up, 'We should get that for our baby.' Whenever we went out and there was a baby in the vicinity he'd potter over and have a chat with the little one, always mindful to be tender. Not every small person is good with smaller people, but Sonny was always great with tiny babies and very good at making them smile. Sonny's strategy worked – maybe we should have another one? Richard was up for it, and so I found myself pregnant with my second baby at twenty-nine. I was very lucky that I fell pregnant quickly and everything initially seemed fine. The day I found out I was having another baby coincided with our first night DJing. We had set up a club night with some friends called 'Modern Love'. Richard and I still DJ now. It's fun although it's actually the main time we argue. Richard is a total control freak when it comes to the buttons and it drives me mad . . . that being said, I have the upper hand. Sean Rowley, who used to run a club night called 'Guilty Pleasures', told us that when it comes to the playlist it's all very well and good to play music that the cool kids will appreciate but they will just stand at the bar and nod their head. What you want is the girls on the dance floor. Then the boys will come and dance. This means the final say of what songs R and I play goes to me . . . although for the record I am intent on raising five boys who can dance so that they, too, will be first on the dance floor.

So I found myself, at twenty-nine, a novice DJ and newly pregnant. I felt confident that I was in better shape than last time to carry a baby to full term. Since Sonny, I'd discovered exercise which I had literally never got into before, but now I was pretty hooked. I write this with the guilt of a woman who has not been exercising very much at all these days. My body likes it, but I don't. It's pretty boring but I guess at some point it's a horse I'll have to get back on. Maybe by the time this book comes out I'll be a gym bunny again (I write hopefully). When I was pregnant with Kit, my pregnancy came along at a time when I was going to the gym three times a week, twice for conventional workouts and once a week with a nice trainer who seemed permanently a little stoned who taught me Krav Maga – a martial art used by the Israeli special forces. I always think it's pretty absurd that the only time I practised this martial art was between my third and seventh months of pregnancy. I used to look at my reflection in the gym mirror and think that I didn't look particularly threatening. My trainer said to me at one stage, 'How far along are you again?' 'Six months,' I answered. 'Oh,' he said slowly, 'I thought you were about three!'

For the most part I felt pretty good. After having had such a headachy, puffy, rubbish first pregnancy, my second felt much better. I was fit and shiny, having sorted out my overactive thyroid and feeling much more athletic than I had been when I was in my early twenties. Richard and I were happy and I'd got to the other side of my first album release as a mum. We still had a bit of stress as we decided it would be good to move house, but it was a manageable stress. I'd been working a fair bit and was keen to keep going throughout the pregnancy. Life was OK.

I was having regular checks to see if everything was all right with the bump and baby and I crossed the midway point with no trouble. Looking back, I was carrying a much smaller bump but I just thought that was better than the extra swelling I'd had first time around.

As I approached the last ten weeks I was asked to go and sing in Russia. 'Can I do it?' I asked my consultant. Heading to Moscow would mean I needed a medical letter to say I was fit to fly.

'You can on the condition you come and see me the day before you fly so I can do a final check on the baby.'

As it turned out I could have just skipped this bit as my doctor sent out the medical letter anyway, but I had given her my word so on a snowy week in February, Richard and I headed to the hospital to get checked out. Good job I did, or Kit would have had a Russian passport by now.

I was in a good mood, relaxed and feeling well, so I expected everything to be dandy.

It was not dandy.

My blood pressure was through the roof and I had protein in my urine. A sign the pre-eclampsia was doing its thing again.

'I probably shouldn't let you go home, but I'm going to let you collect your things and you must use a home blood pressure kit to see how you go. Also fill this with all the water you pass for the next twenty-four hours.'

Gubby handed me a massive empty plastic bottle and off Richard and I went, in a state of shock, to get my hospital bag packed and to phone our parents to let them know that, once again, their new grandbaby would be here soon.

The days between seeing Gubby and being admitted to hospital passed in a blur, not least because the pills I'd been given to try and rein in my blood pressure were so insanely strong. They turned me into Eeyore. I spent the whole of Wednesday packing one small bag and baking a pie. It was like trying to make the pie underwater. I couldn't think fast or act fast. I was too drugged to find this panic-inducing.

During that day I kept putting all my wee in this massive plastic bottle. My thinking must have become quite warped due to not feeling well because when I accidentally forgot to wee in the bottle one time, meaning I had to start all over again, I cried.

Again, I had hoped for a natural birth at the cosy birth-centre-style hospital, but now that was out the window, so it was back to Chelsea and Westminster Hospital with its amazing baby care wing. I was admitted the next day, Thursday, and knew what lay in store. Steroid injections for the baby's lungs and drugs for the mama to keep me pregnant as long as possible. Kit was delivered on a Saturday at thirty-one weeks and weighed only 2lb 6oz. So incredibly tiny.

I felt much more 'with it' than when Sonny was born but Richard probably would say the opposite as he made the ill-advised decision to stand up when Kit was delivered. As a result, he saw things he did not mean to see. I know childbirth can introduce a birthing partner to all sorts of stuff if they are down the business end of things, but I think it takes a strong stomach to stand at an operating table where your wife is smiling up at you one end and has her intestines resting on her tummy at the other end. Poor Richard.

When Kit was taken out I saw him for a nanosecond before he was whisked off to neonatal. I'd already decided he'd be called Kit if he was a boy. My mum had an actor friend with a son called Kit, an adult by then. I always thought it was a great name and sat well with Sonny. As he was born around 14 February, his middle name is Valentine. I thought he was so beautiful and he was born to a song by Vampire Weekend, so he had a good song, too.

The truth was, though, he was a very tiny baby. His weight was more like a baby born at twenty-nine weeks. After the birth, my health deteriorated and I was put into a high-dependency unit, as sometimes with pre-eclampsia it gets worse after delivery. While I was there I wasn't allowed any visitors. After lunch, I heard a nurse coming round to say hello to the new mums. I could hear her cooing over all the new babies. She put her head around my curtain, looked around for a baby, saw none and left again without saying a word. She didn't mean anything by it but I cried and cried. I had had a baby, too, I just didn't have him to show for it.

During those early days, I think Richard and I were in a slight state of shock. I wanted to feel brave about it all – after all we had a lovely nearly five-year-old example of how resilient these tiny babies can be – but in truth Kit's vulnerability scared us. He wasn't thriving as well as Sonny had done . . . even from day one he seemed to be less settled. When I held him he cried a lot as though he was in pain.

Day three was the pits. Coinciding nicely with what is termed the 'baby blues day' (when new mums get a rush of hormones that can make you cry all day and feel generally a bit overwhelmed and weepy), the hospital realised that Kit wasn't tolerating his feeds. The milk wasn't going down. When they tried to work out what was wrong they realised that not only was his right lung partially collapsed (which they fixed), but his left was also collapsed. He was immediately placed in an incubator on full respiration. He couldn't have any food or drink, he would be under sedation and morphine, flat on his little back with a machine breathing for him.

It was bleak. The hospital had some cases of norovirus doing the rounds so for the duration of Kit's stay we weren't allowed any visitors. Seven weeks of no grandparents or aunts and uncles coming to say hello. As we had Sonny to look after, we could often only come once a day. Those early days with Kit felt much more serious. I think we both thought he might not make it. One night, while I was still in hospital, Richard told me, 'We've been lucky once. I don't know if we'll be lucky again.'

When I feel afraid, I try not to let my thoughts run away with themselves. Instead, I find people or things around me that steady me – in Kit's case, the doctors, nurses and staff at the hospital. If they are calm then I take my lead from them. I think the worry stays out of my mainframe until after we are out of the woods. It's a coping mechanism to get me through scary situations. Turns out you don't run around screaming . . . you acknowledge it could be worse, acknowledge it could be better, and get on with focusing on the positives and the momentum of coming out the other side. Plus, I talk. To lots of people. That is my therapy . . . friends are wonderful. My mum, dad, Martha, Jack . . . and Richard of course. My goodness, it feels good to share it all. I couldn't get through much without that counsel and I'm aware of how much it means to me. I'm grateful to have been encouraged to find ways to ask for help and support, and I'll be sure to pass it along the chain. It's a lifesaver.

Turns out Kit was made of strong stuff. His discharge notes told of his collapsed lungs and sepsis, but he came home. Hospitals have to make room for newer, sicker babies so Kit was discharged weighing only 3lb 10oz. I'm not going to lie, I was terrified. He was so small and vulnerable. One night I couldn't make him warm. I phoned the unit. They told me to put the fire on at home and pile the blankets on him or use body heat. The image of tiny Kit in his Moses basket with the fire on and five blankets on his tiny frame is still so clear in my memory. Plus I struggled to keep up with his feeding. I felt as if he was always hungry, crying for more. I managed to get to four months before I admitted defeat and switched to formula milk. I know it's not important, but at the time I felt as if I'd let him down.

For the first couple of years, Kit was a happy baby, but I think it took me a while to get over the fear of his vulnerability. I was so happy when he got bigger and stronger. He did bob in and out of hospital a little though . . . several bouts of bronchiolitis, which is inflammation in the lungs and something I'm sure a lot of early babies are susceptible to. The worst memory I have of all that was one night when Kit was the noisy, crying, unhappy baby on the ward. He was miserable and I couldn't soothe him and all the other babies were being kept awake. By morning, I felt rubbed raw and deeply unpopular. I went into what I thought was the parents' or visitors' kitchen and made some toast. Two nurses walked in and started to tell me off. Turned out it was the staff kitchen and the visitors' one was next door. I burst into tears. Sleep deprivation is an amazing tool for making your skin feel like tissue paper.

As far as having two kids goes, it's fair to say it was a lot harder than I had anticipated. I thought it would be easy to go from one – hey, I've done the hardest bit surely? – to two, but two really did feel like double the work. It's harder on a couple, too, as you're constantly delegating. Richard and I can have days where 90% of our conversation is asking each other to sort out things for the smaller members of the family. Plus we did the classic thing of having Kit and then moving house. When he'd been home for only two months we packed up all our things and moved to where we now live. I've blocked out a lot of it but I do know it was so stressful that I promised myself I wouldn't move again for at least a decade. Our nanny Claire was with us the day we moved and, as the daughter of a builder, she was good at noticing all the bits of our new house that needed work. I can laugh about it now but at the time I had a sense of humour failure when, at 9.30 at night when we finally sat down, surrounded by boxes, to eat our fish and chips, Claire remarked that the low fence in our new garden meant that in all likelihood people would lean over the fence and steal the kids.

Now that Kit and Sonny are grown, I'm not sure you'd pick them out in a line-up as premature babies. I never wanted them to be labelled so I didn't really talk too much about their beginnings when they were small. As they've got older it's become obvious that they both learn in a way that isn't typical. Sonny struggles with maths and has something called dyscalculia, which is like dyslexia for numbers. It's not very well known, which has meant it's been hard for us to find him support. Kit is very dyslexic. I adore the way both Sonny and Kit think about the world and being conventional is really overrated, but it has meant that school has been quite tough at times.

I didn't realise until I became a parent how much our education system is designed for the most typical of learners. Of course, it makes sense when you have hundreds of kids to teach – it's hard to make learning bespoke – but I do wish there was a bit more scope in how children are taught. The arts have been so devalued and there's too much stigma attached to getting the 'wrong' answer. School should show you how mortgages work, how to budget, how to keep a check on your mental health. If you learn best while dancing or drawing, let's do a bit of that, too.

When kids do fall outside of the lanes I was surprised how tricky it was to get extra help. We are lucky – I can afford tutors and to pay for educational assessments, but what if you can't? I wish that the end goal of learning was to get kids equipped with employable skills in a more open-minded way, rather than being assessed only on strengths in maths and English. I can google the answer to an algebraic equation, but when computers take over the world, it's the creativity in us that they won't be able to replicate. Anyway I'm getting fired up because I got chucked into all these issues from day one . . .

It turns out that premature babies are more prone in the long term to learning challenges and I honestly don't think I realised that when I took my little babies home from hospital. I think it would have made primary school a little easier if I'd known what to look out for. I didn't realise the extent of Sonny's struggles in maths until he was eight or nine. That's a long time for a kid to feel like they just aren't 'getting it'.

His experience has taught me a lot. I think I was quite a 'typical' learner but I'm raising a few that aren't. I know with all my kids that once they get out the other side of the education system they'll be fine so long as their morale is intact, but it's quite a journey while we travel through it. If I had more time I would campaign to rethink school in a wider sense. I'm not saying kids have to find school wonderful every day, but there's definitely room for a bit of modernising how we teach and what we teach. Anyway, that's a whole other load of plates to spin but watch this space as it is something I get fired up about, as you can probably tell.

15

MUSIC: Songwriting – 'Music Gets the Best of Me'

Here I am writing Murder on the Dancefloor, *which I wrote when I was 6 (this is untrue).*

Well this is a funny one; songwriting can be a strange muscle to flex. The American actress Rosalind Russell said about acting that it was 'standing up naked and turning around very slowly'. I would say songwriting isn't far off. It can either be the easiest, most fun and exhilarating thing ever – or it's downright painful and embarrassing.

I primarily write with other people. When I write on my own I can't edit very well or decide if it's good or not. Having someone in the room with you, someone you may have only met that morning, really makes you choose carefully what you voice.

It's hard to explain the process of songwriting to those who haven't done it and I guess it sounds pretty excruciating. The early sessions certainly were. A typical songwriting session will go something like this: it's me and one other person writing a song. We've never met before so the first hour is mainly about settling in, making a tea, small talk. Then I might either play them songs I've already been writing or maybe something I've been listening to that I find inspiring. Then the other person (rarely me as I'm not very good at playing an instrument in front of people) will either grab a guitar, or get some beats going, or sit at the keyboard and start working on a bit of a (cringe) 'vibe'. Yep, we'll say things like, 'Yeah ... I like the vibe.' It's important to get over your squeamishness early on. (Just so you know, the folk I tend to work with now do not talk in this way, but I'm painting a picture for you, no?)

Once we have something in a vague musical shape – as in, a possible verse or chorus or both – it's time to put down some ideas. I'll be singing little noodly ideas all the while so that when it's time for me to suggest my ideas, I will have a few things ready to contribute. I saw an old interview where I compared songwriting to Michelangelo's thoughts on sculpture – that with the block of marble he had to find the sculpture within and that similarly with writing a melody it's like finding the melody that sits just right within the instrumental. Big kudos to whatever journalist that was for not running with the headline, 'Pop star compares her songwriting to Michelangelo'. Honestly, I was spared looking a total twat with that one.

When you write with familiar people, like songwriters you get on with or, even better, friends who happen to be musicians, then the whole process is fun and you can laugh about the bits when you can't think of the right lyric. I write all the time now with Ed Harcourt, and we often get into fits of laughter coming up with stupid lyrics which rhyme but aren't helpful . . . the other day we had to rhyme something with 'you', and all we could come up with was 'hardly had the chance to sit alone with you . . . maybe it's because I have so much fibrous tissue.' See? Songwriting can be fun!

Also, when you are actually in the zone and loving the conceit of the lyric or the way the song is sounding, it's exhilarating and exciting. You stop thinking about the time or making another cup of tea or changing the subject . . . you're just in it and you know something special is being written. Whether or not that comes to pass is not the point, it's worth it all to touch the sides of that feeling and sometimes, you're right. Its great and you love it. I'm sure Michelangelo felt just the same way about the sculpture and that he was distracted from making another espresso or whatever got him through the day.

When I was in theaudience (how my spellcheck loves it when I write my band's name), I didn't write at all. Billy wrote the songs. He was good at it and he enjoyed making teenage me say things I wouldn't normally say like, 'I can't believe you keep in touch with computer brood, even if we're so unctuous, what have you got to lose?'

I wasn't very interested in songwriting then. I was happy to interpret Billy's words and it became so key to the sound of the band that the songs were written by him and sung by me. When the band got a record deal and a publishing deal soon after, it was Billy's publishing they wanted but they also wanted me to sign. Looking back, I do not remember having any idea what that deal meant. I didn't know it was quite unusual to sign a publishing deal when you don't write but obviously from the publisher's point of view it was a guarantee of sorts that for as long as Billy and I were in a band together, I would be the singer.

As it turned out, the deal became crucial in giving me any sort of future as a singer. When theaudience disbanded, I was in the wilderness. I was fairly sure my biggest successes in music were behind me. It was in late spring 2000 that I was thrown a lifeline from someone at my publishing company. As I mentioned earlier, I was a bit offended to have been sent a dance track but I ended up writing some of the top line and so it came to pass that the first song that ever had my name on the songwriting credits was 'Groovejet'.

When it came to my first album, I think I felt the need to tell people I was a writer so that they wouldn't think I wasn't making any decisions for myself. New artists can come up against cynicism and it mattered to me that people took me seriously. Perhaps I was also a bit defensive as pop was such a dirty word in 2001. Pop meant manufactured bands and songs written by formula and I wanted to try and distance myself from all that. I was twenty-two and kept talking about how I was making 'sophisticated pop that didn't talk down to people'. My first single, 'Take Me Home', was a cover of a (fabulous) Cher song. I had changed the lyrics and to make sure people knew I'd co-written the new lyrics (and I'm so sorry about this), I lied and made up a story that Cher didn't like my new lyrics because they were too sexy.

I am still a bit shocked that I was believed at all! I mean, Cher, who is amazing and who did a video in a bodysuit while straddling a cannon, thinking my lyrics were risqué? Ha-hah.

I promise I haven't lied too much over the years but come on, that's a good one. When I told Richard he was very confused.

'Why did you lie that Cher didn't like it?'

'Because I thought it was funny?'

When I made my first album, I was still learning what worked for me as a songwriter. The collaborations were mainly set up by the label based on who they thought I might work well with, or who was having a lot of success in my genre of music at the time. I'd also add in my own wish list of folk whose music I liked, just to see if they might want to work with me. I always think it's worth asking people – even if they are unlikely to say yes – just because the worst they can say is no and then you're only where you started, anyway.

Ordinarily, I don't write lyrics first. It's not my style and while I might jot down some ideas, I find it easier to let the melody dictate what it needs. I loved making that first album as I cast my net far and wide with the collaborators and it was so much fun. Working with Moby in New York was an adventure, writing with Alex James from Blur was a pleasure – I'd grown up such a big fan of Blur.

As I wrote, I gained confidence in my ideas but here's the real gold – I'm never the most talented person in the room. That sounds like a humble brag, but it's true and also reassuring. I can pull my weight pretty well, but most of the time even now I'm still learning and being around other folk who are so brilliant makes you want to do better. It's a good feeling – even now I still get that little fizz of excitement that maybe I'm about to write a song that will change my life. Some of my songs have been part of my life so long they are now old enough to vote, or drive. Who knows what new songs I'm going to add to that collection?

That being said, there's just no rescuing a bad song and believe me it's excruciating when you're writing and you go past the 'Oh wow this is the best song ever!' to the other side of the wheel and the 'Oh, no . . . it's not is it? It's terrible.'

The most intense songwriting period was definitely for my third album. After the lukewarm reception of my second, the pressure was on from the label, but much closer to home was the fact I'd now had my first baby and so this album was the new mother version of me. I took as long as I needed. I knew time away was the same difference whether it was six months or two years. My dad had said to me what I think is true, that if I could get the third album right then I'd have a career . . . otherwise I could just go back to doing something else. So I worked super hard to get the best songs I could for that record.

Well, I did once I was ready but I did have one hilarious songwriting experience when Sonny was only three months old. A rather pushy American writer was in town. I explained I couldn't write as I had a small baby and wasn't doing any work. Somehow he persuaded me to have him over to write for a couple of hours. He turned up in a suit with a feather in his hat and a little keyboard under his arm. I don't know why but we sat in the garden to write. He had woken early due to jet lag and had watched the riverboats on the Thames in the morning. This, he decided, was perfect fodder for our song and so I found myself with my baby in my arms singing a (crap) song about riverboats in the garden of a house I'd only moved into four weeks before. All I could think was, 'I hope my neighbours don't think what I'm singing is any good.'

Six weeks after Richard and I got married I took our toddler Sonny and nanny Claire with me for a month-long trip in America. I was writing for ten days in New York then two and a half weeks in LA. I'm not gonna lie, it was very full on. I had no days off and New York was particularly intense. They have a different work ethic there compared to LA. In New York I was expected to work until late and I wanted to be able to clock off at 6 p.m. to put Sonny to bed. Still, I had fun. I've always enjoyed collaborating with left-field people whose work I love. I've written with some of the best pop writers; people like Glenn Tilbrook from Squeeze, Andy Partridge from XTC, Par from the Wannadies and then in New York, Fred Schneider from the B-52s. All were lovely. Fred was full of energy and eccentricity and we ended up partying in fabulous clubs after the writing sessions. The song we did is called 'Supersonic' and it's pretty much as camp as they come, a song about love in space. Perfect.

When we got to LA things were much more relaxed. The Californian way is a bit more my way of doing things. We'd work for a bit, then break for a healthy lunch somewhere under the sun, then back to finish the song and be done for 6 p.m. It was ideal as it meant I could then play in the pool with Sonny. Nanny Claire was brilliantly helpful not just in looking after Sonny and being my date for a couple of nights when we got the chance to head out, but she recognised the names of some of the writers who had been performers too. One of them was a singer called Matthew

Wilder. She saw his name on the schedule and said, 'Oh, he wrote a song called "Break My Stride".' I couldn't think of it at the time but the next day I met with him. He was friendly and nice but his tale about how his touring life had meant his marriage ended in divorce was an unusual one to tell a newly married pop star away from her new husband. Sitting at his keyboard, he started playing a few chords before breaking off, pointing at me and asking, 'Name that tune!'

' "Break My Stride"?' I said.

Broadly smiling, he confirmed it was indeed his 1983 smash, 'Break My Stride'. Thank you, nanny Claire. It is a good song, to be fair.

*

In the end I had a huge pool of songs to choose from for the record. I'm really happy with the way the record turned out. It's a largely joyful, upbeat record and I think it represented well my relationship with pop at that time. The first single was a song called 'Catch You'. We made a video based on one of my favourite movies, *Don't Look Now*. Essentially, my favourite films are either classic horrors or wholesome musicals. *Don't Look Now* is up there with *Rosemary's Baby* and *Jaws*. I think *Jaws* might just be my favourite film of all time. I watched it too young and was scared to swim in swimming pools thereafter. I could even imagine the shark swimming round the corner of my bedroom door. On the other side of the cinematic favourites coin, step forward *Mary Poppins*, *The Sound of Music* and *Grease*. I watched *Grease* so much as a child that I would turn the sound off and recite the dialogue. I thought the girls in it were soo cool. Confusingly old teenagers, but cool. There's a part where bad boy T-Bird Kenickie is in a car with head Pink Lady, Rizzo. He goes to get a condom but it's split. They don't make this explicit – it's a PG certificate. I didn't know what was happening when the snogging pair stopped and Kenickie looked with disappointment into his wallet saying, 'Oh, it broke. I've had it since freshman year.'

I asked my mum, 'What broke?'

'A medal he won for sports,' answered my mother.

To clarify – I do like a lot of films made after 1978, but they aren't in my top six.

With the music video inspired by *Don't Look Now*, I ran around Venice looking wild-eyed, menacing and pointing a lot. I had worked hard to make this and the record as good as I could and had returned after a three-year gap with more confidence than I'd had when I left the music scene. When the video for the single was shown at the label, word reached me that the boss man had, on seeing it, told everyone around the boardroom table that I 'looked like I really wanted it'. When I was told this, I replied, 'Oh yes, it's true, I feel really focused . . .' The girl who told me interrupted me: 'Oh, no, not like that! He said you looked like you really "wanted it".' I felt deflated. All that work and they said something so crass. It gave me a shiver.

That first single was written by Cathy Dennis, and before we'd met, our names had already become entwined in a story. It's not a true story, but that didn't get in the way of that story being told anyway. Apparently I was offered 'Can't Get You Out of My Head' before Kylie, but I turned it down. I didn't actually hear it until it was on the radio, but no matter, it went to the right singer. That song was written by Rob Davis (who co-wrote 'Groovejet' and 'Get Over You') and Cathy Dennis who I was already a fan of when she was a pop star in her own right. I didn't meet Cathy in person until my third record and we didn't write together until my fourth.

When I came to write with Cathy I was finishing off some lyrics I'd written for a melody I'd put on top of a Calvin Harris track. Cathy was writing with Calvin and as we'd already done 'Catch You' together and got on well, Cathy generously offered to help me write the verses. She was working on something else the next day but said if I got to her house for about 10 a.m. then she'd have an hour to spare. When I arrived, I was already a bit nervous. Cathy has written so many amazing songs and I love how she works so I felt a little intimidated. On her wall was a huge clock and as I sat down to write, the first line was something simple which ended in the word 'night' . . . I needed a second line to rhyme and comedically all I can remember is the big clock tick-tick-ticking as the little numbskulls in my head scrabbled around looking for a word to rhyme with night. People, sometimes the more you force things, the harder they become.

I often get asked if Richard and I write together. We now do write the odd thing, but for a long time we didn't, as at the beginning when we tried I found it really hard. I wasn't very easy to collaborate with, from Richard's point of view. I could be tricky – getting frustrated if Richard couldn't read my mind and do whatever it was with the music I thought needed to happen. Now I've learned to relax a lot more. I'm not sure what my previous brittle approach was to do with . . . but whatever it was, I've happily grown out of it now and like doing little musical projects together.

*

I did find some very comfortable and fun writing partnerships during my pop days (I'm not saying I'm out of them, but I haven't written that way for a while). Hannah Robinson and I wrote a lot and I'm super fond of her. It's always the best when it's not like working. I do admire songwriting teams like Xenomania, who write pop music in a more methodical way. They wrote songs for Girls Aloud among others and would write seven or eight verse ideas, and the same for bridges (the bit between the verse and the chorus) and choruses. They then put lyrics to these ideas and whittle it down until you get the cream of all the work. It makes for good pop records but despite the method in the madness, for me, the madness is too exhausting. I know different techniques of songwriting get the results – but my favourite way is to not be too serious about how you do it even if you're very serious about doing it well.

That brings me to my current-day collaborator, Ed. For years I dreamt of having one main collaborator so I could flesh out ideas and scope a project. The problem with the more classic pop writing is you tend to write with lots of different writers and they are all looking to get their track on the record, ideally as a single. With Ed, I've been able to write the kind of albums I want to make, albums that tell stories. We'll know what we need to paint the scene. We will intentionally write the sort of song that we picture opening the album or provide a good contrast to the song that's gone before. It's more rewarding and more sure-footed. With *Wanderlust* we introduced ourselves to characters then went back to them to see where they had found themselves for the next album, *Familia*. The runaway bride character from 'Cry to the Beat of the Band' on *Wanderlust* was now waiting for her new lover on *Familia* in 'Don't Shy Away'. The mad witch in 'Love is a Camera' was now living with ghosts and being driven mad in 'Hush Little Voices'. It's so richly inspiring to write that way.

When we have an initial conceit, I can almost see it in my head like a silent film. I just need to give each scene a soundtrack. Because we work together, we don't have to write in the usual 'pop' way of trying to write singles, so you end up with an album of songs like girls in their prom dresses, lined up against the wall where the prettiest ones get asked to dance in the charts. Now I make albums where we keep an eye on the colour palette and write according to what colour we need to use next so that when we step back, the album is balanced. It's relaxed and fun. Maybe one day I'll revisit the pop school in that way but if I don't go whole hog again then my fourth album, *Make a Scene*, was a good place to leave it. But I'm a kid in a sweet shop when it comes to music so knowing me, after Ed and I have finished the album we are doing at the moment (inspired by Japan and more prog/synth than its predecessors), I'll probably want to run in the other direction. If the dance floor calls my name, I know how to find my way back.

I once went to an awards event where the artist Badly Drawn Boy was giving an award to someone and he told this funny story about how once he had written a song, and it was amazing. After writing it he felt on cloud nine and full of confidence. He went for a walk and was smiling at everyone. He bought stuff from the fruit and veg stall outside his house and felt so up that he chatted to the guys on the stall. He'd seen them before, but thanks to the new hit he'd written he felt like he was buzzing and it made him confident enough to chat. Then he went home and listened to his masterpiece and . . . it was crap. It wasn't amazing, he hated it. The point of the story is – isn't it funny how making something new that you think might be great can change your whole world and make everything, if only for a while, so happy and bright? That's the thing I'm always chasing when I write. Who knows what song is out there waiting for me?

In the studio recording Familia with Ed Harcourt and Richard,
with 13-week-old Jesse along for the ride.

16

MUSIC: Live Stuff, Good and Bad
– 'Cry to the Beat of the Band'

This day was a good day, on the road for the Song Diaries
tour with baby number 5.

I have now reached the glorious point in performing where I truly don't care what people think. I do want to do a good job of entertaining, but the fear that people might think I'm crap has left me. It's flipping wonderful. I think that's why spending my time singing karaoke from my kitchen in an old ice-skating leotard has brought me so much joy. I've screwed up and been slagged off so many times, and I've also had the most wonderful live gigs and even danced a Charleston complete with backflip on live

TV. My inhibitions have pretty much vanished and now I just don't fear much on stage anymore.

The truth is, the times when I've been singing on stage have been some of the most magical moments of my whole career but there have been some truly traumatic times too.

I always think of gig audiences like a date. You can get a good idea after the first song or two if it's a good date (happy, smiley, responsive crowd, they do what you hope – quiet in the quiet bits, loud in the loud bits) or a tricky one (distracted, rude, noisy in the quiet bits and quiet in the bits where you want them to sing along or cheer). My job is to turn every gig date into a 'I want to see this girl again sometime' date.

At the beginning, I felt fairly stable when I was actually singing, but incredibly awkward between songs. In an indie band, when the music plays, not much is expected of the singer. In fact, any movement at all is an unexpected delight. You can stand very still and look moody and that will do the job nicely, thank you. Now, I could do moody while singing Billy's lyrics, which were wordy and dense. I didn't always have a clue what I was singing about, but it sounded gruff and intellectual and studenty and I could inhabit that space so long as I didn't have too much expression on my face.

Between songs I would make stupid knock-knock jokes or tell a little anecdote if I felt bold enough. My love of onstage jokes is probably (definitely) something I have inherited from my dad. I always have a little joke up my sleeve and it doesn't have to be very funny. How kind I am to myself. I remember early on my dad telling me I should talk more. 'The audience want it from you, they are ready to listen.' Good advice, but I wasn't ready to talk. I was still very nervous and afraid of ridicule. I do remember playing one of our tiny early gigs at the back of a pub in Camden and asking the crowd if my dad was there yet as he was late. When he arrived ten minutes later they cheered him hello.

As theaudience fizzled out we did our last live gig at the Electric Ballroom in Camden again. It was a headline show and I think it went well but unbeknownst to me it was my last gig for three years until I was a signed solo artist with Polydor.

In the autumn of 2001, a month or two after *Read My Lips* had been released, I did a one-off show in North London. It was a showcase gig with lots of bookers from TV and radio invited to see if the label could entice them to book me for stuff when I did promotion. The musicians that were booked for that gig were seasoned session players, all a lot older than me. They were more experienced and quite world-weary when they played for newly signed artists. Universal had spent a fair bit of money on the preproduction of the gig, even building a giant image of my face to form the stage, which led me to quip that it was 'the first gig I've done standing on my head'. I've loved jokes and puns since time began and anyone who has seen me live knows I have to have a joke or two up my sleeve. I've got a lot of Papa Bextor DNA in that way.

The gig was nerve-wracking but I got through it. I had panicked at the last minute about what to wear and had decided on a black fitted top with a long black wrap skirt, which I then safety-pinned at each corner so it was short at the front and long at the back, along with little net fingerless gloves and frilly knickers in case they got seen (they did a bit). I don't know why the label spent all that money on the stage and not on a stylist for me, but that's how it happened that night at the Scala, in King's Cross.

However, what I didn't realise was that a lot of journalists had been invited too and the show was reviewed, fairly harshly. Well actually they kind of massacred me. In the name of being thorough I googled some of the reviews and wow, they actually made me howl with a sort of horrified laughter at the brutality. Laughably, one broadsheet starts with 'She must have an army of stylists' before saying I looked 'nervous, amateurish . . . truly embarrassing'. One from a credible music paper starts with 'SEB is a pop star. Discuss. She sings pop songs which aren't very popular, was involved in someone else's number one . . . and is the daughter of a woman who used to appear on children's TV 20 years ago . . . her songs are shit . . . she doesn't possess the personality to carry her first live gig . . .' Yada, yada, yada. The line which the journalist must have been so proud of is near the end: 'The crowd only clap because it stops them from yawning.'

To be honest this view didn't necessarily go away. After watching me sing at Cornbury Festival in 2014, Sonny, then ten, told me afterwards, 'There should have been a climbing frame.'

'For me?' I asked.

'No, for the crowd when they got bored.'

The thing is, I was petrified the night of my first solo show. So, so nervous. I didn't know I was going to be reviewed but I did feel vulnerable singing to a sold-out 1,000-strong crowd of tricky Londoners when my last gig had been three years before as part of my band. I felt freaked out and I didn't know the guys in my session band well enough to be able to interact with them at all. It was all a bit terrifying and I don't doubt I was crap.

I think in theaudience I was probably a bit of a contradiction on stage. Performing as a band does allow you a little more time to grow. You're up there with people you know (hopefully) and you can reassure yourself you share the limelight with others. Even if the frontperson gets the lion's share of the attention you know there will be fans of the lead guitarist or the bassist (obviously I'm a fan of the bassist) watching. The pressure for the singer is diluted. Although obviously, I still used to get so nervous I couldn't really speak. I used to tell knock-knock jokes when there were gaps in the proceedings and be so worried about being criticised for my dancing that I hardly moved. In a weird way this gave me a bit of a different vibe against the backdrop of dance music when I performed 'Groovejet', but for theaudience I was just super still. Funny to think of that now, as these days I can't stand still.

The first time I watched a recording of myself on stage I cried and those tears made a few more appearances over the years, but by and large

I was happier once I had my own band with me once I was working as a solo artist. It also meant I had people to share the experience with. Of course there was also the serendipity of being introduced to the man I would later marry.

Generally speaking, the gigs where it's my show with my name on the ticket have gone OK. I've had some blokes crash the stage and the odd technical hitch, but overall the shows have been fairly textbook affairs in the sense that I haven't felt as if I've been forced to face my fears up there.

But elsewhere, blimey. Aside from the fire alarm going off in my first ever gig with my band, I've had some real clangers live. Singing 'Groovejet' in the clubs of this land saw me perform on some very wobbly stages. One time as I leant back to sing, the heel of my shoe went through the stage and I nearly fell off. I am touching wood as I say this but I have googled singers falling off stage and laughed at some of the videos, so I know karma is coming for me.

The first real clanger was with 'Groovejet' at a radio roadshow in Germany. As was the norm throughout promotion of that song and my first couple of singles, it was expensive for the label to fly out a band (and when I did my first few singles I didn't have my own band) so in the UK I had what was known as my 'TV band', which was basically a miming band for any performances I did. Coming from the indie world, I always found this pretty embarrassing. I knew what it felt like to be surrounded by playing musicians and it felt babyish to have people pretending to play around you. But that was how it was. Landing in Germany, I was introduced to my TV band there. Lovely guys who spoke little to not much English. I was just going to do the one song. It was an overcast day in Hamburg but I was quite excited to be in front of a pretty huge crowd. We walked out to applause. I thought, 'Yeah . . . here we go!'

'Hello, Hamburg!' I said.

Then waited for the track to start . . . and waited . . . and then it began and the band started miming and we were all grooving and then . . . it stopped again. We were temporarily miming and dancing to nothing. On stage when things go wrong, seconds feel like hours. I looked at the crowd, who all spoke a language I could have learnt but at my school it was either German or Latin and I'd chosen Latin. Stupid choice.

After a minute or two it became apparent that nothing was going to happen. No music was coming to save us so I thought, 'What would a great performer do?' And tried to get the crowd to clap along while I sang acapella. When you try a ballsy move like that in the movies, it results in a magic moment where the crowd appreciate the purity of the human voice and show that appreciation by smiling, clapping and singing along. The reality was, that on that grey day back in 2000, as I sang a song hardly anyone seemed to know, they all just looked bored/confused/ started chatting to their mates, so after a verse and a chorus I kind of petered out and left the stage. It wasn't the masterstroke I'd imagined.

Still, it was less embarrassing than the time I was in Amsterdam to promote 'Take Me Home'. I was on a TV show where I had to perform on an ice rink as dancing skaters twirled round me. Leo Sayer was on the same show and I recall at one point in the day his trainers had been left in my dressing room by mistake.

We had had a full rehearsal for the show, although as I would be miming to the song it was just a camera rehearsal really. We couldn't do it live as the rink was very echoey so I would have struggled to sing in time. The plan for the performance was this: I was to head to the back-stage of the rink just before my track played. I would climb onto a little round stage, complete with a microphone on a stand and remote-controlled wheels. This little stage would wheel me out to the middle of the rink ready to be danced around. The rehearsal went well, and I headed back to my room to get ready. I was due on stage at 7.15, and I was ready by 7 but no one had come to get me. Usually when you perform or do anything on TV they like you ready ages before you're needed, but occasionally they have a more relaxed team running the show so it wasn't hugely concerning they hadn't got me . . . or maybe they were running late? At a minute or so before quarter past, there was a knock on my door. Behind it was a slightly sweaty and panicked-looking runner who had come to fetch me to take me to stage. 'We have to run,' he said.

The stage was a way away and I had heels but we went as quickly as we could to the backstage. As we neared the ice rink my song started to play. Miraculously I didn't fall over as I trotted across the little bit of ice to get to the remote-controlled stage. I hopped on and it started to move just as I looked around me to see . . . nothing.

No stand, no microphone.

The curtains opened and I was in front of an audience of happy ice-skating fans and soon I was surrounded by a flurry of dancing ice skaters.

Now, this was in the era of Cher singing 'Believe' on *Top of the Pops* with no microphone. I thought it was genius, actually. It always looks a bit weird when someone is singing a song when the vocal is clearly filtered and fiddled with, so in a song like 'Believe', where the vocal had been auto-tuned to make it a feature of the song itself, I loved the fact that Cher didn't even try to pretend it was a live vocal. I thought that was very cool. With that in mind, in the middle of the Dutch rink, I thought, 'I've got to style this out,' and began miming away as if that was always the plan. I probably had the wild look in my eye of someone who is not feeling super relaxed, but I gave it my all. Except that, halfway through the track some poor sod scuttled out from backstage, scurried across the ice dodging the dancers, ducking down low, as if that made him invisible, and offered me a microphone. I waved it away and kept going but felt like even more of a moron.

After the show I went back to the hotel, where I was so embarrassed I didn't leave, even though I was supposed to meet with the label. Nowadays I'd shrug it off, but back then I felt humiliated.

But, the fire alarm, the lack of music and the lack of microphone were all small fry compared to the biggest humiliation of all, in front of 10 million people on the BBC New Year's Eve show where we'd say farewell to 2006 and hello to 2007.

This show was a big deal. Big in terms of being booked on the live NYE broadcast, big in terms of potential audience, but in personal terms a big deal because it was my first TV performance after having my first baby. I was excited to be back. I'd taken ages to write my third album and I was ready to launch the new music. It was exhilarating. Again, I was performing with a band but I was singing live. I was due to sing just after the Big Ben chimes and the fireworks. What a way to start the year! This was going to be great.

I had a great crowd with me including my brother Jackson on drums and my friend Laura on bass and another good friend, Mara, on keys. Happily, too, Richard's band The Feeling had been booked for the same show and they were on just before midnight. The whole thing was being broadcast live from a gorgeous location – Somerset House in London – where there was an ice rink and fairy lights and Christmas trees and festive scenes all round.

As the show time approached I felt surprisingly relaxed. I was singing the first single from the new album, 'Catch You' and I was just feeling really happy. I was with lovely people doing a great TV slot with new music. I felt good in my skin, had a great metallic gold dress to wear and my husband there to cheer me on. After work was done we had a plan to meet our mates at a brilliant gay club to dance away the rest of New Year's Eve.

Life was good.

It was time to head to the stage. There was a live audience of around 300 – including Richard and Dan (the singer of The Feeling) and my best friend Maria. They were all smiling up at me as the band and I took to the stage. Natasha Kaplinsky was presenting and she did the live introduction. Then the song started up and 'Catch You' blared out of the sound system.

I started singing and . . . you've probably guessed it . . . nothing could be heard. When you sing live there are two options for how the band hear themselves, either wedge monitors (old-school huge wedge-shaped speakers you have near your feet that play back your voice and whatever mix you want of the other instruments) or, more commonly now, in-ear monitors, which are moulded to fit in your ear and again, you can have whatever mix of instruments you want playing in your ear and you can control the overall volume on your pack, which you clip on or wear in a pouch on your arm. Nowadays I only use the in-ears, but back then I used a mixture and on this particular performance I was using wedges. This had been fine in soundcheck. I could hear myself perfectly. But for some reason, now we were live, I couldn't hear myself at all. I could tell from the confused expression on Richard's face in the crowd that he couldn't hear me either.

It must be the microphone. That was what I thought. If I can't hear me and the crowd can't hear me, there must be something wrong with the mic and any moment now someone is going to come running over with a spare mike and I'll sing into that and everyone will clap their hands in joy that the big broadcast is back on technical track.

Only . . . no one came. I got to the end of the verse . . . still no one . . . and as I sang the chorus the realisation hit me – they are not coming because whatever I am singing into the microphone is being broadcast.

There is no issue with the sound as far as TV is concerned.

Now, I don't know if you've ever tried singing along to a song you love with headphones on, but if you recorded what you were singing and had a listen, chances are it wouldn't sound exactly the same melody as the song. It's pretty hard to sing anything in tune when you can't hear a note you're singing. But oh, lucky me, this was exactly what 10 million people at home were listening to.

Richard, meanwhile, was storming through the crowd to the sound desk.

'She can't hear herself,' he told the monitor guy. He shrugged, 'Nothing I can do, mate.'

Richard – who had finished his performance and so was enjoying a pint of Guinness – then threw that over the sound guy in frustration.

I was up on stage singing like a rabbit in headlights. If it had happened a few months down the line, after I'd got back into my flow, I probably would have said something into the microphone to make it apparent that I couldn't hear, but I was newly back to work and just went on a weird kind of autopilot.

The song finished and I was met off stage by my TV plugger Sarah who uttered, 'Its's a fucking shit show,' as she hurried me back the dressing room.

When things go wrong like that, it's the moments after which are the hardest. When the performance is in its spiral of 'going wrong-ness', you don't have time to think. You're full of adrenaline and focused and you're just getting through it. Afterwards, though, when you have time to reflect and see what went wrong, that's when you can feel angry or regretful or bitter. For me, I was just sad. I was so excited and it should have been such a triumph and it was so, so horrible.

I found out that I'd been given the wrong microphone. When I was singing, I was using the microphone the previous singer, Jamelia, had used. The microphone I was supposed to use, the one linked to my wedges, had been swapped over by accident.

No one from the production came to speak to me but the presenter Natasha Kaplinsky was sent to my room to apologise. A bit weird really as it was nothing to do with her.

I joked, 'At least I'm wearing a nice frock.'

'Actually,' she said smoothly, 'that's really important. Viewers notice 70% what you look like and only 30% what you say.'

'But I'm a singer,' I said pathetically.

Anyway, it was time to wash the performance out of my hair. Dan and Richard cornered me after and gave me a little pep talk. Yes it went wrong but somewhere not too far away a club dance floor was calling my name, as was a bottle of tequila behind the bar. Off we all went – band in tow – into the night to party the hours away and it worked well as a tonic.

Obviously lots of people saw it on TV and I got some horrible comments about my singing, but, hey, life moves on.

Luckily for me, just around the corner from that terrible performance experience was one of my most treasured and significant. Before the release of my first single from the third album, I had a show booked at GAY. I hadn't done a live gig for years at that point. I'd been squirrelling away making *Trip the Light Fantastic* and spent as long as I needed finishing it. Now it was time to get back out there. It wasn't my first performance at GAY and certainly my relationship with my LGBTQ fans was going from strength to strength, but to use my dating metaphor, it was this particular show on this particular night when I think we started going steady. I'm allowed to see other crowds, but this one has my heart.

On the night, I was petrified but excited. It had been so long since I'd sung for a crowd and this London club was a well-seasoned venue for big pop performances. I didn't just want to be 'OK'. I wanted it to go well. I had a cute little outfit of a short black vintage dress customised with a red net underskirt. I planned on taking it off to reveal a red leotard and sparkly pants. This wasn't my usual style but I think my inner quirky sparkly leotard lover was starting to take hold (see pretty much every weird and wonderful thing I wore for the Kitchen Disco. I even have a drawer of clothes in my wardrobe – aka Mickey's bedroom – marked 'ice skating'. I don't skate, but I love the vintage costumes). As I walked out on stage that night, I was met with a wave of love in the form of cheers and whistles and smiley happy faces. Every nerve went in that instant and I performed in a way I never had before. I interacted with the crowd and kneeled down to meet them. I shimmied and shook my sequinned pants and felt alive . . . I felt like ME. Afterwards I felt a little out of my body. I went to see Richard, and Dan was with him. They were super complimentary and supportive. I knew something had changed in me. I think my gay fans have helped me more than they will ever know when it comes to truly accepting – no, celebrating – myself. My kids probably hope that some of my true self might have stayed a little more under wraps but hey, in every Kitchen Disco I dress as if I'm headed out to a night at Sink the Pink and it works for me. Sink the Pink started as a little nightclub where anything goes and it's now huge . . . clubs nights, festivals, drag-queen tours . . . but at its heart is the same ethos for why I do what I do: finding your tribe and feeling good about yourself. The kids that go to that club night spend ages getting their look right. They all look fabulous and strong, no matter what insecurity is challenged to bring that look to a reality. How wonderful is that? Everyone can benefit from a little of that, even a forty-two-year-old woman like me.

*

I have definitely learnt a lot through the times when things have gone wrong. I know that it's easy to become attached to safety blankets when you perform. Tiny rituals you follow before stage which, so long as they go OK, mean it's going to be a good show. But, I've actively tried to push that away. I don't want to have a wobble if I forget to put my stage clothes on in a certain order or don't have thirty minutes uninterrupted before a gig. I'm almost guaranteed to have those plans be rumbled, and then I'll be a singer in a state of anxiety, which is a horrible feeling. The closest I've come to that was when I did need to have space and quiet before shows and my manger came in before one big gig saying I had to go through the budgets. I found it really stressful and it was like all the energy I'd stored up for performing was being let out of the canister. I was worried I'd arrive on stage a deflated balloon of a singer. Now, having toured with so many people and got ready in all manner of back stages, sometimes with my kids round my feet and only thirty minutes before I go and sing, I've just had to relax or I'd pop. I'm chilled with it all now, but I guess you have to go through the stressful bits to get there.

There are two types of show which have really helped me hone my craft on stage: the support tours and the corporate gigs. Of the support tours, the most challenging was the longest – thirty-four dates with Take That. There's nothing that sharpens the senses quite like walking out on stage to an arena filled with 10,000 (mainly) women who are waiting for four men to arrive.

I toured with them in 2008 and it was so much fun. The thing about supporting artists and bands is that you can tell within about an hour of joining the production what kind of tour it is. You can gauge the mood. When I supported George Michael for eight shows it was a fairly serious and sad mood. He performed beautifully every night and his voice was incredible, but one of the crew had died of a short illness not long before I rocked up with the band, and it was clear that everyone was shaken. Plus I think George was going through something, too. I don't know what but I felt as if everyone was being extra sensitive and careful with him. His dressing room had a built-on tunnel so you couldn't accidentally see in, even if the door was open, and he was very private. He did ask to meet one night but unfortunately it was the only night I could get home in time to see Sonny, who was still only a toddler. So, as it worked out, I never met him.

The show itself saw me and my band only allowed to perform on one little side stage of the production. That's not unusual – headline acts can limit the support's sound if they want to and definitely have full control over whether or not they use the main stage. Behind our stage area was an enormous video screen so if I did a little shimmy and turned around, I could see my wiggly body, bum and all, and the band facing out, smiling at the crowd. One night as we played the rain was coming down in sheets.

We got on with it, getting drenched as we went. I could see my lovely smiley bassist Laura grinning away at the crowd but as she swayed, her skirt was being pulled up by the bass. With every move it got higher and higher until the gusset of her tights was on show. Trying to be discreet, I turned around and mouthed to her 'Pull your skirt down', only I'd forgotten about the video wall. As she lipread my message, blushed and pulled down her skirt, I could see it being beamed ten foot high behind our exchange. Luckily, she found it pretty funny.

The tour with Take That was pretty funny, too. If you have to be the woman on stage first in front of those men-hungry fans – and I do mean it, there was one section of the gig where TT would walk through the crowd and they'd quite often emerge with the shirts ripped off their backs – then you've got to accept your role as warm-up is just that. To warm up the crowd, ready for the main act. I don't quite understand artists who become massive divas and if you've done lots of support and private gigs it's pretty hard to keep up the pretence. The role of a performer isn't so different to the old court jester. I am there to keep you happy and entertained and that's the rung of the ladder I'm on. It's healthy to remember that, I think. For every single one of those shows I had a clear objective – to win over the crowd as best I could, to persuade them I was friend not foe, then leave them ready and willing for the headline.

It's also great as a support to watch the main show. I've learnt so much from standing at the side of stage. I can honestly say every gig I've ever seen anywhere has taught me something, even if it's what doesn't work.

But watching certain people has changed the way I perform. I once saw Grace Jones performing at a rainy festival and she was awesome. I only knew a handful of songs but she performed every single song in the set as if it was the hit, and the confidence worked. Never be apologetic. She also hula-hooped through the last song, which was skilfully eccentric and I love a bit of that. With a similar dose of confidence I once made a crazy trip to Australia not long after I'd had my fourth baby, Jesse. He was sixteen weeks old and I had two club shows to do so we set off with a tour manager and Jesse's brand-new passport. We left England on Wednesday, landed in Sydney on Friday, where I sang that night in a club, flew the next day to Melbourne where I sang on the Saturday night, then on Sunday we flew from Melbourne to Sydney, Sydney to Singapore, Singapore to London. I was only in Australia two nights in two different cities. Both nights I was sharing the bill with a drag queen called Alyssa Edwards who had been on RuPaul. I watched her perform and was transfixed – she was brilliant, lip-syncing her way through her song choices with complete conviction that went from the top of her head to the tips of her fingers. It taught me you have to give it your all when you are telling the story of a song. It's mesmerising when folk get it right.

But the band I've seen the most is of course The Feeling and – I know you will say I'm biased – but honestly, they are always brilliant live (and Richard will tell you I am actually honest to a fault with this stuff. I can't really hide how I feel). They have played live together since they were teenagers and you can tell. They play really cohesively together, it's so natural and Dan is a great frontman. He's warm and funny in between songs and dramatic and bold when he's singing. Richard is relaxed on stage and a brilliant musician and I have to say it's always really attractive to see your other half being so great up on stage. I've never really understood the idea of being jealous of the one you love getting attention on stage. Since The Feeling began, I've always been in the crowd thinking, 'Surely all the girls must be fancying my husband?' It's OK, he comes home with me.

Richard has been in my live band for the last seven years now. He was there at the start but after we started dating and The Feeling came into being we stopped for a few years. It's been just right having him back in the band. I love that we can share the experience together and he's been onstage with me at all my favourite shows. We can also turn any work trip into an adventure and I know we're so lucky to be able to do that. We only had a very short honeymoon when we got married, as we didn't want to be away from baby Sonny too long, but that's meant every time we have a trip for work somewhere amazing, we manage to take a bit of it just for us. Last year, just as the pandemic was in its infancy, I had a show booked in Tel Aviv. The gig got cancelled at the last minute but the plane tickets had already been booked, so we went anyway. Three nights away just following our noses to see what we could see. It's the best.

*

The times that have brought me the strangest experiences as a performer, the weirdest and sometimes most wonderful, are definitely the times I've played private shows. I am a singer and I'll sing pretty much any place that wants me. I've done children's parties, weddings, bar mitzvahs . . . you name it. One children's party not too long ago saw the stage invaded by the small people and I basically became the singer/childminder while the parents went to get themselves another drink. The private shows have sometimes been really fun or touching – if someone has happy associations with your songs and books you for their birthday or wedding, that's lovely – and in fact I'm happy to sing anywhere where the crowd are receptive and happy.

But that's not always the case. I don't take it personally (maybe I should but I don't) as I've sat in the audience of many an event where I've watched the music act and sometimes the timing is a bit off and what the crowd really want is to talk or just sit rather than stand and boogie along. Still, I believe in a bit of karma (except for the googling of funny times people have fallen off stage) and if I'm somewhere where someone is performing I'll always try and be the kind of person in the crowd I'd like for my own gigs. I've done enough rubbish corporate gigs to know that sometimes you have to play for the gig you wish you were at in your head and then fake it until it's true, but lockdown gigs have been a whole other tribe. So that's my trick. I try and sing just for the pure love of singing and dance about like a looney just to reassure the crowd – 'Don't worry, I'm fine up here' – and generally they come and dance with me pretty soon after they stop feeling self-conscious. So far I've never done a gig where I didn't get a dance floor going . . . well that was true until I played GAY during lockdown restrictions when the crowd couldn't stand, dance or sing along. That felt very peculiar and when I sang 'Like a Prayer' and danced like a crazy woman, I felt as if I was taunting them with my wild abandon.

Even though I've had so many strange experiences (like the time the client tried to get my band to start the gig on a stage suspended forty foot off the ground with no safety harness; or the time when I sang my ballad 'Young Blood' as a lovely Ukrainian woman pole-danced behind me; or the time when I sang to the rudest birthday girl on earth who kept her back to me the whole time I was singing after her husband booked me as a surprise for her party; and the most Russian thing that's ever happened to me – the time when I sang inside the Kremlin for the Aeroflot ninetieth birthday party wearing the complete Aeroflot uniform, which is gorgeous), my most memorably peculiar was also my first.

Having private bookings in amongst the festivals and tours is pretty standard for most performers, but when I was asked to sing for a Russian client in 2006 for a dinner party of thirty people, I hadn't ever had a request like that before. I know I was nervous about it. How would it work? They'd all be eating as I sang? Yes. I was to do a thirty-minute set with my band while the guests were having pudding. And all this at a private house in the south of France – a beautiful big house with real Salvador Dali paintings in the loos and party planners who had spent a fortune (a real fortune) on garden lights and a firework display.

The whole party was thrown in honour of one of the guests: Bill Gates. The host was a spectacularly rich Russian who had booked me,

Christina Milian, Cirque du Soleil to perform an aerial show and the Gypsy Kings.

Sometimes at private parties you are very much 'front of house' – invited to sit and dine with the other guests and see and be seen. Other times you're hidden away and you make your entrance through the kitchen.

For this one I was invited to join the party and my band was, too. We seemed to be the main people having fun. We ate the food and drank the drink and did our show. When I sang 'Yes Sir, I Can Boogie', everyone danced and Bill Gates did a move which saw him push his hips backwards and forwards as he clapped in front of and then behind his moving pelvis. Quite the mover.

After us, Christina Milian sang and we danced around. The rest of the party was pretty restrained but we went for it. Next up, we hopped in the golf buggies that were parked all over the gardens of the gorgeous villa. At one point my brother crashed his into a tree. Two security men ran over. 'Uh-oh, we're about to get kicked out,' I thought. 'Here you go, sir, take these keys to the other buggy,' they said as they wheeled away the crashed one and led him to a fresh buggy. The night ended with Richard accidentally knocking some champagne onto a beautiful girl who was sitting with the host and the Gypsy Kings performing 'My Way' on acoustic guitar as Bill Gates sang the words.

I ended up being booked a few more times by the same host at various parties, until the time he leant close to me and whispered, 'Next time, no husband.' There was no next time.

Of course, the latest bit of my live education has been our live-streamed Kitchen Discos. What a crazy thing . . . last year when I did *The Masked Singer* I thought that that programme would be challenging in terms of the restrictions I had inside the suit. I was not able to make eye contact, or express myself with my face, or move normally, and had reduced vision and hearing (when I first put on the suit I joked that it was like coming round from a terrible accident). But actually it was nothing compared to the challenge of performing in a lockdown when you're given the biggest restriction of them all – no audience.

When lockdown first started Richard and I felt like most people. A bit freaked out, stressed by the heaviness of the news, discombobulated by the tilt our world was now on. We'd started 2020 with a very full diary of gigs all the way to December and suddenly overnight they were all gone. Not only that, all our kids were suddenly off school and they were a bit unnerved too. Meanwhile, I was looking online and seeing so many talented musicians performing songs for people, accompanying themselves on piano or guitar and sounding lovely. I had such a strong urge to do something fun and creative that we could put out there. Richard felt it too and suggested we do a live-streamed gig on Instagram and see what happened. We chose that platform as it was the easiest without needing complicated streaming rights in order to transmit music live.

The first gig we streamed was pretty ridiculous. I put on a sparkly catsuit and our youngest was only fourteen months old so I kept having to warn Richard when he was about to walk backwards onto our crawling baby. The kids ran riot and Sonny was on hand like a nanny/bouncer, keeping an eye on Mickey while also occasionally breaking up fights occurring between the middle three kids. I did my thing and shimmied about and embraced the absurdity, as did Richard, who joined me on his Millennium Falcon bass (the best Christmas present you can buy a bassist who loves *Star Wars*. It's a genuine *Star Wars* Millennium Falcon toy which has been custom-made into a working bass. I bought it for Richard five years ago and I cannot now top it as a gift) and he wore an animal mask.

Afterwards we wondered a bit what the hell we'd just done. We'd always been pretty private about our home and we'd never put the kids' faces out into the world, but in the midst of the pandemic and the whole world gone wonky, none of that felt important or relevant anymore. The

223

desire to connect with folk, have some fun, alleviate some tension and distract ourselves won out.

Still, I was genuinely expecting a lot of ridicule. I was a forty-year-old woman in full sparkle singing pop songs surrounded by her offspring. I assumed people would make fun of me.

But they didn't. I think the intensity of the news meant daftness was in short supply. Plus, who doesn't love a dance around to let some of the stress go? Also the cartoony strangeness of the sequins and the sprogs was like a caricature of what so many people had been experiencing when trying to work and feel like themselves in their own lockdowns, whether surrounded by kids or not. Music has always been our family's way of flipping the script. We play music to celebrate or dance about and be silly, to shake off tension or to make each other laugh. It doesn't always work (I'm pretty sure all my kids will leave home relieved they won't hear me singing around the house anymore) but when it's good, it's great.

Our playroom already had all the elements ready for the disco anyway. Sequin bunting, giant disco ball, laser lights and a smoke machine. One friend said when she saw me singing during one of our Kitchen Discos that I looked the happiest she'd ever seen me. Lockdown has been down-right awful sometimes and I've shouted/raged/resented more than normal, but the discos themselves have been pure joy and I hope the kids will look back fondly. One time during the Halloween disco I found myself singing 'Wuthering Heights' to Kit who was wearing a brown bear mask and dressed in a black gown. His spooky outfit had come with a scary mask which he'd discarded, so now, with the black robe and the bear mask he looked like some kind of clergyman. As he played ursine Heathcliff to my Cathy, I did wonder how on earth I'd come to be singing that at him, in my home, as I wore a ringmaster leotard, fishnets and heels whilst Richard filmed and broadcast it round the world. Strange times, my friend. But I have felt such enormous affection for all who've been over to our house, virtually. What a lovely community of dancing people. That's the best way to get through strange, sad times . . . with a group of people who shimmy their way through it. I'm glad and proud to be part of the party and it has reminded me yet again the importance of joy for joy's sake and silliness and music as a tonic for the soul.

17

MUSIC: Me at Thirty-Four,
Part 1 – 'Young Blood'

I felt so proud of the success I had with Wanderlust and I share that with Ed and this great band. (Left to right: Ed, Seton, me, Richard, Phil.)

I was talking to Richard the other day about a podcast he likes to listen to on which he'd heard the (very successful male) musician being interviewed say, 'See, the thing is, the main bulk of what people want to talk to you about is the first ten years. That's the bit . . . the first ten years. That's when the main stuff happens. The bit where you are discovered, or you break through, and then have your biggest breaks and successes and that's the bit that defines your career.'

I thought about that a lot. On the one hand, I totally get it. It's true that the first ten years of my career were defining – it's when I did the majority of things that people know me for. But what interests me in other people's careers is what happens after that first flush. What did you do when you had to find a way to make a career last beyond those first ten years? That's the bit that actually is pretty revealing. When you're riding high, momentum is your friend and you have lots of company. The saying is true – success has many parents and failure is an orphan. So how do you push on and keep the love affair going whilst you grow up and need to plot your own map through the Mountains of Diminishing Returns and the Forest of Not Very Successful Ideas?

I wonder if it's a male/female thing a tiny bit? For a woman, chances are, at some point in or just after those ten years, she's going to think about whether or not she plans to be a mum. Or maybe it sneaks up on her, unplanned. Either way, that's a big deal. I know men can have that same conundrum, but they can become a dad in their seventies if they want to without it stopping play, as they can still tour and work without pregnancy, childbirth and all that coming into the equation. There's also the fact that for women, getting older can complicate things. It's one thing to have your first flush as a younger woman but giving yourself space to grow in a way that incorporates your maturity can be tricky.

My last single of my twenties was a clubby dance record called 'Heartbreak (Make Me a Dancer)'. Even now, I love singing it live. It was written with the Freemasons and is so tough and insistent that when it's played with the full band and orchestra, I feel like a disco superhero. When it went to radio, my second baby was only a few months old. The song was B-listed at Radio 1 so it should have been getting some fairly decent plays but it was being played at weird times like 2 a.m., so not really getting much support. My manager Derek asked me, 'Why do you think they are not playing your music anymore?' 'Because I am nearly thirty and a mum?' He nodded.

I didn't feel sore about this. Makes sense that a young radio station might not see me as working for their demographic. The harshest thing really was that I'd worked so hard on the record and worked with some amazing people and it felt sad that all that work was just going to sink down to the bottom of the Pop Ocean (the Pop Ocean is where I reached on my map after the Valley of Britpop and the hazardous Record Company Drop). When the second single of the fourth album didn't connect either, it was time for Universal and me to part ways.

Happily, the album and its singles did really well abroad. This introduced me to gig after gig in Eastern Europe. I was thrilled and relieved. Richard and I had found ourselves spread very thin financially when we bought our home (the one we're still in) when Kit was only four months old, and it was incredibly stressful. We were worried we'd completely messed up, in fact. A blip in moving accountants (and it's very British I called it a 'blip' as it was actually terrifying) meant that money I thought I'd paid to people, I hadn't. I owed tens of thousands and had to carefully work out how to pay that and still have the mortgage. In short, we didn't have it. We moved in July and I remember calmly saying to Richard that we would muddle through to September and if things weren't better then we'd have to sell the house. The last time I'd been so down on my sums, I had not been a parent. Now, I had two small children so I just knew I had to take any and every job that came my way.

The day Derek told me Universal wasn't continuing with my contract I remember so well. I'd just been out somewhere singing 'Bittersweet' and I was now at home, sitting on my kitchen countertop in sequins I'd borrowed from somewhere. After Derek left, Richard and I got fish and chips and tried to plan the next bit of our lives. It was a bit scary to go without the safety net of a huge company like Universal and on that day, I only had one gig in my diary. I am a simple soul and I can hang a lot of good morale on not too much to look forward to. I remember thinking that I would always just need something on the horizon. One bit of work.

And slowly, slowly the work did come. With 'Heartbreak', 'Bittersweet', 'Not Giving Up' and 'Can't Fight this Feeling' all doing well in the Russian, Ukrainian and Polish charts, I started to get invitations to come and sing there. I said yes to every single one. The gigs started coming quicker and quicker until I was away at least twice a month and sometimes doing two or three shows per trip. There was a stint where, in the lead-up to Christmas, I was away every weekend for eight weekends on the trot. And then I kind of . . . hit a wall. I came home from the airport and the house was silent. Kids and Richard not home. It was a Sunday afternoon and I'd been away two or three nights. I was tired as had left the hotel at around 2 a.m. to get a 5 a.m. flight. From our strangely empty house I phoned Richard who was out with some friends and the kids on a walk, miles away from home.

After I hung up I slumped on the floor and cried. I was so exhausted and sad to be missing out on so much family time. I knew I was lucky to have been working so much, but I felt a bit empty. The gigs I was doing were mainly private parties and whilst they were easy, they were also kind of soul-destroying. Something had to give.

One of the first things I did was decide that now was a great time for another baby. Clearly, this is something of a pattern for me. In the summer of 2011, I decided one more was a wonderful idea and so that is why Ray's middle name is 'Holiday'. During my pregnancy I started to think about making another record. I think pregnancy is quite a natural time for me to think about being creative as there is no chance I'll be too rushed about getting the next album out into the world. I have a bit of time to think. I think back to my pregnancy with Ray and it was the happiest pregnancy (aside from my constant moodiness for the first few months) as I was so content to see my tummy get bigger and bigger.

Make a Scene had been a very dance-y album. I loved making it and I'd done proper clubby songs and even trance with Dutch DJ Armin Van Buuren. I'm not someone who's ever really listened to trance but I was seduced by the track I wrote with the gorgeous and bonkers identical twin sister DJs, Nervo. We had a lot of fun doing that. Almost as a reaction to my headlong run into the club world, I decided I wanted to write something totally different now. In fact, the first song I wrote for *Wanderlust* wasn't even planned as a song for a new album. I was just doing it for fun and to try something different.

Ed Harcourt was already a good friend of Richard's and mine. He's one of the most talented musicians I know but luckily for me also a generous and fun person to write with. When we first sat in the studio I had no idea how it was going to go. Sometimes working with friends doesn't work out. You need a bit of a spark and a complementary way of working. Ed and I talked about what we might do together. 'I want to write about the sort of stuff I normally can't write about.' That was the starting point. I had written song after song in the '4/4' time signature with a four-to-the-floor beat and an objective that was clear – get the listener to the dance floor. Don't get me wrong, I love disco and dance but I'd had my fill. Four albums of disco pop and I needed to be able to do something else. The thing about dance music is, it thrives on the instant. It lives in the world of the heady and the immediate. Love, lust, jealousy, desire . . . it'll eat that up. Reflection, storytelling, introspection . . . not so much.

Ed and I decided to write a waltz about a spooky witch who lives on a hill and when she takes your photograph, she steals your soul. A cautionary tale with a folky Eastern European slant. The song was called 'Love is a Camera' and I wasn't sure it would ever see the light of day, but I knew I loved it. Meanwhile I was having conversations with Derek about a new record and he was encouraging me to make a themed album of some kind. He kept talking about a Paris album, but I didn't really know what he meant if I'm honest. I don't think you can force a feeling or an atmosphere. I think he essentially meant making a record with its own feel and one set apart from my previous album, but I had to find it for myself. I had never had the chance to make a record completely under my own steam before, but once Ed and I wrote that first song together, I knew we were on to something. Ed and I talked it through and decided to write an album with an Eastern European feel. My travels to Russia had been rich inspiration. Moscow is only four hours from London but a whole world away with the look and feel and the culture. As a child I had a book of Russian fairy tales I loved and this all helped me frame the record. I sank myself happily into the songwriting. Ed and I wrote songs two or three times a month with no pressure and the record came together very easily. So much so that instead of my previous technique of writing song after song until I had around thirty before choosing my favourite twelve, this time we only wrote the songs that ended up on the album. It felt sure-footed and fun and cohesive and grown-up. I felt as if we were writing for a film and I could see the landscape of the characters' worlds so clearly in my mind. I loved being able to tell tales and I loved being able to do it all without anyone offering opinions.

Around halfway through the process, when Ray was safely in the world, Derek raised the idea of maybe having an A&R man to steer the ship with the record. We met with a guy who suggested I record a cover of 'Humans' by The Killers. Now, I don't mind that song, but the suggestion was so far away from what I was doing and I was a bit sick of the idea that every album I made had to have some bloke in the background telling me what I should be doing. I'm done with that. I said to Derek, 'I don't want to employ that guy . . . I feel it in my gut.'

Derek had always been very supportive of me. We've worked together since I was making my third record and I love the fact he's an old-school strategist of a manager. He worked for a long time with Elton John (and is working alongside Elton's management company again now) and Derek had been there in the days of John Reid and the court case. He's got anecdotes for England . . . except he's Scottish. I've even been by his side when he was temporarily arrested at Heathrow one morning. We were flying to Estonia – for me to support Elton there in concert, as it happens – and it was one of those chronically early 6 a.m. flights. As we walked down the gangplank to the plane, two very aggressive and out-of-puff airport security guys pushed Derek up against the wall and put hand-cuffs on him. 'We know you've stolen the laptop,' they wheezed. Turned out that Derek had accidentally put another man's laptop in his bag at the security check and had forgotten to put his through the machine, so he had two laptops. Eventually, they let him go but not until I'd already had to fly on to Estonia alone. The trip had a surreal flight home, too. Elton had kindly offered Derek and me a seat in his private plane to get us back to the UK straight after the gig. I fell asleep and woke to find a tracksuited Elton watching me sleep. He later told Derek I had a good aura. We flew home with such speed I was back in my own kitchen by midnight the same evening.

But in the days of *Wanderlust*, Derek did not quite understand what I was up to. All I knew was that, with the support of Ed and Richard, who was unfailing in his ability to buoy me up and make me feel that the fight was worth it, I had to make the record I wanted. I knew it was a tricky sell but I didn't care. I was thirty-four and felt too young to settle into a career just singing for oligarchs and not giving myself anywhere to go. Halfway through recording *Wanderlust*, the penny dropped and I realised that, for all its Ukrainian strings and Bulgarian choirs (recorded at the Bulgarian Embassy one dark night in London), the whole album was a huge love letter to my home. I wanted to have a foot back in England and be able to tour and sing there again, rather than stumble my way through my back catalogue all the time.

Recording the record was the most joyful time. We used a small studio in Richmond called State of the Ark – just one live room and a little kitchen. I could squirrel myself away and not bump into other bands in reception. I paid for the album and refused to use any kind of crowd-funding. Obviously, this was a privilege but also a risk, but mine to take ... I wanted to be answerable for the whole project. It felt so empowering. I loved it, and the success that followed the record was all the sweeter.

One of my favourite moments in the studio was when we came to record a song called 'Young Blood'. It's the most romantic song I've written, inspired by a conversation I had with my mum. She told me that when you fall in love with someone, no matter how many years go by, a part of you always sees them at the age they were when you first met them. Of course she was talking about her relationship with John, but I could see that in my relationship with Richard, too. He's so incredibly supportive and loving. He taught me what it really means to love someone fully. When it came to recording the song, as I sang I could see Richard knocking around the studio kitchen through the glass. He didn't know I could see him but there he was, eating humous on toast in his socks while I sang a love song to him the other side of the window. (I've made it sound as if he was ONLY wearing socks, he did have other clothes on too.)

After the music was recorded the budget was super tight for getting all the artwork and first video done. For the entire budget, I had less than the catering must have cost for my first video. I have made many friends over the years with the creative people I work with and this time, I couldn't pay them anything like the amount they would usually receive for their talents. Happily, each and every single person I asked said yes. How amazing is that? Whilst I didn't have the huge pay cheques, I could offer creative freedom and fun while we were doing it. Happily again, the people I've ended up working with a lot are kindred spirits who love what they do, so we had a brilliant day out in blue-skied Essex. In one day, we managed to get two videos and all the artwork and press photos done. What a great day out we had and I love the technicolour off-kilter Canvey Island photo story that emerged.

The cover of the album was shot in a little mobile home in a trailer park. The chap who owned it had done the whole thing up in tones of burgundy, white and crystal with giant lilies everywhere. They became a symbol of the album and for all four videos ('Young Blood', 'Runaway Daydreamer', 'Love is a Camera' and 'The Deer and the Wolf') I had those lilies feature and I wore the same white dress. I think for me with that fourth album the penny dropped that all the time I'd spent chopping and changing my hair and style growing up was necessary for me, but not for the audience. People don't always see every single performance you do, or every video. Keeping the aesthetic consistent helps to tell the story, so after that I simplified everything and I prefer life that way. The same goes for my stage clothes. One look for the show and stick to it.

MUSIC: Me at Thirty-Four, Part 2 –
'Murder on The Dance Floor'

With my granny, Sybil, on set at Strictly, just after I'd danced my foxtrot.

After *Wanderlust* was recorded I was asked if I'd like to be a contestant on *Strictly Come Dancing*. I'd been asked year after year and I'd always said no without too much thought. Going on a programme where I showed people whether or not I can actually dance didn't seem particularly smart. When the question about taking part rolled around again, I happened to have my old school friend Helen round. As we watched our one-year-old babies play on the carpet, I told her I'd been asked about doing *Strictly*. Helen's body language immediately changed. She literally waved her hands about, jazz-style, eyes wide with excitement.

'Oh my god you HAVE to do it! It's amazing . . . what if you got to Blackpool?! Oh my god what if you did a foxtrot or a quickstep . . . that's my favourite! Oh wow you just HAVE to do it!'

I was really surprised. I had no idea Helen was such a fan.

'Not just me! Becca is a fan, too!'

Based on this unexpected *Strictly* enthusiasm from friends I've had for decades, I told my manager I would be happy to meet with the producers.

It was all very 'secret squirrel', which I found amusing as, whilst I knew the show was huge, I'd never watched it and neither had anyone in my family. I met two of the senior production team and I was asked to do a little dance lesson so that they could get a sense of my skill level. Then it all went quiet while they deliberated other options and I got on with whatever else was going on in my life.

When the *Strictly* team had made their decision, manager Derek called me. I was with Richard out for the day. We were actually flying in his little plane. When Derek told me I had been offered a place on the show, I asked him if I could have a little bit of time to think it over before I said yes. I knew enough to know it was going to be a big thing to commit to, even if I was knocked out straight away.

That evening, with the kids in bed, Richard and I were in the garden lazing in a hammock we used to have. I knew we had to make the decision together. We talked it through and decided that, yes, we could handle it. I've thought back to that night many times . . . I'm so glad we decided together. The whole experience of the show makes me think of that Dickens quote: 'it was the best of times, it was the worst of times'. It sums up my feelings about the programme so well. Some of the show was pure joy and exhilaration. But some of the show was intense, and even for a strong marriage like we have, it gave our foundations a good old shake.

After being comfortable with my work for so long, I knew I needed to challenge myself. To see what else I could do. To embrace the risk. It turns out I have an appetite for doing things that scare me. I always think if the reason you're not doing a thing is that it makes you a bit nervous, do it. Making a folk record, spending my savings on it, was something I felt I had to do. Commercially successful or not, I pictured my feet crossing a stream and the next stone I needed to land on was that.

Strictly was a whole other thing. I did it because I couldn't really think of a solid reason not to, it looked like fun, I could dance all day (heaven) and learn a new skill and do something properly terrifying (honestly, the nerves I felt before I danced a Paso Doble in the semi-finals has now set the benchmark high-high-high for anything nerve-racking I ever do in my professional life, ever) but even now I feel I paid quite a price for that privilege.

Strictly is something people adore to watch and I am not about to dismantle that. I get it. Watching Deborah Meaden smile as she danced around the floor showed me in one moment the magic effect of the show and what people love. But the show can be cruel, too. I think the majority of its cruelty could be sidestepped with a little more internal infrastructure. A bit of focus on the participants' emotional well-being. The thing is, it makes you press hard on the edges of what you feel comfortable putting out into the world. That is not all bad, but sometimes you take that new-found questioning outside of the dance floor, too. I found aspects of it traumatic and saw close up some long-term relationships disintegrate while the programme carried on. There's that stupid 'curse of *Strictly*' myth which, can I say, is not helpful when you have signed up to a show that you and your husband haven't watched and then when you tell people you're doing it they turn to your partner and tease them, 'Oh so your wife is going to have an affair, eh? *Strictly* curse and all that!' On that topic, I do have a rather daft and long-standing tendency to say yes to participating in shows I haven't seen. It's the impulsive streak in me and possibly a self-defence mechanism. What you don't know can't hurt you, and all that.

I'd argue that the *Strictly* effect on relationships might be not just about the fact you're 'sexy dancing' with someone else but might also relate to why you signed up to it in the first place. If everything in your life is hunky-dory and busy, chances are you're not going to say yes to doing a show that sees you committing so much of your time to it.

But maybe I'm being naive . . . there are certainly a lot of boundaries that get pushed early on and that's not a smutty double entendre for the waltz hold, but it could be.

My baptism of fire with *Strictly* arrived on the first day. On the launch show we were all dolled up but backstage was reserved for only the *Strictly* team and participants. Normally when I do any TV I am allowed to bring anyone I want with me, be it management or family. That wasn't the case at *SCD*. Richard and whoever else was my guest was on one side of things, either waiting in the bar or sitting in the studio, while I was in make-up or wardrobe. That all makes sense, of course. It's a big show with many people involved and a live one at that. Risking lots of unnecessary folk backstage would be messy and potentially problematic, but it also created a physical divide between your usual counsel, the people you like having along for the ride, and the new *Strictly* family you found yourself in.

On the day we got partnered up, I was terrified. I had met the pro dancers at the group dance rehearsals but seeing them on the red carpet, their natural habitat, was another world. They looked incredible. The female dancers were wearing little sparkly gold outfits and looked amazing. Seeing them do their dance routines, at the speed that those dances were designed to be danced, was hypnotic to me. I adored watching the big group numbers and would find myself smiling away as I watched them. There's nothing quite like the pure joy that comes from watching a brilliant dance routine. I know aspects of it are cheesy, but it's such a happy and uplifting thing when the choreography and the music come together.

I and the other contestants were revealed to the press via a hydraulic stage. We literally appeared like Michael Jackson rising up from the floor. It was already very exciting. The hair, make-up and wardrobe team are flipping phenomenal. I adored them all from the get-go. Smart, savvy, supportive and talented, I clung to most of them like a rock when the *Strictly* waters got hotter and hotter around me as the season progressed. The production team was amazing, too.

It's a juggernaut of a programme, bigger than the sum of whoever is the show at the time. I was in the last year of Bruce Forsyth, too. He was lovely and kind. Ever professional, part of that generation of broadcasters. He had a little plastic screw-top pot in his jacket pocket with a menthol sweet in it that he would lick in between his lines to keep his mouth lubricated. When I did the *Strictly* Christmas special the following year, I saw how the public loved him. We were filming in Leicester Square and everywhere he went, people were so happy to see him.

In the group routine there was a part when I had to be lifted up into the air. James and Brendan carried me. Just before the show, my friend Louise had said to me that when she used to go salsa dancing, sometimes when she danced she would have what she called a 'love explosion'. Obviously I found this hilarious and a bit ridiculous, but as the group dance was being filmed and the crowd were clapping away, the live band playing, the confetti cannons doing their thing, and I was being lifted high up into the air . . . I forgot my normal embarrassment at being lifted by two men I didn't really know, and I felt it. I felt that heady explosion in my heart and I knew what Louise meant. When it all comes together, it's amazing.

In the launch show where we met our *Strictly* partners, I look absolutely terrified. It wasn't that I was terrified to be paired with Brendan – I liked Brendan. We'd got on when we'd met learning the group dance for the launch and I secretly wanted to be paired with him as he was the only professional to be married and a dad, so I knew this would give us things to talk about other than footwork. It was more that I found the whole thing of being paired a bit mortifying. I felt uncomfortable that there was a slight weirdness in forming a new 'couple' when you're both two married strangers. In the show, I found that kind of thing just didn't sit too easily with me – even though Brendan was a complete gentleman throughout. Why do they fetishise the 'couples' aspect so much? Dance partners, yes, but a couple has a different nod. I had found this really innocent when I'd read it in the papers, but when it was me, with another man, and Richard watching on amidst a sea of smiling grey-haired audience folk (when I was nervous before a dance, I'd find any particularly kind faced old lady in the crowd and pretend I was just dancing for her), I didn't find it quite so innocent. As soon as we were paired and the show stopped recording, Brendan went straight over to find Richard in the crowd to shake his hand. Brendan had done the show since the first one so he knew inside out how weird it was for the family outside of the programme. He had good advice for me, 'If you want this to work well, involve your friends, involve your husband.' It was good advice and I think it did make a difference.

I had a lovely group of people I did the show with and there was never any drama with the other contestants. We were pretty supportive of each other and the weird little *Strictly* boat we found ourselves in. It's funny, whenever I meet anyone who did the show – regardless of which year they did it – there's definitely a shared semi-trauma you all relate to. Some of it is pretty personal. I am not a touchy-feely person and I'm not very flirty or bawdy, so when I had first been paired with Brendan and he strutted into the make-up room and boomed, 'Where's my strictly wife?' I had to hide my prudishness. Abbey Clancy, who ended up winning *Strictly* in my year, was a lovely dancer and very good at quickly being able to do what I called 'dancer face'. I found that really, really hard. On my way to the first ever rehearsal with Brendan for the waltz, our chosen dance in week one, I suddenly remembered when I was in the taxi on the way there that I actually didn't like dancing with men where they could touch me. Insert 'gritted teeth' emoji here. This might sound a slightly ridiculous thought process en route to the first *Strictly* rehearsal, but I can be impulsive and make big decisions without giving a moment's thought to the small details. You might argue that being touched when you dance is not a small detail in *Strictly*-ville, but that is just how my mind works and that's that. In fact, it took me until maybe week three for me to be able to look Brendan in the eye while we danced. I just found it too intimate, too intense. I was open about it, though. The dancers would chat about whatever choreography we were finding hard and then Brendan would grab one of the female dancers to get her to demonstrate to me what I should be doing – he'd flip her around and she'd end up with her leg round his head or whatever. 'You know this isn't normal, right?' I'd say. 'You know normal people out in the streets aren't just grabbing each other and swinging one person over another? It's not normal!'

And I had to cling on to that for the whole show. So much of it was outside not only my comfort zone, but the norms of how most people interact. When I did the Argentine tango I was criticised for not making it sexy enough. Backstage, judge Bruno told me, 'Darling, you just have to become like a fucking slut.' He was saying it half joking, but the truth is it was supposed to be sexy and I knew my granny was watching. And my husband. I couldn't suddenly leap into that character just to do the dance. It would have been too much for me. My mum gave me such brilliant advice when I started to feel a bit in over my head. 'Just enjoy it and do it the way you want to do it. For the rest of your life it's just going to be a nice thing you did once.'

I carried that like a mantra.

Some of the show was incredible. I loved that first waltz. Brendan's choreography was always beautiful and I think the waltz we did to Audrey

Hepburn singing 'Moon River' was so sweet. There's an innocent romance to ballroom dancing which is so pure. I have to say, of all the things I've done in my professional life, my grandparents loved *Strictly* the most. I'm glad got to share it with them. Surreally my favourite memories of each of them see us at TV studios. My grandpa (mum's dad) was in my team with my mum, brother and sister when we did *Family Fortunes* and my granny was my dad's date in the front row at Elstree studios when I danced my foxtrot on *Strictly*. She loved my sparkly frock with the feather trim – it would have suited her. I adored my granny – my dad's mother and someone I always felt was a kindred spirit in the family. She was funny and a little mischievous and loved to dance. Having her with me at *Strictly* was genuinely very special. Sybil Bextor – you are missed. Thank you for giving me my love of dancing and my love of slightly naughty humour. Plus she was, by the end of her 91-year life, gloriously and beautifully wrinkly but still twinkly. That's how I want it to be for me, too.

I have to confess as well that from that beginning dance, for all my awkwardness about having to cling onto another man for the dances, I was hooked and addicted to the show and the ride. My real highlight came when I did my second dance, a Charleston. Brendan had never danced one before on *Strictly* and together we watched loads of footage of old Charleston dances. So many cool clips. Brendan took our favourite bits and created such a fantastic routine. I even did a backflip and felt kind of fearless as I loved the spirit of the dance.

On the day, fellow dance pro James watched the rehearsal and said to Brendan, 'It's the best dance you've ever done.' The two of them had a real banter-led friendship and so I thought James must be taking the mickey. I got all paranoid; there was a bit of the routine where I literally had to come up through Brendan's legs – my head emerges near the pants region – and I thought, 'Oh my god I'm about to make a complete idiot of myself in front of millions,' but by then it was too late to change it. We did the routine and . . . the audience went crazy! It was an incredible feeling. What a privilege to experience a moment like that. I felt as if the *Strictly* team had given me such a brilliant *Strictly* moment. It's not just a great routine . . . it's the lighting, the music, the little gold playsuit and the glitter into the champagne glass at the end. The whole thing is lush and if I watch it back my favourite bit is how happy we both look when we'd finished. It's a shame no one has made the Charleston fashionable since 1927. It's one of the only dances I can do.

I never cared about winning and there were so many good dancers in the celebrity dancers. But from the start I knew that if I was only going to do the show once then I wanted to have a go at all the dances. Like swimming lengths at school, I wanted to collect all the badges. Making it to the final meant I got them all.

So it feels a bit of an awkward juxtaposition to have had this exquisite experience on one hand – learning all these gorgeous routines and being put in fabulous sparkly frocks with amazing hair and make-up – to then have a downside . . . but there was. Richard started to struggle with my involvement from the launch show onwards. He knows I'm writing about this so I'm not being candid without his say-so. It was so hard for him that I can remember wondering if they'd ever had a contestant walk away from the show before they'd even danced their first dance.

It was like living a double life. At the TV studio everything was adrenaline-fuelled and exciting but at home things were strained and I knew I was finding it hard to give Richard the reassurance and support he needed. My head was overloaded. The schedule is like this – Monday afternoon you start a new dance, rehearse Tuesday, Wednesday, Thursday (whilst also filming the behind-the-scenes stuff, interviews and getting together the little video they play at the top of the dance), then Friday you had to be ready to rehearse at Elstree with the cameras and then live on Saturday night. Sunday we didn't do anything but some couples trained then, too.

The physical closeness was something I struggled with throughout but by the end a lot of things I had thought were odd at the beginning – like the 'couples' holding hands or gripping onto each other for the results show – I was used to and it seemed as if, by doing those things, I had crossed another *Strictly* hurdle. But with the dances, I didn't feel I could be totally unselfconscious until very near the end.

In a lot of ways it was good for me. I became a better performer on stage by doing the show. I loved pushing myself and trying new things and seeing what I was capable of. It also changed my relationship with my body. I realised I was stronger than I knew and my body lapped up the exercise. For a brief moment I had what I call a 'dancer' bod, and though I knew it was on loan, I loved it while it lasted.

The show was with me from August to December . . . thirteen weeks (my mum used to joke it was the closest I've come to having a proper job) and whilst I got used to the shape of things, it didn't leave anything for anyone else.

Meanwhile, back at home, my head was distracted. I'd get home, exhausted, and while listening to what had been going on with the kids, I could feel my thoughts getting foggy as I went over and over some step I was finding hard. Some of it was a good lesson to learn – if you're ever stressed about trying to learn something and you think it's not going in, just trust in the process. Your brain is pretty amazing and it's processing information even when you're not actively trying to learn something. But I feel bad that I was so absent. Especially at Christmas time as the final approached. The number of people still in the show dwindled and the intensity ramped up. For a lot of it I was just the observer. I could see some of the other contestants' marriages and relationships were under strain. There were three marriage break-ups in my year and two *Strictly* babies have been born from fellow contestants and their dance partners. That is not meant to trivialise any of those incidents. I have no idea what was going on in the marriages that broke down, and hey, working together is sometimes how you meet people

– just like Richard and me. But the concentric circles of these real-life situations, changes and developments definitely started to change the atmosphere of the programme. I can't think of any word other than intense. The fun and laughter of the first half of the series was diminishing by the week. It was getting more serious and competitive. By the final, I was done. I can remember standing on the side of the dance floor with Abbey and we were both saying how ready we were to go back to our husbands and our normal lives.

All the while, Richard was feeling left out in the cold. He was worried he was losing me. Not that I was going to run off with anyone – he liked Brendan and knew that nothing was going to happen there – but I think he thought that something was awakening in me and he felt he wasn't part of my future anymore. I never ever felt like that but I couldn't convince him. He could see that I was completely wrapped up in the show and consumed with the intensity of it and the constant learning, learning, learning which you share with one other person – your dance partner.

Richard became unusually insistent on knowing where I was all the time. If I didn't reply to a text, he'd spiral. Supporting me in all that I do usually came so easily to him, but with *Strictly* I think he was just waiting for it to end. He'd message me all day when I was rehearsing, extra keen to know my schedule. We would argue when I was home about how distracted I was and about whether or not I'd get through to the next week. He just felt as if I might slip into a new life that left our family behind. I have no such desire but was too spent at the end of the day to give him the reassurance he needed. I think the only real reassurance could come with the show finishing.

I feel terrible that I did that to him and at Strictly Towers there was no one to help. There's no emotional care at all – aside from the wisdom and make-up-chair counsel of the folk working backstage. For the dancers, too, they have to be choreographer, dancer and occasional psychiatrist. It starts off with you just being keen to show you can do the right heel or toe footwork for Len, but then later your confidence in your ability to act or be sexy gets tested, and that is more emotionally challenging. I do think they should have a counsellor, just to check in with the contestants. Richard started seeing a counsellor after I'd been in the show a month or so . . . he wanted to try and rationalise why he was feeling so threatened by the show, and it really helped. Perhaps I should have too. To find ways to help him. If all this seems a little dramatic just for a show that teaches you to jive, I couldn't agree more. It's too much. For all the glitter and sequins and stagecraft it taught me, I had to pay quite a heavy price, and Richard, too. Luckily what Brendan said was true, if you start off happily married, you'll leave that way too . . . but it wasn't immediate.

The day of the final was three days before Christmas. On the camera rehearsal day each finalist (I had a brilliant finalist family . . . all women and we were all supportive backstage) was taken to a little studio to do our interview, which was then edited to slot into the last show. We were asked questions like 'Is this the best thing you've ever done?' 'What has Brendan meant to you?' 'How incredible has your dance partner been?' 'What will you do to fill the hole after *Strictly*?' And I had the epiphany that, oh my god . . . it's like a cult! Trigger words and the constant repetition of how much it must mean to you. I looked to my left and right and all the finalists were being talked to as if we were in barrels about to go over a waterfall. One of the cameramen even said to me on the day of the final, 'You're going to love this. Best day of your life. Better than your wedding day!' And I thought, 'No it is not. You're not getting me. This isn't the best thing ever . . . it's been great, but this isn't better than my wedding day and the reason I sing is because that's the thing I love doing most. Not the foxtrot.'

The day of the final went smoothly and I actually felt the most relaxed I'd been throughout the whole thing. When Brendan and I did our show dance, I felt as if it was the final song before the end credits so I danced just for me and had a ball. I began the routine forty foot above the stage sitting within a giant disco ball. I was supposed to wear a little harness round my wrist so that I couldn't fall and I was worried I might struggle to get it off smoothly when I danced so, sitting high above the live studio audience's heads, I took off the harness and sat on the edge of the mirror ball. It did occur to me that death by falling from a disco ball live on telly in the *Strictly* final would be a pretty spectacular way to go. Murder on the dance floor, indeed.

Final conclusions on the Church of *Strictly*, then? I'm glad I did it and dancing the Charleston is one of my favourite things I've ever done and thank you to Brendan for making the whole show lots of fun. We never argued and I'm proud of that, but I'm prouder still I didn't cry or anything. I kept part of myself back and no matter what I was asked to do, I never did more than I meant. It took more strength than you'll know but hey, it's just a nice thing I did once.

After the show finished, I felt done in. Rinsed. That Christmas I felt removed from everything. Part of me was terrified – what if my feelings didn't return? – but more of me felt calm. I told myself to just go with the flow. And slowly, I did return to myself. Richard and I took care of each other. We went away, just the two of us. A lot of it wasn't spoken about. We didn't really talk about how hard it had been for a long time . . . not properly. It was too tender. We never doubted our love for each other but I think Richard worried that I just wouldn't want our life again, but of course I did.

Together we looked forward and now it was time to release *Wanderlust*, the curve ball. My strange little folky record seemed even more left-field after I'd just done such a piece of big mainstream telly, but my heart was still very much in it and I was proud of it.

The first single was 'Young Blood', the love song for my mum and John, but also for Richard. The album campaign started off OK but then we had a turning point when Radio 2 decided to A-list the song. Now, I've been lucky enough to have a few songs do well on radio but I can honestly say nothing has meant as much as that song being supported like that. I'm not a big major record company singer and Ed and I had written something from the heart. Having the opportunity for people to hear it like that was so special. The album did so much better than I anticipated and it was honestly my favourite thing I've ever done in my career. Everything just lined up so perfectly. It felt as if every single person that had a hand in bringing it to life was part of its success. A little *Wanderlust* family. It was the best present I could have ever given myself. This love letter album to home did bring me back. The gigs came back. The songs and the record were supported and I did things I hadn't done for years, like being welcomed back at Glastonbury. The whole experience reinvigorated me and inspired me. *Wanderlust*'s little sister, *Familia*, was born a few years later (after I'd had another baby, obviously) with some of the characters from the songs on *Wanderlust* continuing their story there. It taught me that you can make some crazy wiggly-path choices in your career but if you're doing it for the right reasons, people can cope with the twists in the road. I should have known that, really, having gone from indie to house in one year back in 2000, but along the way I think I forgot that you can be experimental if you fancy. Thirty-four was a weird old year – folk and foxtrot – but overall I put my feet where I meant to, most of the time.

Len Goodman's advice for me (given to me on The One Show)
just before I started strictly. I did, of course, start with a waltz.

18

MOTHERHOOD: The Other Three Pregnancies – 'Birth of an Empire'

Pretty sure this is the night before Ray entered the world, but it might be Jesse.

So sorry to Ray, Jess and Mickey to lump you all in together but I feel I must in the interests of not boring the dear reader to death (if I have not already done so).

See, the thing is, after having two early and tiny babies, I started to get a bit better at producing chubby full-term ones.

An obvious question might be: why so many babies? Some people say, 'Ah, you must love the baby bit!' And I do . . . but that's not why there are so many kids. I think it's a combination of things. First, as I've mentioned,

I had good early associations with babies after my brother Jackson was born when I was eight, which marked the end of a tricky period in my life.

But the other reason there are so many is that I really like getting to know my kids and helping them along their way. I love the contrast between my day job (make-up, microphones and sparkly clothes) and having a young family (nappies, uniforms, learning the theme tunes to all their favourite TV shows and keeping up with whatever matters to them). It is good for my head. The problem-solving suits me. Seeing them evolve and grow. Trying to figure out who they are and then help them get there with morale intact. Chaos, noise, mess, laughter, drama . . . do not have five kids if those things don't appeal but hey, I like it. And once I'd had two and could see how different they were, I couldn't wait to see who else was out there – numbers three, four and five – all different and quirky and interesting. I say all this as I write in a quiet house. Obviously, once they are all home I would also add 'annoying' and 'too noisy' to the adjectives. I think I've had their hearing tested after most holidays we've had. Why are my kids so loud?!

Looking back at the dramatic pregnancies and first few months of being Sonny and Kit's mum, I surprise even myself that I was so gung-ho about having more babies. I don't know exactly when it occurred to me that three was a good idea, but I do know that the powerful feeling I'd had when Sonny was born – that even twelve kids wouldn't be enough – was still doing its thing in my psyche.

I have five very different little personalities and each one brings something different to the party. In fact, I'd say wanting Ray was the first time I've properly felt broody. Sonny wasn't a planned baby (but Sonny – you know that you were always wanted) and with Kit, I felt it was probably a good idea to have number two, but with baby number three it was a more intense feeling. I had it before Mickey, too. It felt as if, no matter what I was up to, my brain was obsessively thinking about having a baby. All thoughts, all roads led to that. One hot August, while we were away, I managed to convince Richard that it was the right time for the new Jones Jnr to be part of the tribe and Ray Holiday Jones began his journey to existence.

Once pregnant, I found myself sitting talking to the lovely nurse at the hospital who is head of what they call VBAC – Vaginal Birth After Caesarean. I still wanted to have a natural birth and I think I've watched an unhealthy amount of *One Born Every Minute* not just because I love how they tell each story but because I am fascinated with labour. I wanted to see what was possible. My consultant talked me out of it eventually though. 'Thing is,' she told me, 'as you had early C-sections, the operation was more intense. We had to cut through thicker tissue and that might make you haemorrhage and get very sick if you had a natural birth.' I can be as stubborn as the next person but the idea of being very unwell whilst being mum to three small people didn't sound like a good gamble, so the date was set for the operation.

Meanwhile, I counted the weeks. Kit was now nearly three. I had been so intent on Kit being three when his little sibling was born (my brother Jackson is three years older than Martha and I think it's a good gap) that I actually factored in a security window of two months in case the baby was early, hence Ray and Kit are three years, two months apart.

I've been incredibly lucky to have fallen pregnant easily but I do know that not everyone can plan things this way. Richard and I have been incredibly lucky with having the children we wanted to have and we've only had one unlucky experience: our fourth pregnancy ended in miscarriage, but I count myself as so fortunate as it was very early, I didn't really 'feel' pregnant and I found myself pregnant again with Jesse soon after. Still, for the short while that the test was positive for that short-lived pregnancy and for the time after when I was going to work and trying to do all the normal things while miscarrying, it was an insight into the silent sadness that affects so many.

My own mother had ten miscarriages throughout my teenage life and that must have been unbelievably tough. I was so lucky that, for me, it was over before I'd even really had a chance to register it . . . I know it could have been a very different story. I send so much love to anyone going through any pain or sadness trying to have a baby. It just isn't fair.

As the pregnancy progressed and I got bigger and bigger, I absolutely loved it. There's something comedic about the shape of a very pregnant woman but I loved the ripeness of my huge tummy. I stopped exercising with that pregnancy and I have a little theory that keeping my stress levels and heart rate down helped stop me developing pre-eclampsia again.

Ray was born on a rainy Wednesday in April 2012. I didn't mind if it was a boy or a girl, but I was hoping for a boy because I thought the name Ray Holiday Jones was so fantastic. I could name many more kids. Picking the names is the fun bit. For Mickey, I found the list of names I'd kept and one of the girl names is my pet name for him. 'You OK, Sue?' I ask him. A boy named Sue, for sure.

The operation for Ray went smoothly but I found having a scheduled C-section without the drama of my health deteriorating kind of weird. My fattest baby was born to 'Rocket Man' by Elton John. Ray weighed more at birth than Kit and Sonny added together. I felt so clever that I'd produced a baby with curves. He had a chubby bottom and everything (premature babies have no bum). He was so beautiful (says his mother) and I loved the fact that, for the first time, I could hold my newborn from the get-go.

There's a line in a song by Athlete called 'Wires', a song all about the singer's premature baby, where he says, 'First night of your life, curled up on your own'. It was playing once in the car and Richard and I found ourselves boohooing away by the end of the song because that line really got us. Of course it's just the way things go and I know we are so lucky in the Western world to have access to incredible medical care, but the significance of holding Ray in my arms during his first twenty-four hours on the planet meant a lot to me. That bond is still there and he's the one who gets into my bed for a cuddle every single night, even now.

After that, apart from some incredibly painful breastfeeding (I now understood that those breast pumps, if they are to mimic a newborn, should basically be pretty much going round the clock. Wow – newborns are machines!) which, after a meeting with a breastfeeding consultant, we started to get better at, things were pretty smooth. I could see that all that time we'd spent in hospital with Sonny and Kit was not typical and I'm grateful we had it that way round, so that with them we simply didn't know it any other way.

Ray may have been my third boy, but he was brunette so that showed we could have a little variation on a theme. Poor Ray told me over the weekend that, on account of his non-redhead status, Kit had spread the cruel rumour at primary school that he was adopted.

Because I had been expecting Ray to be premature, I had foolishly said yes to a DJ booking which I had thought would be when he was three months old. As he was born on time, he was only six weeks. I'd completely forgotten about it and only saw it again in the diary two days before. I didn't have time to sort Ray's passport so I had to leave him for the night. The night before I left, I sobbed and sobbed. I felt as if he was being ripped from me like Velcro. Sometimes when I go to work abroad, I wear what I think of as metaphorical heavy boots. The tug of leaving can be so hard. My mum once told me it's as if there's a forcefield of a couple of miles' radius around your babies and when you're outside it, it's easier to be away. I'm not sure that's always worked for me but it's a comfort. I do know that when I work abroad it can be fine so long as I don't go anywhere I know they would have loved . . . then it's really tricky. However, I love it when they are old enough to come away with me on a one-to-one trip. It's lovely to have a little adventure with just one of them and good for them to have a story of their own to tell.

When Ray was three, little Jesse Michell Jones appeared on the scene. Another completely different character. He was 7lb 7oz of chubby good-ness and born in November so he had that month to himself (Ray, Richard,

Sonny and I are all April. Kit was due then too but sensibly chose February). The pregnancy had gone smoothly and when Jesse arrived he was another gorgeous redhead (as the tally stands I have 4/5 flame-headed children). All was fairly textbook and I was feeling as if I should be a dab hand at babies by now. A word to the wise: you can still make mistakes and experience is not always the same as expertise.

When Jess was only two weeks old and we were still in the flurry of visitors coming all the time to say hello to him, we had a day when he just wasn't quite 'right'. His feeding was down, he was snuffly and sleeping a lot. I remember my friend holding him as he slept again and saying 'What a good baby! He's so relaxed,' but I was not relaxed at all. I took him to the GP who told me he had a cold, which would make his appetite diminish, but that he was fine. The next morning he still wasn't eating much. Back to the doctor and on the way Richard suggested maybe we take him to A&E. I felt that was too dramatic and I didn't want to bother them with a baby with a cold. The GP checked him again and saw his nails were still pink so he must be getting good oxygen. 'But if he's still not eating by evening, maybe take him to the hospital to be safe.'

By 6 p.m. we were standing in the A&E at Chelsea and Westminster watching as a team of doctors took over and monitored his oxygen. He was frequently stopping breathing and it was 50/50 whether he'd need a respirator. Luckily, after a week in hospital, he came home again. The moral of this story – trust your instincts and if in doubt, go to the hospital. They will never tell you off for bringing a potentially sick child their way.

Once the drama was over and life was getting back to its new pace with baby number four in the world, I felt a bit more confident about making choices with work. I'd joked after Sonny that I was going to alternate babies and albums for a while and it had ended up happening that way. After Sonny came the record *Trip the Light Fantastic*, after Kit came *Make a Scene*, after Ray came *Wanderlust* and after Jesse it was time to make *Familia*. This was my second album with Ed Harcourt and we recorded it when Jesse was thirteen weeks old. To be honest, even though I look back and wonder how I got it done without a big meltdown, I was actually very productive after Jess. I was feeding him, recording the record and cooking for the band and engineers every night. It felt wholesome and happy. I even recorded one song while feeding tiny Jess in the booth. I couldn't have done it without the lovely people I was working with, including Richard. Working together probably doesn't suit every couple but I think it's been so good for us. We have very different roles so we don't tread on each other's toes but having him in the studio with our tiny baby felt great.

If someone had told me when I had Sonny that one day I'd be able to get on with so much with a tiny bubba, I wouldn't have believed them. Not only was I physically knocked for six after my first two babies, I also found it emotionally more overwhelming. Not that it isn't profound being a mother for the fourth or fifth time, but it's just not as scary to admit what you can't do, which in turn gave me the courage to try and do more. I had a safety net and I wouldn't have beaten myself up if I'd admitted it was too much. Plus I did feel more confident about looking after a newborn. The bit when I would really struggle is if I had to get anything done with a toddler (for reference, see the last twelve months of my life). I could have seven kids or one, but if that one kid is a toddler then I ain't getting much done. Mickey is a beauty but he's busy and bold and swings between Angel of Joy and Dr Destructo in seconds. It's a good job I don't own anything of value because nothing is safe here.

I had some of the happiest days of my career when pregnant with Mickey. I had started the pregnancy feeling a bit 'what have I done?' As with the others, I'd been lucky enough to fall pregnant as soon as we'd started trying, but I suddenly felt panicked. I had very much wanted a fifth baby but I'd had to be a bit stealthier getting Richard on board. I know how that sounds – I did not trick him into fatherhood for any of our smalls – but I do think he'd have probably stopped at three if I hadn't been so keen.

The very day I had Ray I had asked the consultant if I would be safe to have another. I started off pregnancy number four telling people, 'This is the last one,' but halfway through, I wasn't so sure. Then when Jess was about eighteen months, I felt that familiar broodiness creeping in. Working out every day when I'd be due if I got pregnant that month. Factoring in how work would be. I was approaching forty and trying to turn the volume down on that desire. Why was I so keen to have another? I'd been lucky enough to have four healthy babies, even after four C-sections and two premature babies. Why did I want to gamble with another pregnancy? I could see the logic in stopping, but as anyone who has wanted a child will know, logic sometimes doesn't get much of a look in. I almost felt as if the intensity was increasing, probably because my baby-making years were running out.

I spoke to Richard and my mum about it and both of them weren't sure it was a good idea. Richard worried a lot about the health implications of another operation, and I think my mum was concerned about that, too. But I felt as if I could put the decision in nature's hands. I would give it three months and see what happened. If I didn't get pregnant, then that was that. Of course, whether I really had any control over those emotions isn't something I can know. Easier said than done, I suspect. And then, just like that, I was pregnant. My first thought was for all my girlfriends who were trying to conceive and struggling. It's a cruel lottery. I felt as if I'd been greedy to want another. What if this baby needed more from me than the others? Had I gambled with our family's equilibrium?

After telling Richard (who was his usual matter-of-fact and calm self – happy but measured) I phoned my mum in a bit of a panic. She had, as ever, brilliant wisdom to impart. 'There's a reason why pregnancy is nine months long. By the time the baby is here, you'll feel more prepared.' That's good advice for anyone who is mildly freaking out at the prospect of a new baby.

This state of Zen was going to take a while to find though. Almost as soon as I'd started to get used to the idea (but before I could tell anyone) I had a meeting with my manager Derek about how to take my new album on the road. I'd been making an orchestral record and it was proving tricky to find a smart (i.e., cost-effective) way to tour an orchestral record with a live band, too. I'd messaged a man called Ollie Rosenblatt, who was experienced in putting on orchestral shows, about how we might make it work. Ollie more than gave advice, he offered to get involved and help me move out of the traditional rock venues and into beautiful theatre venues which would make the orchestral tour really work. Derek told me, 'Ollie is proposing we do the full tour in spring but we do a big one-off show at the Royal Festival Hall in September.'

'Sounds great,' I said, smiling in a fixed way whilst hastily working out I'd be six months pregnant by then. Six months pregnant and doing the biggest gig I'd ever done on my own with a forty-piece orchestra.

Sod it, it was happening, so I'd better just get on with it.

As it happened, and the pregnancy progressed, my mum was right. I started to relax about the idea of the new baby. The other kids weren't so sure, though. Sonny had been away on a school trip and when he got home, I told him. He started crying. 'Why did you do that? I've only been gone a week!' Rather than correct my fourteen-year-old's sketchy grasp of the biology of pregnancy, I took a softer approach.

'It'll be OK, darling,' I told him.

'But there's only two of you and so many of us already.'

Poor Sonny. Little did he know that Mickey would actually be a good little mascot for helping Sonny through the midst of teenage years. Those two are really close.

When I told Kit, he laughed and said matter-of-factly, 'So did you guys have S-E-X last night?' Another future biologist in our midst.

Ray and Jess were just sweetly excited.

As the gig approached, I started to feel more empowered. The funny thing is, now when I'm on stage I sort of lose sight of how I look anyway. I feel strong and liberated, even if I know I also look a bit daft sometimes. I was determined to do the gig in my own way and I know I'm not the first pregnant woman to dance about, but it's still something that can make you feel vulnerable. I felt as if I wanted to celebrate. I have often felt lucky with my work, but standing on that stage, with that gorgeous huge orchestra in my five-inch platform heels with a sequin jumpsuit, in a band that included my husband, was pretty special. As ever, I asked the kids if any of them wanted to come and I had two hands go up, so Sonny and Ray were there, too. It was such a happy night. I didn't even feel nervous, just happy.

After Mickey was born, the album came out. At one point they had the same release date (!) but in the end it was baby, then album. I promoted the record with Mickey in tow. Sometimes I'd feel as if I had an album and was promoting a baby, he got so much attention everywhere. I was on the lovely fuzzy hormonal high. With Sonny, I had felt so much love for him, but back then I had found new motherhood isolating and daunting all the same. By the fifth baby, I just felt pretty darn clever to have been lucky enough to have another gorgeous bubba to love. Mickey has really cheered up the whole family. I think whoever comes along, you end up feeling that they are exactly who the family needed. Mickey is a smiley, cheeky little boy and he absorbs the love from his brothers every day. It's addictive, I tell you, but luckily that crazy broodiness hasn't sparked up again in me (yet). Mickey might always be the baby of the family, who knows?

And now a brief word from my sponsor – the breast pump. Breast pumping and breastfeeding is more talked about now, but when I had Sonny I had no idea about any of that stuff. Premature babies do not know how to suck and I left hospital with a hospital-grade single breast pump. Single in that I could do one side at a time. I was immediately into the schedule of expressing milk every three to four hours. This was, dare I say it, more knackering than my experiences of waking to feed a baby. I'd have to get up, fetch everything from the steriliser, do twenty minutes each side, bag up and refrigerate my milk (rather sweetly my dad and Polly bought us a little cute fridge for the bedroom so I didn't have to go up and down stairs all the time), then wash all the bits before going back to sleep for two and a half hours, and then wake up and do it all again. But I did it because it connected me to my new baby and aside from the milk there wasn't anything could do for him while he was in hospital.

By the time I had Kit, pumps had evolved. I had loads of choice, not just the massive single-sided hospital one. I now invested in a rucksack called something like 'Pump and Go', so I pumped and went! Everywhere. I was now getting back to work while Kit was still tiny so my pumping skills were pretty amazing. Back of cab? Easy. Train carriage? Done. I figured out a way to do it without anyone knowing and if there was white noise in the background then no one could hear the telltale milking sound. When I filmed my video for 'Heartbreak', when Kit was ten weeks old, my friend Ruth was milkmaid. She'd fetch me every three hours and filming would stop and I'd do my thing and then get back to set. I know I'm not the first to do it, but I felt connected to my baby and happily unselfconscious. With Ray, I'd stopped using the massive rucksack part and I just took the motor with me in a handbag, wrapped in a cardigan to muffle the stupid noise.

For Jess, I needed it when he was ill in hospital. Even though I had so much experience I still found myself panicking about milk supply when he was ill and I had to keep the milk going. I find I'm almost unable to think about much else when I'm feeding a baby. It's as if I don't get my brain back properly until I stop.

Finally, with Mickey I found a quiet little wireless pump that fits in your bra. Evolution! It means you can walk around and feel clever and slightly disco boobs when it's in your top and silently doing its thing with the lights on.

I know there are other barometers for how the perception of motherhood has changed from my first baby to the last, but the pump is a pretty good metaphor. It's gone from a massive, medicalised, conspicuously noisy thing to a discreet, slimline, silent thing you can chuck in a handbag. We have learnt that new motherhood might be something you want to be moulded to fit you, not the other way round. It's funny, just the other day I found a tiny bag of milk at the bottom of my freezer. I would have cried back then to know it wasn't used. So thank you, breast pump. You've made a lot of difference.

Family photos. They are all a little like this.

19

MOTHERHOOD: It Takes a Village – 'Come With Us'

Me, Sonny, Father Christmas, nanny Claire and Uncle Jack. All but one of these grown-ups have helped raise the kids. I'll let you work out who.

On a good day I feel like a great mum. Exactly the mother I hoped I'd be. I'm calm, witty and gliding through the chaos with style.

This is not how I live all the time. It's just a fragment, not real life.

On a bad day I feel like a shouty, nagging, frazzled failure.

Most days are neither good nor bad, but rather a mixture of all emotions. In a busy house like ours it's par for the course but it doesn't mean I find it easy.

I have inherited a similar mothering style to my mum, and mostly that is a good thing. I'm very close to my mum and think she's raised us all well. She's a strong matriarch who has encouraged us to all band together. If Martha has a big day at work, my mum will message me to remind me to send her a supportive text. If Jack needs our support, same thing. I have memory after memory of my mum giving me pep talks when I was a child, to encourage the best in me. Now I do the same with my kids. I have told them (warned them?): son, I can do the pep talks for years. I've got the patience.

When I was naughty growing up, my mum didn't shout so much as use a low, serious, steady tone, which meant I had really pushed it. I use this too but my kids don't seem to find it so scary. The next voice is usually less calm as I will have lost it and will be having something similar to a tantrum. I'm not proud if it and it's often when my lovely pep talks and wisdom get ignored. I want to raise nice, decent, kind kids and when it goes wonky – particularly when they are mean to each other – it can make me feel as if I've really screwed up. I've found this particularly hard over lockdown.

Ninety per cent of the decisions I make with the kids go through the counsel of my mum, Richard and probably a few other people, too . . . friends who have kids, friends who haven't, professionals if needed, our nanny . . . I'm a big fan of talking things through. My mum is the one I listen to the most. She has helped me feel less guilty about work – 'It's OK to be selfish for yourself,' – and to worry less when I'm in a predicament – 'You are headed towards the answer and sooner or later you will know what it is,' – and sees the children as individuals, which sounds a simple thing but helps them feel 'seen' too. I have a lot of kids, but they are not one amorphous blob and none of them 'chose' to be in a big family, so I try to give them their own space in the flock. I am fairly confident in my decision-making and, with Richard, we are equals. If he doesn't agree with me, I can have the strength of mind to still do it if I feel strongly. With my mum, if she didn't agree with whatever course of action I had chosen then I'd have to feel extra sure to go ahead with it. I hope to have this effect on my kids, too, if I'm honest. I guess with parenting you're really playing a long game. I won't really know how good a job I've done until they are all fully grown. I'm not always here to be liked and yes, you have to be cruel to be kind, but blimey, it's knackering raising another human.

A friend once said to me, 'The days drag but the years fly,' which I think is so depressing, but on a bad day it pops into my head.

I seek solace in a few things. Even though I think my ma is great, she wasn't perfect. She missed the odd ballet recital and left nits in my hair until there were thirty-two of them (we counted). But the big, broad brushstroke stuff was always there in spades.

I also have the benefit of younger brothers and sisters to help me on my way. Not only are they brilliant now at providing another sounding board, or someone the kids can talk to when they don't want to talk to me, but also I saw them grow up so I can see a little of how kids respond and react and change as they experience life and all it throws their way. My brother Jackson and sister Martha are now in their thirties, but as is often the way, the dynamic between us and the way we are together has been set since childhood. In fact, I have to remind myself Jack is not nine anymore and Martha is no longer six. Jackson is a talented musician – a really brilliant drummer – and I'm so impressed with him when I watch him. It's endlessly wonderful watching people you love being good at stuff, isn't it? It's also lovely that we can work together and chat about work stuff as a common ground. Jackson is a calm presence in my life and in the kids' lives, too. He's very funny with a dry humour just like his dad, and good at keeping a close eye on our ma. He's open when it comes to discussing things that excite or worry him, and he treats my house a little like our family home in that whenever he's over he's likely to open my fridge just to have a look as he talks me through whatever is on his mind.

I love the fact that both Jack and Martha bridge the generational gap between me and my kids. Uncle Jack and Auntie Martha are both constant characters in their lives . . . always ready with a little day trip somewhere or a good talk about stuff without the parental view.

Martha – not six but thirty – is so impressive to me, too. When she was small she was so happy. A sharp contrast to grumpy Jack. (He's not cross now, but all my early memories are of a comically grumpy Jack. I now have a child of my own with a similar temperament and it's comforting to cite Jack in my mind as an example of how moody small folk can become measured and relaxed big people.) But from the get-go, Martha was always smiling and social. Confident and capable and charismatic without being a show-off. Both she and Jack have lovely groups of friends around them as proof they are lovely people themselves. Martha is the self-professed 'white sheep' of the family. Jack and I both finished our education before uni, but Martha flew high enough to not only emerge from Oxford with a First but also a Masters from the Courtauld. She's now involved in the art world and has such a brilliant knowledge of modern art . . . I'm extremely proud of her and she's still that gorgeous ball of beauty and confidence that she was at only two or three.

I'm so lucky to have such brilliant siblings and because of our age gap we've never had a single argument. When my stepdad John died, all that family support really came into its own, meaning we could ride the tide of all that was going on without any tension or things left unsaid. Even in the midst of the initial shock and sadness, I could see how precious that was. I know it's not always the case.

*

Having other voices in my children's lives is reassuring . . . I am not the only person giving them guidance, advice and sparkling wit. When I had Sonny, I knew that sooner or later I'd need help with childcare. It never occurred to me to stop work and I was lucky enough to be able to afford a nanny. I know this isn't usually the case for a twenty-five-year-old first-time mum. When I'd been a little girl my parents had used a childminder for me until I was five and then I had a series of nannies – some I adored, like Jenny, who then moved back to New Zealand after looking after me for a year. When I was seven my mum hired Christine, who became our nanny until Jack and Martha were old enough to not need one anymore. Christine became like part of the family and I was determined to try and find someone like her. Practical, reliable, kind and caring.

I put an advert in the *Lady* which, for those not familiar, is a magazine where people advertise things like lovely countryside cottages for holiday rents. You'd find it in the pile of magazines at a Harley Street doctor's. The advert said:

Musician parents with one four-month-old baby seek live-out nanny. Forty hours per week. Hours may include weekend work due to parents' job.

I had billions of replies. Turns out, finding a nanny for one little baby is not hard.

One person I really liked was Claire. When she came for the interview she spoke mainly to tiny Sonny, who gurgled back happily in her arms. Claire was already a very experienced nanny fourteen years my senior who was straightforward and funny. I hired her virtually on the spot. She was due to start in three weeks.

During that time, Sonny developed meningitis and was really pretty poorly. By the time Claire turned up for her first day, Sonny had a little cannula in his arm ready to receive his daily antibiotics intravenously. A nurse would come each day and give him the drugs but occasionally the line would block and Sonny would have to be taken into hospital to have a new cannula inserted. He was four months old but still the size of a two-month-old due to his prematurity.

Richard and I knew no different and Sonny had been in hospital more than out of it at that time in his life. For us, the cannulas and medicine and clinical bureaucracy of hospital life was just part and parcel of having our little man in the world. We'd got so used to it, but poor Claire hadn't. She turned up to find me putting on my trainers and putting Sonny in a baby seat, his baby bag packed. 'His cannula blocked this morning so please can you take him to Chelsea and Westminster Hospital? They know him there and know what to do. They'll put in a new line and he can come home. I've got a session booked at the gym for the first time ever so I have to go.'

I passed startled Claire the tiny baby and headed out. Claire told me later it was the hardest first day she'd ever had.

Claire is very much part of our family now. She was our nanny for eleven years and we adore her. She was so much more experienced than me and I would count her as one of the people who helped me learn how to be a mother. She organised and darned and pureed and fixed. She was capable and unflappable and the perfect mix of being a music fan – so we could get excited about introducing Sonny to songs around the house – but nicely unbothered by the starrier aspects of our life.

I looked to Claire to set the tone on how to do the right thing with a tiny baby. Of course I had my mum nearby, but Claire was my daily expert. I credit her 100 per cent with helping me become the mum I am now. She was so relaxed and straightforward about the feeding, the weaning, the potty training . . . it helped reassure me. I've always made sure that the nannies I've introduced to the family – and it's not many in the last seventeen years, only three nannies (one at a time!) and one au pair – are women I can talk to about any concerns I have about the kids. I ask advice all the time (even if I don't always take it) because they care, too. I can be a bit too close to things sometimes.

Claire's no-nonsense northern views often really made me laugh. I started to think I should have a Twitter account for her called something like 'Nanny Claire-isms' as she's come out with some classics. My all-time favourite was when I was encouraging her to vote. Claire never used to vote for any general elections and this would make me passionately beg her to do so. On one such debate I told her, 'Claire, women died to give you the vote!'

Claire's response? 'More fool them.'

Makes me laugh even now.

The other one I remembered just today (I dropped Mickey off for his first day at nursery this morning) was when I dropped Sonny off for his first ever nursery day. As I walked home with an empty buggy I realised I felt . . . fine. Happy for him, even. I had thought I was going to feel sad or possibly bereft that my baby was starting the next chapter of his life but no, I dropped him and no tears came. I arrived home and told Claire, 'It's cool actually . . . I thought I was going to feel emotional, but I'm fine.'

Claire sniffed a little and said, 'Yeah, but it's the first time he's been anywhere where no one loves him.'

Ha! Got to hand it to her, that one's a goodie too.

Claire suited our family as she was nicely eccentric and we love that kind of thing. Huge Elvis fan (on one occasion four-year-old Kit asked me, 'Why was Elvis so fat when he died?' Claire shouted from another room, 'He wasn't fat, he was just bloated from the medication!') Fun fact: Claire was the first ever visitor to Graceland in the new millennium – and is also a bit of a rocker, Claire loves gigs and music as much as we do. Also cats and bats and anything she can buy on special offer.

Claire was our nanny for eleven years and things were great for so long, but then, whilst I always adored her, I started to feel as if it was time for a change. Heartbreaking (I sobbed when I told her), but sometimes you just know it's something that has to happen in order to preserve and protect all that's good about your relationship. I would say we judged it about right. Claire is like family in every sense. The boys adore her, she comes to stay several times a year, we speak often and we love her. She'll always be nanny Claire and I'll always be grateful for all that she taught me and all the adventures we had. Oh, and small victory – she now votes!

The other extra family members are the godparents. I'm not at all religious (our babies have had Humanist naming ceremonies instead of church services) but the one aspect of the Christian christening I didn't want to lose was appointing godparents. What a brilliant thing it is, to bring your friends into your family. I could happily have another two or three kids just to add in the extra godparents. Some of my friends have been exactly as wonderful as I expected and others have surpassed. Also, it's another long game. You might find you need that godparent counsel more when you're older and that's all good. Not everyone needs to be brilliant at playing with small bubbas. They do grow. My kids happen to have pretty much the 'right' godparents when it comes to their needs, too. This is largely a fluke – but when Sonny found himself struggling a little with his feelings when he was fourteen, godmother Maria was on hand to offer wise advice from her own experience. When Ray discovered his love of music, godfather Ed had already penned a song just for him.

Not every mother is maternal and some of my most maternal friends don't necessarily have their own children. There are many ways to be a part of a kid's life and I think Sonny especially, who was the only baby on the block when I had him, has benefitted from this. He has wonderful and full relationships with some of my childfree friends and they have helped raise him, too. In fact, it was an untold pleasure of parenthood to me to see that you have your baby, introduce them to the significant folk in your life, and then they can grow to have a relationship that's kind of got nothing to do with you, in the best way. Standing back and watching that unfold makes my heart happy.

Since nanny Claire left, we have had three other women in the boys' lives in that role. Jemma, Jelena and Abrar have all brought something new and needed to the family and I count myself very lucky that I know I have such brilliant support. They are all like part of the family and, like Claire, I have an open-door policy with all of them. Jemma was our nanny for two years and she was younger than me with loads of energy – after work she'd head to roller derby training, which I think is pretty badass. Then came our au pair Jelena and nanny Abrar. Jelena lives with us and works for other families but is there for us if Richard and I need to work nights or be away (which with our work is normally pretty frequent). She's like a big sister to the kids, is loving and upbeat and makes the most delicious food. Abrar is our daily nanny in the week. She's kind, calm and caring and gives great advice with the kids. I love the fact that the kids are happy to be soothed by Claire, Jemma, Abrar and Jelena as well as me.

I have the word 'family' tattooed on my arm but the essence of what 'family' means is a bit of an amorphous thing. I have friends I would hold under the banner of family, I have blood relatives who I hardly know. What family means to you is yours to own and a deeply personal thing.

Nanny Claire. She's like family now which means I did a good job when I hired her back in 2004.

20

MUSIC: Staying in Music – 'Not Giving Up on Love'

Staying in music has meant learning what all these buttons do (it hasn't, but luckily I know the right people who do).

I have been doing what I do for a while now and there's a characteristic I have that's helpful if you want to keep going in a creative, competitive and unpredictable world like music: I've always been pretty delusional. I've always felt as if the best is still around the corner. A tiny part of me, a kernel, that thinks the impossible might happen and something could turn into a massive hit even when the odds are against it.

I once saw Ed Sheeran talking about why he's made it and he said for him it was all about having no plan B. I think that is pretty vital, too. When I was at school, aged seventeen, we went on a school trip. As we all lay in our hotel room at night, we each took turns speaking into the darkness about our strengths and where it might lead us.

'I'm really good at history and debating and English,' said one girl, 'so I think maybe I could go into law or maybe journalism.'

'Yeah,' we all replied, 'you're really good at those things.'

'I'm good at languages,' said another, 'so maybe I might work in linguistics somehow . . . but then I'm also good at English so maybe that's something, too.'

'Yes definitely,' we all agreed.

I spoke up.

'I'm good at doing make-up, so maybe I could advise on nail varnish colours?'

There was silence then one voice, 'Yeah . . . you're really good at make-up.'

And that was it. Conversation over.

I'd thought they were going to laugh, but maybe all I could do was get myself ready and then sing.

Thing is, I did and I do love make-up, and transformation, and music, music, music. The times in life I've struggled the most are when I realise I don't have any other employable skills. This has happened at twenty when I was dropped, at thirty-four when I was dropped and at forty when the pandemic started. I felt royally useless each time. But then, music pulled me out, together with the hope/delusion that something good will come out of it so long as I had some kind of momentum. I'm quite a simple soul and I just need something to focus on, to distract me, to chuck myself into, and then I'll ride that optimism until I feel I'm out of the darkness again.

Even now, when I start writing a song, I get a little excitement that that song might change my life. Or that tomorrow I might get an invitation to join something or work with someone and that might change everything, too. I try to embrace the uncertainty. It's so easy to complain and get bitter. When I started out, the interviewers themselves encouraged you to be moany. 'I bet you're tired of answering the same questions over and over,' they'd say. After a while it almost became part of the role to be all 'Oh my god I'm so sick of promo,' and I do get it, but I have been grateful for being able to sing for a living ever since I got my second chance. Working hard and not complaining are good traits. If I do complain about something I feel as if I've only got one or two 'goes'. I have to use my complaint tokens pretty wisely.

Also it pays to have a pretty good understanding of where you are in the pecking order. When I turn up to sing for a party or an awards show, I'm led in through the work entrance and the kitchens because that's the side of things I'm on. It's lovely to have the glitzy life every now and then, but essentially I'm hired to entertain and that's what I must do . . . I've had all manner of jobs and some are downright horrible, but in my head I can perform wherever I fancy and ultimately no job is so horrible that I can't love just chucking my voice around for a bit.

They say, 'Do what you love and you'll never work a day in your life,' and I do adore singing. Ever since I was small, singing a song could lift me up and away from whatever was going on around me . . . or it can make light of what I'm feeling . . . or it can provide solidarity in heart-break. When I was first left heartbroken as a teenager, I listened to songs on the radio with fresh ears. Every single love song was suddenly about my horrible break-up. How could the songwriters do that? Go straight to the core of what I was feeling? It was like magic.

When we found ourselves in lockdown, songs seemed to be speaking about that too. In the midst of the stress and anxiety, I found myself singing around the place more than ever. Singing in that first lockdown was actually the cause of one of the campest ways you can break a phone. I was happily belting out a song from *Grease* but one of the kids kept interrupting me. I was getting wound tighter and tighter. As I reached the last couplet I was interrupted again. This time I slammed my phone down on the side and as I cried, 'I just want to finish the song!', my phone screen shattered. I suppose the point is that music was sometimes the only thing to relieve the tension. Singing has been my little pal through it all. So if you hear me singing something, and I seem pretty 'into' it but I'm – I dunno – carrying a tray covered with delicate teacups, don't interrupt me. There's a good chance I'll smash the lot in frustration.

21

MOTHERHOOD: The Kids I
Have – '13 Little Dolls'

*Our 40th birthday (R and I are 4 days apart in age) with our
collection of small humans.*

I am not going to go into long indulgent paragraphs about the intricacies
of my kids' lives and who they all are, but suffice to say there's a quote
in *Lost in Translation* where Bill Murray's character says that your kids
turn out to be the nicest people you've ever met. That resonates not
because I am raising little angels, but because every time they do something great, I feel amazing. It is an easy source of joy to me that my eldest
boy, now seventeen and six foot and gorgeous, is around in the world. I

feel immensely proud that something I have birthed is now a near-adult. And how brilliant that he's a lovely boy, too. Empathetic and gentle and wise. He signed off his last birthday card to me with 'love, your counsellor' and it's kind of true. I go and see him at the end of most days for a bit of a debrief and he gives witty comments in response . . . until he looks at me blankly and waits for me to leave his room.

Caitlin Moran once said a wise thing about raising teenagers – to get them to open up to you, you have to moo at them. Turn bovine and a bit dim and you can be doing lots of subtle steering underneath, but to the naked teen eye, you are a slightly daft benevolent spirit who means no ill. I realised that had been my tactic for a while already. To maintain good communication – which is flipping vital – I'd turned myself slightly buffoony. OK – even more buffoony. I also ask Sonny to help me out with things. When he started spending a lot of time talking to a new group of friends online, I was open with him and told him that, as a parent, we are told to worry about this. To be concerned about who these invisible strangers are. I asked him how he could reassure me – treating him as the expert here, not me – and it meant he could be the one to help me understand rather than me just walking into his room and pulling out the computer and saying hysterically, 'You're not talking to anyone on here until you're thirty!'

I get it wrong all the time of course but I always admit to my kids when I've fucked up so they can see I'm just a human trying her best but not immune from acts of sheer idiocy, like when I got so frustrated the kids weren't going to bed quickly and easily I threw a electric toothbrush across the room and broke it. Parents sometimes have tantrums too. But I am trying my best to model good anger management. I'm not always good at it but it's hard to encourage a happy society in a five-kid house if you're an unpredictable loony.

Mostly the kids get along all right except for when they fight or break stuff and then I have a tendency to stand in the middle of the ruckus and shout, 'Stop! This is what people THINK having five boys is like and I always tell them it's not as bad as it sounds!'

When they are frustrated or cross, I'm trying to get them to see that the feelings are OK but the behaviour can't be bad and that yes, if you want to then everything can be broken. You can literally turn your house to rubble if you want, but part of a loving home is caring about it being a lovely place to exist and play and feel good, so let's not destroy it.

And mainly, it is that. I love our home. It's full of knickknacks and colour and weird and wonderful crap. Richard has been incredibly tolerant of my penchant for weird shit someone was selling on eBay. I want the home to represent a safe place for the kids – and for Richard and me – to really express and be ourselves. If Jess wants to spend all day dressed as a cowboy, fine. If Ray wants to paint himself blue, fine.

Actually, when Ray was about five he was continually dressing up. Not just in a playful way, in quite a meticulous way. He would find a character from a film or a book and want to dress up then do a photo where we would split-screen it with the original to see our accuracy. One time, Ray's dressing-up resulted in my all-time favourite quote from him. He wanted to be a cartoon character of a boy with what he called 'a boiled head'. He meant bald. The character was a ninja with a samurai stick. I didn't have a bald cap or anything like that so I set about improvising. First I put conditioner over Ray's hair to make it sit flat. Then I covered that in cling film to keep it all smooth. Then I covered that in masking tape, which I painted a colour to match Ray's face. I stepped back, pleased with my work. Ray hadn't seen it yet so I fetched a little mirror so he could see. He examined himself thoroughly, his face neutral. As he finished looking, a single tear rolled down his cheek. He looked up at me and said, 'You always disappoint me.'

Kit is passionate about film-making at the moment and it's so lovely to see him really driven and inspired. I've got no big ideas of what they should do when they are big but I do believe in watering whatever shoots arise from the things they try and seeing how high those plants grow. Richard and I differ slightly in that I am not someone who is particularly strict about them practising the piano if they don't want to, but he thinks that they should do it if they have agreed to do the lessons. I completely get where he's coming from but when I was little I felt as if I was made to do quite a lot of lessons and holiday courses that I didn't want to do, so I only encourage things where there's fundamental enthusiasm. I can see it both ways. I don't want them to say to me later, 'Why didn't you make me learn the violin?!' But I also think that if they are not bothering to put in the work, we should just cancel the lessons.

People say that the main thing you want for your children is for them to be happy, but selfishly I'd like it to be a happiness I can relate to. That would be great. Mainly, I want to raise kind people who are true to their hearts and bold and resolved so they aren't looking outside of themselves too much to feel good about themselves. Being funny is a very welcome extra. I get very upset when one brother is mean to another and makes fun of something he's into. I feel the world is cruel and this home should a place they always feel they can completely be themselves without ridicule. If I can help them find exactly who they are supposed to be – by their own standards, no one else's – then I'll be happy with that.

As their mum I sometimes feel a little overwhelmed by the sheer fact I have five small people to get to adulthood, but mainly I love it. Luckily for me I like problem-solving and find the humour in most things that go wrong. I laugh a lot generally. It's probably quite annoying. When I was growing up my mum was the same and it used to drive me potty as a teenager, and now of course I do it. Then again, the boys all know that if they make me laugh then they can get round me in an instant. Whilst I am not overly strict I do have boundaries that must not be crossed in terms of how we speak to each other, and the kids know not to cross them. I love the fact we like each other and I love their company but sometimes I have to be the person they don't like in that moment, in order to be the better mother.

One thing I am super proud of is having a family of open-minded guys. I think it's partly their generation but a lot of it comes from them, too. They have a natural instinct when it comes to what is right and wrong and I think a moral compass can't really be taught. I'm not saying they don't screw up and I have definitely had to say the warning: 'If you do that when you're older then you'll end up in jail,' but when it comes to calling out gender inequality, racism, sexism, homophobia . . . any sort of societal bullying, they call it pretty quickly.

It probably hasn't escaped your notice that I have five boys. It's amazing how provocative it is to have given birth to five children who all have willies. It's evoked a lot of extreme reactions. For my first baby, no one seemed too bothered whether I gave birth to a boy or girl. As I'm quite feminine in my choices of what I wear and how I present myself, a lot of people thought I'd have a girl. It's said in pregnancy books that women carrying female babies don't look as blooming and lovely as those carrying males, so when people used to guess I'd have a girl I always thought it was a thinly veiled reference to how terrible I looked. But no, I had a little chap and suddenly when your baby is here all other ideas of who you might have had pop like bubbles in the sky. It becomes irrelevant, all those musings of another baby because you had that one – of course you did. Silly to think it would have been anyone else.

I didn't really have any strong thoughts about the fact I'd had a boy. It was only as Sonny grew that the clothing options for boys and girls started to make me feel as if, if you had a boy, it had to be a certain type of boy. I found it puzzling that even animals were gender-specific. Girls – you get horses, kittens and unicorns. Boys – dogs, bats and dinosaurs. Girls – you get stars, rainbows, whimsical statements like 'Dream big' and the colours pink and lilac. Boys – tractors, cars, trains, diggers, statements like 'Hear me roar!' And the colours blue and red.

Now of course, if your little bloke loves those things then that's wonderful, but if they don't that's OK too. I always shop from both sides of the shop floor and put the kids in whatever I think will look cute on them. Similarly I let them play with anything they fancy, and that is why to this day our home is filled with Barbies, Power Rangers, dolly push-chairs and superheroes. I don't care what my kids pick up, but I want them to know every option is OK.

When I had boy number two I guess I probably had the first rumblings of 'I guess you'll be wanting number three so you can have a girl'. My answer since then has remained – the best thing about having a girl would be that folk would stop asking me if I'm trying to have a girl. And of course, just because I have five of the same gender, I do not have five of the same child. One of the most mind-blowing things about having your second baby is how flipping different they are to the first. I honestly feel I have all aspects of the spectrum covered with my brood . . . kids from big families are pretty clever at spotting the gaps in what has gone before and filling that gap. Essentially, there's a big play for parental attention . . . you can go loud or quiet but you will find a way to have your own space.

I suppose the fact I have five very different people brings home to me the strangeness of why people would want to have one gender over another so badly . . . to say, 'I want a boy,' or 'I want a girl,' then you must be imagining a little of who that person is. Maybe to you having a boy means having a kid who will be, let's say, into football. If that's true then my lot might disappoint you. Gender and what that means is open to interpretation . . . if you want a certain gender, what are you expecting them to be like? None of the boys are into football (despite their grand-fathers trying to shake that tree), and so this brings me to the next reason I've never been bothered if they are male or female – I don't want my kids to feel they've been born with their mother wishing they were some-one else. I love the surprise of finding out what makes each one tick. It's addictive.

By the time I got to baby three the comments about whether I would have a boy or girl were still relatively low on volume . . . the worst was probably when I went out for lunch with my beautiful three-week-old baby and a woman I didn't know very well came and had a look at him before pulling a sad face and looking up to say sympathetically, 'Did you already know it was a boy before you had him?'

The fun really started with baby number four. I went to our local GP and told her I was about seven weeks pregnant so could she please help me with booking in at the same hospital I'd had my first three? She started to fill in the online paperwork before laughing and saying, 'That's odd . . . they've asked me to fill in whether you're having a boy or a girl?'

I shrugged, 'Might as well put boy . . . it probably is.'

'Well then,' she replied, 'you'll have to get a bitch dog.'

'Sorry?'

'A bitch dog . . . a female dog, to even out all the boys.'

'Ah, I see . . .' Only I didn't really.

The wacky comments continued so I actually started a list. I was intrigued about what folk thought it was fine to say to me. I just dug it out for you now. There are some crackers in there:

- 'I hope it's a girl . . . not wanting to dampen your hopes but my friend had to wait until number five for her boy after four girls.'
- 'Ooh . . . is this the little girl we've been praying for?'
- After I'd said I thought it was another boy: 'Aw sorry – I know you don't mind but I just really wanted you to have a girl.'
- After I'd said I just want a person, I didn't mind what kind: 'That's a great attitude for someone in your situation, but for Richard I hope it's a girl. I underestimated the love I would have for my daughter. It's the best.'
- 'Ah, Richard must not be able to fire the X or Y or whatever it is!'

- Drunk man at a party: 'You should have had a hot bath before sex . . . kills the male sperm.'
- 'Ah, you'll have a football team!' (x 50)
- 'Are you hoping for a girl?' (x 50)
- 'You need a girl!'

After being surrounded by all this rubbish for years on end, I had a revelation. None of these people had met or would meet my kids! None of them will ever know them . . . it doesn't matter what I go home to, they just like the idea of Mum, Dad, boy, girl and that's that. In short, if you're sitting next to a bore at a dinner party and he has an opinion like this on any aspect of your life, just ask him what he would like you to be going home to, then lie and tell him he's right. He's happy, you're happy and you can both move on.

Maybe because I've had a ton of chaps, they are – particularly my eldest – pretty aware of gender politics, toxic masculinity and the importance of being yourself in whatever guise that makes sense to you. I'm proud of how open-minded and unbothered they are by sexuality and the gender stuff. They've even taught me. Sonny has a teenage friend who is trans, currently transitioning from male to female. I asked why it was necessary to change gender . . . why not stay a boy who is very feminine? Sonny answered calmly and clearly that yes, that was an option and that worked for some people, but it didn't feel right for his friend. That made total sense to me. I do wish these kinds of conversations had been on the table when I was growing up.

It's an unexpected loveliness of raising people that sometimes they teach you and wow, how lovely when they get to near or actual adulthood and they are a nice person. Good to hang out with. Wish me luck though cos I've got to do this five times over. You think the little kids bit is complicated? Oh me, oh my, no . . . the bit when they are small is fairly straightforward but come the big kid bit and there are many forks in the road and some of those roads have hidden bear traps . . . you'll be down in the ditch before you know it! But for now I'm still on the road and we are much better, our generation of parents, at understanding that kids don't mind us being human and making mistakes so long as we acknowledge it. If in doubt, I let my kids be the leader for a bit or I rely on the fact I am only their mum. I am going to screw it up a bit, no matter what, and so long as I love them, love them, love them, I cannot be getting it too wrong.

Still, wish me luck!

This is a side of motherhood I adore . . . the relationships they
form with each other that have nothing to do with me.
This is biggest (Sonny) and smallest (Mickey) who still cuddle a lot.

22

ME/MEN: Modern Traditional –
'The Distance Between Us'

It is fun to have fun, but you have to know how.

S o, I find myself at forty-two a happily married mother of five who sings for a living.

So far, so good, as long as you're cool with the fact your husband has picked the same job so the two of you are at the mercy of your next big idea and both of you have a part of you aged seventeen completely encased in amber because if you're a musician, you don't really have to grow up at all if you don't want to. So far, so good, so long as you don't run around screaming at the prospect of having to bring one, two, three,

283

four, five people up to adulthood in a way that leaves them non-feral and capable of being employed, capable of loving and being loved, able to dance and cook and to phone their mother every other day or so.

So far, so good, so long as you don't run around screaming at the idea of having a job that is completely unreliable and where you have to create your own momentum and at any point it might be pointed out to you that it's not a 'real' job.

There have been a few times in my life when I've wobbled on all of the above.

I adore my children and the chaos our house is partial to. It's a place where there's never a dull moment and – in the words of Madness – 'always something happening and it's usually quite loud'.

However, it can be relentless and knackering. This year I realised that I'd done a bad job of giving my work much space in the house. Being a mum can be a bit like working behind the scenes. No one turns to you and says, 'Thanks so much for doing all the laundry. My socks are perfectly clean and dry thanks to you.'

I am in a modern relationship with a modern man, and yet sometimes I'm so surprised by the traditional trappings I find myself in.

My kids want things from me constantly – of course they do, I'm their mum – and I feel as if I have to give them as much of me as I can as it's not their fault I decided to have four other brothers besides them. I don't want them to look back and think I overlooked them or lumped them all in together.

Plus with Richard I am likely to feel, as the mother to our offspring, I should be the one to get up in the night if they need me or do bedtimes when they want their mama as he would have probably been fine with two kids . . . I'm the one who wanted so many and as I always wanted a big family I sometimes felt I couldn't complain too much about finding bits of it hard in case he decided we shouldn't have any more because I wasn't coping. I can see this might sound ridiculous but I'm just being honest. I am the one who wanted a big family so I have to be able to deal with it all, else why on earth did I take it on?

Essentially, I sometimes feel I can't complain about being knackered all the time (I am knackered all the time) as no one else decided to have all these small people but me.

Also in my head is a little family who live there. This family is very similar to mine except they maybe have one or two or extra children, the woman achieves a lot more with her day and she is all round a Better Mother. She and her family been living there, comfortably, in my head since I had my first baby. The mother in my head is really nice, a good friend, great wife, wonderful mother. She's organised and has time for making the best of herself but is also always there for her kids. She's never grumpy and is measured and calm in a crisis. She coped brilliantly with lockdown and her polite and impeccably mannered kids were amazing with their home-schooling.

I've realised I am a far happier and more relaxed person when this woman is on mute in my thoughts. I cannot live up to her level. She's amazing.

The worst thing I've done for myself – and I've only realised this in the last year or so – is that I have consistently played down my work. I've often called it 'a job that's not a proper job' or 'a bit silly' and of course when I'm doing a job for Heinz that sees me sitting on top of a giant tin of baked beans for a PR shoot, who's to disagree with me?

But of course the fact of the matter is, when I've found myself doing the jobs I've done – some good, some bad (and believe me the beans one was actually in the 'good' camp. I like baked beans) – I have not always had the luxury of choice as to whether or not I should do them. If I've found myself doing something less than wonderful to bring in the cash then chances are the fact I have mouths to feed is at the heart of my decision-making, so I really shouldn't be so dismissive. There's nothing wrong with working for a living, right?

At the start of the pandemic and lockdown, I was recording the first of my podcast chats. Speaking to other working mums, I found myself banging on and on about the fact I didn't have any workspace at home that was just my own. When the lockdown was in full force, this became a deafening noise in my head. I know that there are probably lots of people who work elsewhere and come home to have no space of their own, but for me I have always had to do bits and bobs from home. Richard has a studio, but I will squirrel away and work wherever is quiet. During lockdown there was no quiet and it drove me a little insane, and because I'd always been dismissive about my work I struggled to give it any weight within my four walls when I talked about needing to get things done. In short, I've had to really think very consciously about owning and valuing my work so that my family – and that includes me – know to give it space. It's not nothing. I'm not pratting around. Yes, I am lucky enough to do something I love but I still have to work hard, be self-motivated and give it a little respect.

When I spoke to Yvonne Telford, a businesswoman who runs a clothing company called Kemi Telford, she spoke with a lot of wisdom and was so cross with me when I told her I sometimes said I was stupid, or an idiot. I do this all the time. 'Oh my god, I'm such an idiot, I forgot to email the school!' 'Oh no! I'm so stupid I haven't remembered to get milk while I was out!'

Now I *do* sometimes do stupid and idiotic things, but I'm not an actual idiot.

'Why would you call yourself an idiot?' Yvonne said. 'You're basically telling people to think of you that way.'

She's right. Now I correct myself if I say it and I make sure my kids never say it about themselves. It's never too late to learn new ways to help yourself get things done. I still don't have a room of my own at home, but I'm better at asserting the importance of the work I do and, in turn, I'm helping my kids. I used to think it would make them feel bad that I am putting work ahead of doing something with them, but that's never the truth. If I have things I need to do, then by telling them I respect it then they in turn will be respectful of the work they have to do.

This might be all super obvious to you, but I'm still learning. Turns out people can cope with you asserting yourself a little more, so if you're like me and always playing it down, just stop. You work hard and you're a good parent/partner/sister/daughter/friend, too. All deserve to be valued and I'm going to tell that little perfect mother lady who lives in my head that it's time for her to move out. Move on, little imaginary Stepford Wife! See ya!

The fundamental thing is – we like each other. It's an underrated relationship quality but pretty darn important.

23

ME: Why Spinning Plates? – 'Keep in Touch'

Working mama . . . roller in, make up on, babe in arms.

Have you ever started a project and at first you're not exactly sure why you began, but the further you got into it the more the answer revealed itself? I've had that happen quite often – partly because I am not one of life's big planners (see – my first baby) and I am also pretty instinctive about my decision-making.

Earlier this year, I followed the advice of my friend Chris Salmon and I started recording a podcast. Nothing so remarkable so far (the world and his wife has a podcast). I called it *Spinning Plates* because I felt it was an appropriate analogy for this time in my life. Arguably, I've never been busier. I still have the day job – songwriting, singing, performing – the other jobs that come with that – endorsements, photo shoots, promotional stuff like telly and radio, and the other bits I do to keep the momentum, like doing up the house, writing this book, recording the podcast.

Only there's another massive element of my life – raising my five sons. I sometimes joke that it's like the film *Gremlins*. I had one cute baby back in 2004 and then I accidentally fed it one time past midnight and he multiplied into five. My children, as I write, range from two to seventeen and as any parent of older kids will tell you, the teenage bit is where the parenting really ramps up. Sure it's not school runs and weaning, but the complexities of helping your small person become a young adult are nuanced and bespoke and sometimes very complicated.

The podcast was initially going to be speaking to other working mums about how they balance it all. How they manage the sleepless nights with a baby when they are also starting a business or writing a book. I set about booking guests and happily my long-term friend, Claire Jones, was able to produce. Claire worked for Radio 4 for decades, knows her stuff, is supportive and encouraging and – as a fellow working mum – was the perfect person to start this project with. I found each conversation with my guests fascinating. These women were impressive. But as time went on I realised the conversations weren't really about whether or not you breastfed and how your birth was, it was about how we, as women, as mothers, kept our sense of self. How do you not lose yourself when you are at the mercy of your new baby? Are you the same person you were before you became a parent? Do you pick up where you left off with work, yourself, your priorities . . . or do they shift?

It's a different story for everyone and obviously this process will unfold whether you are a parent or not. In my life having a baby at twenty-five made some things harder and gave other things more clarity so that's why I have focused on working mothers. I'm interested because, for me, it's been kind of a big deal.

But I do think these conversations resonate whether you're responsible for a small person or not. I know that priorities and sensibilities change even without having kids and sometimes it might have nothing to do with them, but it's hard to disentangle. Change will come with growing up; it might come with leaving a bad relationship; it might come with grief; it might come with falling in love; it might come with being made redundant . . . any one of life's big moments could cause you to sit back and think, 'Who am I here? What are my dreams? What decisions do I make based solely on what I want?'

One thing I do know is, I'm still learning. I am not the best mother in the world and I'm never the most talented person in the room at work, but this is actually a bit of a secret life hack. I adore my friends and the ones I work with are incredible – their talent makes me want to do better, too. Nothing I do is in isolation. I am lucky enough to have tons of support, not least from my amazing husband. He has always supported and loved me no matter what and it's incredible what that can do for the soul. He was the first man I dated who told me he fell for me when he saw me without all the make-up and heels. It made me feel seen and accepted. That's the good stuff, isn't it?

The podcast may only be a podcast, but the chats I have had have encouraged me to be more forgiving of some parts of myself, more ambitious with my goals and ultimately to be more amazed by what people can do. Honestly, women are AMAZING. Every story has surprised or impressed me and there are so many more stories out there. And so many are not like me – they don't run around on stage seeking praise – they are just getting on with being strong, resilient, multitasking, wondrous beings. It's been so great just to sit and listen and occasionally be a little nosy. Plus pressing 'record' on my little Dictaphone is the best way for me to have an uninterrupted conversation. It's worth recording a podcast for that alone.

24

ME: Are You Pregnant? – 'Get Over You'

*R and I heading out . . . I'd had a baby 5 months before. Felt a
little self-conscious hence the handbag in front of the tummy.*

My whole adult life, there have been so many occasions when
someone has thought I'm pregnant when I'm not. Why is this so
mortifying? After all, women's bodies are designed for it so it makes
sense that it might LOOK as if you're in the early stages of pregnancy
when you're actually just hanging in your usual, non-pregnant state.

I suppose it comes down to body image and feeling in control. When I
was growing up I felt so disappointed by much of my physical appearance. I was pretty critical . . . almost marking bits of myself out of ten. I

knew it could be worse, I knew it could be better. Being in the public eye in various ways from an early age, I felt the pressure – not to be perfect as I knew that wasn't an achievable goal or even anyone's reality, but to be able to shrug off any criticisms as if they didn't hurt. I was young and this was before I had even thought about having a baby. I wasn't as strong as perhaps I seemed when articles or even people in meetings would comment openly on my appearance.

I suppose doing a bit of modelling wasn't the best place to avoid that. Even my own booker at the agency – who I liked – once took a photo of me (size 8, 24″ waist) and said, 'Let's take another one where it doesn't look as if you've had a burger the night before.' As it happened, as this was just after my band had split, I was probably a way away from a burger. I had become quite controlling of the food I ate, probably as my life was in a bit of a downward spiral, and I began counting the grams of fat in everything I ate and avoiding carbs. I lost a lot of weight.

Once 'Groovejet' came out, I experimented with doing a 'lads' mag' shoot. I think I just wanted to know how it felt. I wore a bikini (something I never wear in real life) and stood under a waterfall in a studio to get the photos. The results don't look like me . . . it isn't me. I think you've got to have the right look in your eye and 'own' it, which I don't. They airbrushed me to look super slim, anyway . . . no softness allowed. I feel better and more comfortable with myself now than I did back then.

So no, having a little tummy isn't normally shown as a sexy or attractive shape. We're supposed to have flat stomachs, abs even. Is it associated with youth? Being very fit? Is the opposite perceived as a little frumpy and lazy? I don't know. As I've got older it's almost as if that shape is associated with having kids which has, traditionally, been a side of a woman's life she has kept private. Remember, it's not that long ago that putting a pregnant woman on the cover of a fashion magazine was done as some kind of statement . . .

I remember doing a school play when I was fifteen. One of the leads was a girl in the year above. After a show she put on a little pencil skirt which showed that her shape was a bit like mine – a little round tummy. I found it pretty radical and actually awesome that she had accentuated that shape. I remember feeling almost a bit shocked. I know loads of people have a shape like mine, but I just hadn't really seen anyone wear it like that. Not trying to conceal it. It looked great that she had that confidence about herself and I hoped to find it for myself one day.

Of course it's not just your body you feel self-conscious about. I had a very mixed relationship with how I looked. My teens were spent trying to get rid of spots, which covered my whole face. I found it so humiliating. You're at your most vulnerable, and nature chucks a load of acne at you, too. Glorious. I tried creams and even prescriptions pills to make it better. Eventually I grew out of it, but not before one boy even rejected me because he said I was too spotty. Oh, what a time to be alive.

Then there was the shape of my face which I used to hate. I would promise myself I'd get surgery when I could. I'd reduce my jaw and stick back my ears. I know everyone has their insecurities and I was no different, but in a weird way it's done me a favour. Not feeling like one of life's beauties also means I have a fairly relaxed attitude to getting older. I don't expect to look younger than I am and I don't want to risk looking weirder by trying cosmetic anti-aging stuff. No judgement to those that do, I'm just at peace that I'm getting crinklier.

The first time I was accused publicly of being knocked up was when I did my first solo tour. I saw an article which wondered whether I was maybe pregnant. It hurt. It felt like a secret about my body shape was being uncovered. Something I didn't feel good about.

I found an article from 2002 titled 'Bigger is Better for Bextor.' It's a charming little piece which goes on to say that 'while some women struggle to maintain their physique . . . [Sophie just can't] be bothered'. It goes on to talk about my having a potbelly. How lovely.

One way I have learned to feel better in myself is through getting a bit fitter. It's been a revelation to me, as when I was at school I thought 'sporty' was a box I would never tick. I think the way they teach PE at school is pretty barking. The kids who can run, jump, spring and backflip get all the attention but it's the ones lagging at the back who probably need the extra boost of good morale sprinkled their way. Can you tell I was one of the last chosen to join a team when we had to line up? Oh yes. For me the hidden bonus is that a) going to the gym means feeling stronger and more capable – rather than making you a gym bunny – I'm not a gym bunny and b) when you get into shape you can pretty much eat what you want. Guys, it's a loophole. Only slight issue – you have to keep going. I know, it's annoying but true.

Ten weeks after Kit (baby number two) was born, I found myself standing on set for the video shoot for 'Heartbreak (Make Me a Dancer)'. I was wearing heels and a mini skirt, which felt so peculiar on my body after a C-section not too long before. Afterwards, in the edit it was decided it was best if they 'stretched' the image so I'd look leaner. I've felt weird about that ever since . . . who was I trying to kid and what was I trying to promote?

Some years later I had a red-carpet awards to go to when Jesse, baby number four, was about six months. I had decided to wear a beautiful dress by The Vampire's Wife. It was figure-hugging but I felt OK about it. I didn't wear support pants or anything like that as I don't like the way they feel – they just turn my middle into a solid block.

I'd had a lovely night out and felt happy, confident and slightly clever that I'd managed to feel like myself with such a gorgeous small baby at home. Sometimes it takes me ages to feel like 'me' again. Sometimes I find myself and then lose 'me' again shortly after.

We'd had the awards and had gone for drinks when a woman I don't really know put her hand on my tummy and asked, smiling, 'Are you . . .?' Then, 'Oh god, you're not are you?' So we're both standing there, in a little group of folk, her hand still on my tummy in shock from the faux pas.

I reassured her, 'This is just what some women look like after a baby. It's fine.'

But I didn't feel good anymore. Maybe I was being oversensitive, but I suddenly felt foolish for thinking I was looking anything like my old self. I don't mean just physically, I mean emotionally too.

Richard was really reassuring but I felt as if I had to 'own' being OK about it so I posted something online along the lines of 'Sometimes this is what a woman looks like when she's had a baby and that's cool.' It helped a little but I still think we've got a way to go to really feel positive and truthful about the way your body changes.

The most recent time I was asked if I was pregnant was just a few months ago. I made a video for my version of 'Crying at the Discotheque' where I went round different venues in London – all lying dormant at the time because of the pandemic. I won't name him directly as that would be a bit harsh, but a male member of my team phoned me after seeing the video and asked me, 'Do you have big news?'

'What?' I was cooking supper for the kids and didn't have a clue what he was getting at.

'Well, I was watching the video and I wondered . . . you know, do you have big news?'

The penny dropped.

'Are you asking me if I'm pregnant?'

'Yes.'

'No, I'm not.'

'Of course you're not! I knew that. OK, OK, all good.'

So this percolated in my head a little and I decided, no that's not OK. Here's the email I sent back.

Hello numpty, (pretty sure that's how it started)

    Our conversation yesterday has upset me and I feel I need to clear the air and also make sure we don't find ourselves in this situation again.

It is actually not the fact that you thought I looked pregnant. I don't really mind that. I know my shape very well and I've had that many times over the years. I've never had a flat stomach and after five children am not really interested in chasing one. Every time I go on stage in anything that shows my shape, I know some people might think I'm pregnant.

I think the worst thing for me was being asked outright if I was pregnant, based solely on the fact I looked like I might be.

The fact of the matter is that as a woman it is completely mortifying and deeply personal to have to confirm or deny to someone if she's pregnant if it's only because someone has had a look at you and wants to know if their hunch is right.

Let's imagine I was or had recently been and had had a miscarriage . . . if I stood in a sequin catsuit ten days ago filming a video and knew I was pregnant/had been and decided to say nothing to anyone about it, chances are I don't want people to ask just because they think I look like I am.

Anyway I don't really expect to have to talk about all this with you. Even my own mother wouldn't call me and ask if I'm pregnant by saying, 'Do you have big news?'

Onwards, as usual, but let's not have this ever again.

(NB – This would have been a more brilliant and empowering moment if I hadn't thought after writing, 'Hey I'll blind copy in my mum and Richard as they knew I'd been upset and a bit angry about all this and they will be amused by my answer.' However, I accidentally copied them in so my poor recipient not only got a real telling off but also had my husband and mother copied in. Palm face emoji to be inserted here.)

I guess the relationship we have with our bodies is a constantly evolving one. But there is a common inclination to look back at our younger selves with such tenderness and forgiveness. Why was I so hard on myself? We can be so self-critical. I don't want to be like that and life is too short to worry about 'moment on the lips lifetime on the hips' bollocks. The lady I mentioned before, Yvonne Telford, who was so smart about telling me not to say I was an idiot, also spoke about her experience of learning to be happier in her own skin. It sounds a bit 'Oprah' (and in fact, came out of her watching a bit of *Oprah*) but bear with me. On this show, Oprah's guest was talking about how every day she looks at herself in the mirror and says 'I love you'. It took Yvonne seven months to do the same thing for herself. I'm not saying we all have to stand naked and say 'I love you', but we should try to be kind to ourselves as we are in the here and now. The resulting self-worth will keep you visible.

*

It's easy to disappear – to lose yourself in busy career stuff or the demands of parenthood. These can become unhelpful shields that make you invisible. So keep an eye on yourself. Wear the bold colours. Be seen. Hey, why not take it a stage further and get a sequin catsuit? Let's be celebratory about ourselves. Sure, you might occasionally have someone think there's a bun in the oven but I've given you the email to copy and paste back to the fool. I promise, once you slip those sparkles on, you'll find a twinkly superhero smiling back at you. And if all else fails, if you stand outside on a sunny day, the resulting reflection of laser beams shining out from your apparel will ensure any short-sighted bystanders get their eyesight back to 20/20 in an instant. C'mon, give it a try . . . you'll love it.

25

ME: You Go Ahead, but Wait for Me
to Catch Up – 'Death of Love'

*Early days of having a stepdad. Back then I always said
his hair was like moss. A cute chubby Jack here, too.*

M y stepdad John died recently. It's been hard. The English language
is wonderful in so many ways, but in other ways it's just lacking.
I want another word for sad. Losing someone you love is so sad. It's hard
to adjust to the new life without that person and to accept that the world
as you knew it is gone. My grief is my own but I want a word for the
sadness you feel seeing a loved one grieving. My mum has written
publicly about her own grief and it's beautiful and raw and takes my

breath away. I wish I could make things better for her and I hate to see her so full of sorrow. I understand that it is what has to happen, but it's not easy. I'm not very good at not being able to fix things and without a plan, I feel useless.

Death is heartbreaking and tricky to articulate but I also feel I want to shake any remaining uptightness I might have about the squeamish topic of talking about it. Your loved ones were here, they existed. Let us speak their names. We have to be able to talk about it if we want to, because as we all know, death is part of life.

The first person close to me who died was my grandma on my mum's side. She was only fifty-eight and I was eleven. I had known she was very ill but I did not understand she was dying. The last time I saw her I had a sore tummy – nothing significant, just one of those Wednesday after-school moans, but I remember on the way home my mum telling me, 'You mustn't complain about minor aches and pains in front of Grandma, she's in a lot of pain herself.' As it turned out, my grandma died that night.

Some children might feel the sadness of a loved one dying very keenly, but at that point I didn't. I remember when my mum told me the news I had just woken up and I thought, 'I'd better look sad,' so I screwed my face up. I didn't cry even though I had loved my grandma.

Now I have children, I know that my reaction was pretty normal. My kids have all dealt with losing their grandpa in different ways. They all adored him and spent so much time with him, and I don't need to see them cry to know that they miss him.

Not too long after my grandma's death, I was at my dad's house reading the end of a book I had loved. It had a sad ending and I was crying when my stepmum Polly put her head round the door. 'Oh, you're crying. That's good to see because we thought you couldn't cry.'

Looking back, Polly probably meant that the book had unlocked something in me, but at the time I thought it meant there was something wrong with me. I must be cold-hearted and numb . . . how could I not cry about my grandma? Memory is a slippery thing and it's possible that my little old brain has knitted together my grandma's death, my lack of tears, crying at the end of a book and someone observing that I was emotional and made it into . . . what? Not sure really but it was made of guilt and worry.

John dying has changed my opinion of all of that, which I guess shows you how long I carried that feeling somewhere in me. Probably goes back to my early worries about being seen to be sad in public, too. Golly, we're so complicated sometimes, aren't we? Now I can see that grief is like a cloak you wear and when you are monumentally knocked for six by something then you never question if how you're acting is right or proper or 'sad enough' or 'too sad'. One of the most special but also heartbreaking things about John's death is I had no question marks left about any of it . . . not about how we as a family felt about each other, not about anything I needed to hear or say to John. Nothing was left unsaid, no last-minute proclamations or muddiness . . . it's a huge comfort to me that I feel very resolved in terms of my relationship with my stepdad. But it's hard not to see his death as the end of an era of happiness. I see photos of our extended family together and we all look so blooming happy.

John was sixty-three when he died. The sort of age I would have thought was pretty ancient as a child. He lived quite subtly, really. Not an alpha male and not an overly demonstrative man, but he was funny and kind and constant and wise. I can see that my mum saw herself reflected in him and it empowered her. Their relationship taught Richard and me so much of how we wanted our own dynamics to work. No big dramas or shouting, and lots of support from the wings with our projects.

John had been diagnosed with throat cancer four years before he died. He was treated and seemed to make a full recovery but then later some cancer was found in his lung. It was just before Christmas and we all knew what the diagnosis meant. Still, over the next eighteen months my mum and John lived the same way they always had, with adventure and plans. They went to Japan, they bought a little place in Sicily, they went to the theatre (that will have always been my mum's idea) and saw friends.

Even when you prepare for someone dying you can't truly know how you'll feel. I know I was always worried about the idea of my mum on her own. I thought that we – my brother, sister and I – would be round constantly, keeping her busy. We've done what we can but wow, a pandemic was never factored into my thinking. We couldn't just pop over, she couldn't come for Sunday lunch, we couldn't go to plays and museum exhibitions, as I write she still can't travel to the little place in Modica with a friend. It'll all have to wait. I know our story is just one story in millions. Thank goodness for Angela the dog for keeping routine and nature in the mix. There's always a friend ready to have a walk with my ma and Angela. If I want to join I have to get in quick and reserve my spot. My mum jokes it's like she has a dance card and it keeps getting marked before I can get to it.

The pandemic did help us in one way. The week in July when John died, we were all together. Ordinarily, the musicians in the family – me, my brother Jackson who drums and Richard – would all be travelling a lot. With all of our gigs gone, we were able to be there for one another.

John had been getting progressively worse since autumn of 2019. Treatments had stopped being as effective and so by the new year, John was pretty much housebound. The March lockdown masked quite how limited his living had become by then and my mum was already getting used to dog walks by herself. Then with the lockdown the treatments stopped altogether. John's consultant fought hard to get him more medical care and by May he was back in the system and they were trying more things to help him stay alive. But it was all starting to a feel a bit futile and options were running out.

In June, John was struggling to breathe so my mum took him to hospital. Whilst John was there, on lots of antibiotics and after a dose of radiotherapy, he fell in the night. By now he was really quite weak but John was never one to complain and his sense of humour was still lively. As we all stood around his hospital bed he pointed to the whiteboard on the wall where his name was written. 'Every doctor who comes in has a look at that to get my name . . . they glance and say, "Ah, hello John". I'm going to rub it out and write "wanker".'

John came home and the plan was for palliative care but I was still struggling to get my head around the inevitability of it all. There always seemed to be one more treatment to go, one more possible explanation about what was causing the breathlessness that might not be cancer. Another infection? Build-up of fluid? Possibly, possibly. I'm sure this is a familiar tale for anyone who has been through it. You cling on to things and don't want to accept the fact it's probably the end of the road, as you feel as if, once you let that thought in, it becomes the truth.

On a hot week in July, John was admitted to hospital for the last time. The care he needed was too much for my mum and a once-a-day nurse at home. On the Tuesday mum called me to say there was nothing more they could do. I remember sitting in the beautiful sunshine in my garden where the flowers were all out and thinking, 'So this is what it feels like.' I'd known the day would come and I didn't expect it to be such a glorious warm day.

The next morning Mickey and I went for the dog walk with Mum. While we were out, the hospital called my mum. John was asking for her. She said, 'Oh that doesn't sound good,' and we immediately got her in a taxi to the hospital. I took the dog, Angela – adored by Mum and John – home to Mum's then dropped Mickey off before heading to be with the family round John's bed.

That day was one of the saddest and most special I've ever had. We – Jackson and his then girlfriend, Paige, Martha, her boyfriend Gabe,

Richard, my ma and I – spent all day around John's bed. We cried when we needed to, laughed when we needed to. We reminisced. Played music. I'm so glad we had that day. If 2020 had been a more usual shape the chances are at least one of us would have been away . . . but instead we were all together. It's so sad to say goodbye but it was peaceful, too.

We sat around the hospital bed that day in late July, we played Rufus Wainwright's song 'Peaceful Afternoon', a beautiful song about wanting to be with the one you love when you die (go and listen to it please, it's gorgeous), we cried a lot and finally in the evening I kissed John good-bye for the last time. Before I went I asked the kids if they wanted to say anything to Grandpa on FaceTime as they weren't allowed to visit. There was no pressure on any of them to speak, I just wanted them to have the chance if it felt right. John had been sleeping a lot by then and his eyes were closed when they called. I was proud of Kit and Ray. They both said goodbye and told John they loved him. Then Richard and I went home.

The next morning at around 7 a.m. my mum called to say John was gone. By the time I got to the hospital, Jack and Martha were there, too. We stood by John's bed. It was the same mood as before . . . a lot of tears and a bit of laughter too. In amongst the shock you've still got to work out whether or not you bring home the half-used toothpaste from the hospital bedside. And through it all, John was still there . . . and he wasn't there, too. It was him and not him. What a strange thing death is. After we sorted out what to do with his things in the room and did the paperwork, we knew it was time to go. I said goodbye, my brother and sister did the same . . . then it was my mum's turn. She walked to John's body, put her hands gently on John's shoulders and said, 'You were a beautiful carrier. You were so, so beautiful and you did such a good job. Thank you. Now, you go ahead, but wait for me to catch you up.'

It was heartbreaking and amazing. I don't think there's anything much more profound than watching your mother say 'goodbye for now' to the love of her life. It was possibly the most beautiful and sad thing I've ever witnessed. It really brought home that fact that at the heart of all the concentric circles of all that was happening was the love story between my mum and John. If having that love means one day you have to go through the pain of mourning like my ma is with John, I'd still choose it every time.

My grandpa died in 2014 and I remember feeling that love so strongly. We all stood in the church for his funeral and there was so much love in the room. My grandpa wasn't at all demonstrative with his affection. In fact, he was sometimes quite comically awkward. He didn't want to hold any grandbabies and there wasn't an ounce of sentimentality in him. He was my mother's father and an ex-army man turned (quite extraordinarily) prop-maker. As I mentioned earlier, he helped make Daleks for *Dr Who*. He loved creating things and knew how to make a homemade confetti cannon or find a really useful household tool . . . he loved a gadget. He was one of those people who would never say 'I love you,' but when he died I saw so clearly the way he felt about us in everything he'd ever given us. The baby gate he'd made with a little arch for the cat to run through, the hand-made and painted Beatrix Potter bookshelves designed to fit all the books underneath with a little shelf on top, the 'pram pusher' sheepskin gloves, which I still use now when it's cold as they keep my hands unbelievable snuggly, the photos of my great-grandparents he'd had framed for me with a family tree on the back, the Christmas cards and presents he'd already wrapped for us even though he died before Christmas. As we sat in the chapel for his funeral I felt it so strongly – all we really have in this life is the love we make and the love we receive. I think it was his death that inspired me to have Jesse (my fourth) as I thought, 'Blimey, family really is where it's at.' I had Mickey when my granny died. Later, after John died, Richard said to me, 'You know, you can't have a baby every time someone dies.'

Not many weeks after John died, I did a TV programme called *The Masked Singer*. For anyone who hasn't seen it it's a show from Korea where different celebrities – some singers, some not – wear costumes on stage so you can't see who they are. Each week anyone not eliminated sings a song and a panel have to guess who is under the mask. A small studio audience vote for their favourites and the panel choose one to be unmasked. It's all quite silly and surreal. I was asked to take part and I knew John had quite enjoyed watching it the year before so I thought, 'Why not?'

It was a welcome distraction and a bit of fun but also it was work and as any musician knows, 2020 hasn't been great for that. As I went for rehearsals I remember still feeling very raw and bruised. It all felt too loud and shiny . . . I wasn't sure I was ready to put myself out there and perform. In the end I was given a song I liked but I wasn't sure what to do with it, so I put on a stupid voice to try and not be discovered. It didn't work, the judges guessed me and I was first to go. That was probably for the best. When I got in from work I told the kids, who thought it was the funniest thing they'd ever heard. 'Why didn't you just sing as yourself? That's so stupid!' I was pretty teased about it round here.

When I watched the series back it brought back all of those feelings again. The hardest bit was that, after I had agreed to do it, I was given the dates, which were exactly when my mum, Jack, Paige, Martha and Gabe were flying with John's ashes to Sicily. I had to miss the trip and that was hard.

Comically, Kit nearly cost me the contract anyway. He had set me up with a TikTok account (something I was pretty rubbish at) and then when I had something like 4,000 followers he switched the name, photo and all the details to his, so he 'took over' or 'stole' my TikTok account. About a week after I did the show, I glanced at Kit's TikTok to see if he was behaving himself on there and he'd posted a photo montage of shots from my own photo album . . . photos of me in the suit, holding the mask. I phoned him in a panic, 'Kit you have to delete that post from *The Masked Singer* now! I'm not supposed to let anyone know I'm in the show!'

'Oh don't worry, Mummy,' he replied, sounding very relaxed, 'it's been up for a week and it's hardly had any likes!'

That wouldn't have been a great phone call from management . . . 'Erm, you can't be paid because you put everything on TikTok . . .?'

I think John would have found that very funny, too.

On the other side of this camera is my mum
They made each other very happy.

26

ME: Stuff Which Makes the Path a Bit Smoother – 'Today the Sun's on Us'

Fred and Barney would agree with the points I make in this chapter.
Especially about how being cool is overrated.

I am not about to blow your mind with any groundbreaking thoughts here, but these are some things that have helped me along the way and sometimes there's no harm in pointing out the obvious like:

Be nice to everyone
Well you don't have to and obviously this is going to lead to a load of folk on Twitter messaging me about the time I didn't smile at them when our

eyes met in a shop or whatever, but life has a funny way of taking someone who was once a leading character in your life story and reducing them to a bit part (or writing them out altogether), whilst it also quite enjoys making the least likely of folk stay for the distance. Chances are, some kind of weird serendipity of circumstance is going to make it so that someone you went to school with ends up on a work project with you. Best to be nice to everyone just in case your paths cross again. It's a horrible feeling when someone says, 'I met you fifteen years ago. You were horrible.' Obviously no need to be nice if someone is unpleasant to you. Get that gone from your life.

Don't complain too much

Complaining is really off-putting, isn't it? I'm not talking about having a moan about stuff when you're at home with your other half, I'm talking about when you're working. I tell my kids, when you're working and learning your craft, get stuck in and don't complain. Be keen and helpful. That'll get you back for another day, and then when people are considering you for a job they'll go for whoever was nice to be around on top of getting the job done. Sometimes it's hard not to complain. When I started promoting my first album, it was almost expected. Radio DJs would ask, 'Are you tired? You must be sick of answering the same questions?' But hey, there are harder jobs than talking about yourself all day. I think some pop acts think complaining about their diaries makes them look more successful, but it never comes across well.

Don't compare yourself to others

You're the only you on the planet and wanting other people's destinies wouldn't work. You don't know the full 360 of what their life is like and thinking you're entitled to what other folk have just leads to bitterness. Besides, there's room enough for all of us and who's to say you haven't done better than you maybe deserve anyway?

It's good to have a party trick

I can turn a napkin into a bikini top and tie a cherry stalk in a knot with my tongue. The cherry thing is seasonal, but the napkin trick is always a winner when cherries are not available. I learnt the napkin thing from my grumpy and not very funny granddad who unexpectedly and wordlessly performed his trick at a Sunday lunch one day. It's my best memory of him. Even more weirdly, I once had to race Jackie Chan live on telly with the cherry stalk thing as it turns out he can do it too. I beat him, if you're interested.

Being delusional is a welcome attribute

I have learnt to be able to perform gigs as if I'm performing at the gig I want to be at, even if the reality is pretty rubbish. What this means is that if I'm singing somewhere where the crowd are ill at ease, I can sing as though I'm happy as anything and this allows the crowd to relax as hey, I'm happy, I've got this, you can just get on with the business of watching me. For some parts of my career, I've had to be my only cheerleader. My third album was years in the making, and when we came to release the second single there was a mistake made with the digital upload which meant it came out on the wrong date and charted lower than it might have if it had come out on the right day. Now, people don't really care about that. If your song doesn't do super well, they don't say, 'Hang on a minute, the small print says something went wrong.' When it happened, I felt terrible. But the delusional thing kicked in, which meant I was able to get my chin up again and think that everything would get better, even if all signs suggested things had gone pretty badly. I guess it's a kind of warped optimism. I can also sometimes weave the delusion into my emotions. If things hurt me, I can sort of 'tell' myself how I want to feel about it until I feel it. It doesn't work for everything, but for helping shift the perspective when things don't go your way, I'd recommend it.

Compartmentalising is also useful
You can't necessarily choose these things, but if you are someone who compartmentalises, I'm here to say I think it's pretty helpful. It can get a bad reputation as it can seem as if your emotions are tidy and repressed. But when you're a grown-up you realise that being able to focus on work when you're also grieving, for example, can be quite a welcome distraction and might help the process. So long as you allow yourself to feel all the feelings when you're in a safe environment to do so, why feel you have to let people in on the thoughts in your head just to prove you're having them? Do it on your own terms, I say.

Remember to be silly and daft
Simple, but so flipping important. Being silly doesn't mean you can't be serious, but it does mean you will be able to provide a bit of catharsis for the tension in life. Let that stress out with a bit of daft jumping around. I am a professional daft jump-arounder. I know what I'm talking about.

Don't take it all too seriously – but if you do need to,
then don't mind the anger – it's important
We can talk a lot about how anger is not a welcome or helpful emotion, but actually sometimes it's really flipping important to stay angry about the things you feel aren't right or just. Being angry can be the momentum needed to speak up for yourself or make a difference. Plus, suppressed anger finds a way out in other ways. Focus your anger and use it to fuel the fire of change.

Find the joy in anything you fancy
I wholeheartedly recommend finding the joy in the little things. When your heart sings, do the things that make you happy. When you're truly caught up in it you won't even care what other people think of you or

whether it's cool. Our Kitchen Disco agrees with this, so does the Lego house I built in lockdown. I loved making it, it made me happy. Yes, I'm forty-two and no, kids, you can't play with it. The same goes for guilty pleasures. Don't feel guilty about the food you eat, the books you like and the music you sing along to. Life's too short to feel guilty about loving ketchup or 'I Want It That Way' by the Backstreet Boys.

Being cool is overrated

What a waste of time it was, all the time spent worrying about being cool. What an exhausting facade. My teenage self was so bothered by it – 'If you like that band, you're an idiot,' etc. – and then once in a band we had that whole shebang of trying to prove we were 'credible'. Honestly, whole discussions were focused around that. Being credible in a band sense meant that people took you seriously. The opposite was . . . what? You weren't the real deal? How daft. No wonder we always looked so serious in photos with our 'band hair' (although I probably undermined the credibility with my Mr Topper's special).

Anyway, as it turns out we are not defined by each and every choice we make. The coolest people are the people who have found their own unapologetic way to be themselves. It took me years to get to feeling like that myself. I'm not cool, never was, and don't care. It also . . . drum roll . . . DOESN'T MATTER. Honestly. You don't stop and admire blossom in the spring thinking, 'Blossom is really cool.' It does what it does in a beautiful, natural way, and it works so well it stops you in its tracks. The best things rise above the need to decide if they are 'cool' or not. They are just wonderful and make you happy. That is more than enough.

*

I am busier than I have ever been. When life gets a bit comfortable I have a tendency to take on a new project or, I dunno, have another baby. I am not particularly skilled in any area but I do enjoy being creative and the space it gives my head. My top tip is to never be the most talented person in the room. I never am and it leads to a happy life surrounded by amazing people who pull you up, not drag you down.

Ultimately one of the best things to make the path smoother is good counsel and I have that in spades, luckily . . . I speak to my brother and sister all the time and they give me good advice (although still let me wear this inflatable crown).

27

ME: Bonus Ball/Ending – 'Bittersweet'

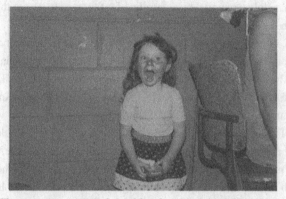

This is me at age 4 or 5 when I'd found my mum's blue stage make up and decided to put it all over my face.

So I don't think a book called *Spinning Plates* should necessarily include a chapter on 'general times I've embarrassed myself' but you're here and I'm here so why not share with you some of the most embarrassing moments I've had, just for fun?

I mean, we've come this far, right?

This is also slightly for protection . . . I have been very honest with you in the pages of this book and this means that if you've read it all and not really liked me, at least I can attempt to claw back some ground with the sympathy card. You might think, 'She went on a bit at times, but I did feel sorry for her when she fell down Esther Rantzen's stairs drunk.' That kind of thing.

So, here just for the hell of it are some of my most embarrassing moments.

*

I am standing on stage in Birmingham Arena. I am facing around 10,000 people (mainly women) who are waiting for four men to take to the stage, but I am the support and Take That are not on for forty minutes.

First, I must do my best to warm the crowd up. It is the second of our thirty-four dates on tour with the band and it's pretty intimidating on stage. The crowd are not necessarily pleased to see me. On walking out to the microphone, it becomes apparent that the microphone stand is set at a comically low height for me. The microphone itself is level with my boobs. The crowd laugh a little as I battle to make it the right height. Do you remember I told you earlier that I like to make jokes on stage? It's the Bextor in me. Out of awkwardness, I decided to speak to fill the gap. I laugh to myself as a thought crosses my mind and I decide to share my thought with the crowd.

'I was just thinking . . .' my voice booms.

No. Hang on a minute, don't say it . . . it's the wrong forum. But it's too late now . . . the crowd are waiting for me to finish so what the heck, here goes.

'I was going to say . . . the microphone stand looked like it was the right height for Mark Owen.'

Mark Owen is a lovely man and a member of Take That and not as tall as me. The crowd boos.

I continue, 'No – I mean, I don't have any issue! My stepdad is diminutive!'

I look round at my band who all have the same pleading please-stop-talking eyes. My brother counts us in and we finish our set before miraculously never hearing of it again. Thank you to the headline for not kicking me off the tour.

*

I am flying over to Australia for the first time. It's 2001 and I am super excited. The label tells me that Ronan Keating, my stablemate (label mate) is in Sydney doing a massive arena show the night after I arrive, would I like to go? Sure, sounds fun! I'm in a new town and my nights are free. I had met Ronan a few times and he's lovely. But professionally, I am an indie kid turned house singer and now doing my pop thing and so when I'd been asked about maybe doing a song with Ronan, I wasn't too sure. I felt as if it wasn't the right thing for me. Seeing as I was going to the gig, might I like to hop up on stage and sing? That's very kind but no. I'll be tired anyway and jet-lagged.

Lisa Laudat is away with me. We get to Ronan's gig a little after the lights have gone down. Ronan is in full flight with his show, with 14,000 fans happily singing along. As the song ends he begins his introduction, 'I'd like to say hello to someone in the house. Hello, Sophie! Sophie Ellis-Bextor is here! I asked her to sing with me but apparently she's too tired.'

I swear my cheeks have never been so pink. Still, a very nice man.

*

I am sixteen years old. I am about to spend Christmas with my mum, but my dad has made a special plan to see me on Christmas Eve as it's the big annual Christmas party of his old work colleague, Esther Rantzen. I have known Esther and her family for years as I grew up with my dad doing *That's Life*. She has children around my age so sometimes Dad and I would go and visit. I have happy memories of jumping in the pool with them at her house in the countryside. But now

I was a teenager and so going to this party was my once-a-year-moment with the family. This year my stepmum Polly wasn't coming so it was just my pa and me. I still remember what I was wearing . . . a brown dress I used to like because it was slightly balconette on the bust and split each side on the long skirt to show a bit of leg as I walked. I wore it with a little fitted black cardie and kohl eyeliner with Mac Spice on my lips because it was 1995.

When we arrived I quickly found the other teens and they were drinking pink champagne. I swear to god I didn't realise it was alcoholic. I thought because it was pink it was fake booze, so when I found myself horribly drunk after knocking back glass after glass, it was too late to pull myself back. We'd only been there about an hour and I was wasted. I am not the kind of tipsy person who forgets things . . . alas whenever I've taken things too far, I can remember every detail. This means I can remember drinking the black coffee I hoped would sober me up, I can remember the blurry haze through which I saw the rest of the night, I can remember trying to sneak four cigarettes from a packet I found up onto the roof for a smoke with the cigarettes sticking out of the straps of my frock, where my dad saw them and was absolutely horrified. (Bless him, he made rebellion so easy.) I told him I'd taken them to give to my friend Ruth. I don't think this lie washed given that it was Christmas Eve and I likely would not be seeing any friends for the next week or maybe longer. I also remember the brilliant conversation I had with my dad where I detailed all the boys I'd snogged.

The grand finale came when, as my dad ended our night early and tried to get me out, I slipped and fell down the main staircase in front of everyone and shouted 'Fuck!' at the top of my voice.

My dad then drove me home in a car with an atmosphere of embarrassment, confusion, shame and drunken adolescence. He dropped me off wordlessly at my mum's, too shocked to speak. We didn't talk about it for years to come. My mum, on having me back at home, was brilliantly tender and supportive, tending to my carpet-burnt and bruised shin and

– was that maybe a little smile at the drama I'd caused my dad? Hmm . . . just maybe.

*

It is 2000 and 'Groovejet' has been number one in eleven countries round the world. I am riding high on its success and out at my first fashion party with my best friend Maria. We find ourselves with the party people in a little snug at the back of a trendy fashionable bar. A man leans over, 'Can I ask you a question?' he shouts into my ear, above the noise of the PA.

'Is it to do with my mum?' I reply.

'No,' he says.

'Is it to do with Victoria Beckham?' I counter.

'No,' he says.

'Fine then, ask away . . .'

'Your friend,' he says, 'is she single?'

Basically – the world doesn't and won't revolve around you and not everyone knows or cares what you are up to. Life can be simpler and more beautiful when you accept this.

*

This is a simple tale but shows the way just one sentence can cause a ripple of profound and excruciating awkwardness for three in a conversation. It is another drinks party for my dad and his colleagues, only this time I am in my mid-twenties and though Polly is again not there, this time I am not drunk and do not get drunk. Instead the embarrassment comes when a man is chatting to my dad and me. After a pause, he asks, 'So, how did you two meet?' My dad immediately says, 'No, this is my daughter Sophie . . . you remember my wife Polly?' And thereafter we all just stand in silence as the horror of him presuming my dad and me were dating unfolds to all three of us.

*

317

I don't come across that brilliantly in this one, but here goes . . . when I had Sonny, I was inundated with offers of free buggies. The funny thing about new parenthood is that not only does it turn your existing life upside down, it also makes you part of a new consumer demographic. I was on both sides of this equation as someone wondering which pieces of kit I needed (not much, as it turns out – a Moses basket, but even that can be substituted in the early days by an empty drawer. You can bathe them in a sink and have them wear hand-me-downs and they'll be fine), but also having companies try to give me bits and the buggy is the big one as it's probably the biggest purchase you make (especially now it's not just a buggy but a 'travel system'). Showcasing the buggy was a good and easy marketing opportunity. We accepted a Bugaboo and I now wish I'd bought shares as those things are everywhere.

Come baby number two and the buggy folk came out again. This time I pondered getting something else . . . we were offered a super posh carbon buggy, which meant it was extra light. The PR woman who emailed me was lovely and we got on well in our exchanges. It was worth something daft like two grand. After putting the new pram together I decided, no – the Bugaboo was still the right one. Now, what to do with the other brand-new buggy? I had no friends having babies and so, yes, in hindsight the charity shop would have been good but I decided to put it on eBay. We sold it easily and that was that.

Months go by and I don't think about it.

Then the PR woman gets in touch. She's heard from a couple in Scotland who say they bought the buggy from me on eBay. They have a problem with a faulty wheel and can the PR help? I do not know why or how they decided on that course of action, but they did.

Anyway, I immediately panicked. Of course, I should have just come clean, but I didn't. So what did I decide to do? For some reason I decided the best plan was to pretend I had loaned the buggy to a friend who possibly had a massive problem with drugs who had then possibly sold the buggy on to get money to fund her drugs habit.

That's what I told the PR.

I feathered it out a bit . . . I was worried about my friend. No one could get hold of her. She was not doing so well.

The PR possibly didn't believe me. She replied with a stern, 'Are you sure because this couple are pretty sure they bought the buggy from you?'

I mean. They had physically come to the house so yes, they would be pretty sure.

I tried a different tack . . . oh, the buggy! Yes, now I remember! It had been in storage with The Feeling's equipment and by accident when they sold on their old gear they had accidentally sold the buggy, too.

The PR had now had enough of me and didn't speak to me ever again.

The saddest bit was that up until then she and I had had lovely little email exchanges, so I felt worst of all that I'd lost a pal. Sorry if you are reading this. I am a bad person.

*

In reference to my chapter on mistaken pregnancy, my apologies to the very drunk woman (in retrospect this was a clue) who I honestly thought was six or seven months gone. 'Congratulations!' I say. 'Everyone keeps saying that!' she slurs. Sorry. I will never congratulate anyone ever again unless they 100% confirm their pregnancy. It's not worth the fallout, people.

*

Richard and I are in a nightclub in Ibiza. It's a place called Woomoon and unlike a lot of nightclubs in Ibiza, I really like it. It's in the open air, finishes at midnight and they play good music. We've been before and it's got a lovely warm atmosphere . . . everyone is smiley and it's more because it's still early on in the evening than because of a chemically induced high – or at least, that's my perception. They have circus performers who pop up around the club at random moments . . . maybe one time a tightrope walker, or a woman dancing in sequins inside a huge lit-up inflatable ball. It's cool because there's always something to see. On the night in question, Richard and I arrive on our own as I have come to Ibiza to sing 'Groovejet' and 'Not Giving Up On Love' on Rylan's Radio 2 show. It's been a hot and happy day. I love Rylan and his commitment to his look meant he did the whole radio show in skin-tight black denim. When I said bye for the evening, he was expecting a big night out. Later he tells me he fell asleep in his hotel room at 6 p.m. and woke up the next morning. Getting fourteen hours of good-quality sleep is not the normal outcome of forty-eight hours in Ibiza.

When we get to the club, Richard and I bump into my friends, Max and Jane. I decide to get glitter put all over my cheeks by the club make-up woman who is working her way through the crowd. The DJ plays this brilliant mix of Pink Floyd's 'Shine On You Crazy Diamond' (one of my favourites, Dad) and we dance and jump about. In short, everything is great.

Then what? The DJ plays 'Groovejet'! This is an unexpected joy. Now, I know I'm supposed to play it cool but it's actually always a bit of a thrill when someone plays my song. There are so many songs in the world. Thank you for choosing mine. Richard, swept up in the moment, suggests I show my face to the DJ. Maybe someone spotted me and he knows I'm here? That's why he's playing it? Still, I'm a bit bashful. No . . . I can't. 'Yes!' Richard encourages me, 'There's a spare mic on stage . . . maybe hop up and sing along?' Emboldened by the enthusiasm of my pals I find myself heading through the crowd to the stage. I wave at the DJ. 'Hey! It's me! This is my song!' The DJ catches my eye, smiles, waves me up to the stage. I hop up, feeling more confident. Hey, they did want me here!

I head to the mic in front of the crowd, but now I can't catch the DJ's eye and, oh, there are loads of the crowd up here already. Maybe he just thought I was some eager club goer who wanted to hop up? The security confirm my suspicions. Holding me by my elbow, they sweep me away from the mic as 'Groovejet' plays on, and the soundtrack to my getting chucked off the front of the stage is my own voice. 'Why does it feel so good?' I sing cheerily. 'It bloody doesn't,' I reply.

*

It is Valentine's Day. The kids are at school and Richard is having a lie-in. I am pottering about in the rainy garden. The year is 2013 and tonight Richard and I are off to an awards do. I will be wearing a lovely dress covered in roses, but for now I am in jeans and wellies and in our garden we have two chickens. This is not a surprise – they are in a little coop which we have painted pale blue. The chickens are Richard's attempt at *The Good Life*. He scored an own goal by deciding that owning chickens was a good thing and then buying them before I agreed, which means Richard does the majority of the chicken care. However, it is early morning and I'm feeling industrious so I decide to tidy the garden while he sleeps. There is a huge green garden bin filled with chicken crap. I don't know if you're familiar, but chickens are pretty gross. They poo a lot. They are reptilian and not cuddly. The only upside is free eggs.

The chicken crap bin is also the new home of a third (deceased) chicken as the night before, Myrtle (a large black chicken) was killed by foxes. Despite their unfriendly ways, I feel bad about Myrtle. The remaining two chickens, Peeku and Chicken-boy, are still happily clucking around and there is something wholesome about the whole thing. I decide to move the garden bin round to the front of the house. It weighs a ton. I start moving it but it's unwieldy. Eventually I give it a huge all-my-strength tug and the bin launches forward, gets one of its wheels stuck in a flower bed, whereupon it topples forward. Alas, I am in its way. I slip over with the weight of it and find myself on the wet patio pinned underneath a bin filled with chicken poo and a deceased chicken. I cannot move.

Pathetically, I call for Richard who comes down in his dressing gown. Once he realises I haven't broken my legs, he cannot stop laughing. He frees me, but now has that image forever in his mind. That night we still scrub up and go out looking glam. There's a moral in here somewhere but I don't know what it is. It's not romance, but it is life. Happy Valentine's Day.

*

So there you have it. I have bared my soul to you. Thank you for coming this far with me and my spinning plates. We are all, in our own ways, juggling the various things we care about and some things we don't. Trying our hardest not to feel too overwhelmed by them and probably, best of all, allowing some of them to come crashing down. It's glorious to smash the plates that represent bad boyfriends, toxic work situations, saying yes to things you want to say no to. Sometimes you drop plates because you are trying to do too many things but when you are spinning them all, wow, you feel like a circus performer. I am lucky enough to share my life with awesome and lovely supportive people but I have also learnt my worth and I have gained the ability to sense with more speed the things that don't or won't work for me. You don't get any prizes for toughing out things which make you sad.

I wouldn't be able to do all that I do without the people in my life who I love and who love me, and all the amazing women in history who have gone before me. They have allowed me the freedoms I have now. Mainly, though, thank you to my ma, who has given me the best example of a wonderful, warm and wise woman.

I've enjoyed writing all this down for you. Thanks for indulging me. It's been nice making myself laugh with my jokes before I read them out loud to my friends and family so that they can laugh, too. Even if they don't, it turns out I can happily laugh at my own jokes several times over. And it's been good to reflect. It's made me realise that it's pretty good to be sitting here at forty-two feeling happier than ever. I'm a lucky ducky. I don't mean that life is always peachy, but I feel I know who I am and I'm more resolved than I was when I was younger. It feels good.

Anyhoo, that's your lot. Now, can you help me move the playroom table? I'm in the mood for a kitchen disco. Any requests?

This is the little light box we used for every Kitchen Disco. I wanted to put this message up for the final one we did, but I couldn't find the 'c' and 'h' in time.

Acknowledgments

One of the hardest things about writing this book has been all the amazing people I am lucky enough to know and work with whose names are not already on the pages. Some of my closest friends aren't there which feels weird, but the good news is I have this lovely acknowledgements space to just go crazy and list them all.

I am lucky enough to know some amazing, supportive, kind, generous folk and they keep me on the right side of things. If you can look at your friends and know who you are when they reflect things back at you, that's a good friend to have.

Over the years I've formed a team of talented women who I work with a lot who are all also friends. Nikki Palmer – who did my makeup and hair for the cover of this book – is such a woman. Tamara Cincik another – glad I brought you out of styling retirement! Thank you to Laura Lewis for the gorgeous photos.

Thank you to my manager Derek Mackillop – who patiently waited to read this until it was past the point of being able to add or change anything which is very lovely of him. We've had a good journey since we started working together all those years ago (just one baby and 3 albums back then). Thanks for the support, perspective and 'onwards' pragmatism. Big thanks as well to gorgeous Sabira Hud and to Kat and Charlotte – the Wallace crew.

Thanks to all the people who support what I get up to – Elaine Foran, Natalie McCain, all at Acast, Joe Mallot, Beth Parnell, Sarah and Thom at Sassy, Chris Farrow and Cooking Vinyl for supporting my recent music releases, and Olly and Sarah at Substance: new to the team and lovely to work with.

Thanks to Adrian Spriggs for being such a good person to have in our corner.

Thanks to the extended family, both Bextor and Ellis, like my uncle Duncan and Auntie Elaine.

Thank you to Ellamae for fabulous artwork for the podcast, to all the podcast guests I've had – I've learnt something from every conversation. Big thanks, to Chris Salmon for his ideas with starting the podcast but also his work with me over the years and especially his support and immense patience when we were putting the Kitchen Discos out in to the world (ditto Chris' wife Alexia – thank you for letting us be part of your lockdown).

Thank you to the old Polydor crew... I made friends there! Peter, Cynthia, Annabelle and Sarah.

Thank you to the wise counsel from my friends Sinead, Lauren and Gary, Ellie and Trevor, Mara, Marva, Julia, Neris, Gita, Arwen, Sarah, Simon and Zoe, Elena, Max and Jane, William and Al. You are all always there when I need you. I send you all love.

Thank you to my band: Jackson, Richard (yep I can thank you both here even though you're throughout the pages too!) Pablo, Ciaran, Phil, Jess, Rosie, Amy, Edie (I know you're not in the band!) and to all the other musicians who have toured with me.

Thanks to Yildiz and Daniel for giving me good chat while I try and get out of training.

Thanks to Raman.

Thanks to David Manero. New to the fold and a patient person who has helped me have the best time doing a radio show. Here's to the music!

Thanks to Glyn for good fun and Sink the Pink. What an inspiration.

Thanks to the godparents who I haven't listed already, Andrew, Jono, Philip and Owen.

Thanks to Jeremy Joseph for the stage and warmth at GAY. So many good memories.

When it comes to this book, thanks to Hannah and all at Hodder. You gave me so much encouragement and infectious enthusiasm. This is the biggest compliment I can give – I never handed my homework in on time before I met you. Plus, I like my book and I don't think I would without your gentle nudges in the right places.

Thanks to Ruth Young and all at United Agents. Such a lovely, smart and supportive team to work with.

Thank you to the talented Ellamae who does such beautiful illustrations for my podcast and who also drew my gorgeous dedication at the front of this book.

Thank you to Millie for being so incredibly supportive.

Thank you to Richard, Jelena and Abrar for taking the kids so I could write indulgently and for hours at a time. I adored the headspace.

Thank you to every woman who helped look after Mickey when he was under a year and I took him on tour. You all let me do what I do on stage feeling very supported and that is a lovely thing. Some of you only met me once I turned up on the festival site and it might not seem much to take a baby for an hour or so, but it's the glue that held things together.

Thanks to the nannies I loved when I was small. Karen, Jennie and especially Christine who taught me the good stuff in life like how to rag roll a bedroom and who would buy me gherkins.

Thanks to all the charities I work with for being so inspiring and tireless. The world gets a little better every day because of people like you. Shoutout to NYT and wonderful Roseby, Emma and the Music House for Children, Borne, Lumos, Save the Children and Mothers2Mothers.

Thanks to all the little businesses I follow on eBay and Insta. You've bought me lots of joy. Especially those of you who make the crazy fun stuff like sequin clothing or amazing homes for dolls. Here's to eccentricity!

Acknowledgments

Thanks to the gals in my local coffee shop, Good Boy. Some of these words were written fueled on your caffeine. That's the good stuff.

Thanks to the people who have supported me with my music. If you've come to hear me sing, or you've requested my song from a DJ, or put a song of mine on a playlist... Thank you. You've given me the amazing gift of being able to do what I love, and I cannot ever tell you how much that means.

Thanks to ketchup, mayonnaise, fish and chips. Gherkins – you rock my world.

Finally, thanks to you, whoever you are. You've given me your time and I know that's precious. Thank you for picking up my book and letting me chat to you for a while.

Lots of love. Sophie xx

P.S.: For those of you who are written about in the book, I know my version of events might differ from yours. Such is memory, I guess. I hope you know I wrote as honestly as I could and didn't mean to offend anyone.

Photo Acknowledgments

P. v Dedication illustration © Ellamae Statham / p. 34 theaudience © Piers Allardyce/Shutterstock / p. 98 Sophie Ellis-Bextor and Spiller © Ray Tang/Shutterstock./ p. 119 Read My Lips ©Dave Hogan/Getty Images

Most of my early childhood photos are by my dad.